Professional WinFX™ Beta: Covers "Avalon" Windows Presentation Foundation and "Indigo" Windows Communication Foundation

Professional WinFX™ Beta: Covers "Avalon" Windows Presentation Foundation and "Indigo" Windows Communication Foundation

Jean-Luc David, Bill Ryan, Ron DeSerranno,
and Alexandra Young

WILEY

Wiley Publishing, Inc.

Professional WinFX™ Beta: Covers "Avalon" Windows Presentation Foundation and "Indigo" Windows Communication Foundation

Published by
Wiley Publishing, Inc.
10475 Crosspoint Boulevard
Indianapolis, IN 46256
www.wiley.com

Published simultaneously in Canada

ISBN-13: 978-0-7645-7874-8
ISBN-10: 0-7645-7874-X

Manufactured in the United States of America

10 9 8 7 6 5 4 3 2 1

1B/TR/QY/QV/IN

For general information on our other products and services or to obtain technical support, please contact our Customer Care Department within the U.S. at (800) 762-2974, outside the U.S. at (317) 572-3993 or fax (317) 572-4002.

Wiley also publishes its books in a variety of electronic formats. Some content that appears in print may not be available in electronic books.

About the Authors

Jean-Luc David is a Toronto-based software developer and consultant. He founded Stormpixel.com in 1998, where he specializes in web design and in developing custom desktop, Tablet and Windows Mobile applications for his clients. Jean-Luc has written many technical articles for companies such as ASPToday.com, C | NET and XML.COM. Jean-Luc has the unique distinction of being the first Canadian to receive the Microsoft .NET MVP Award.

Ron DeSerranno is the founder and CEO of Mobiform Software Ltd. His software development career first began at the Space and Atmospheric Research Group, Physics Department, at the University of Western Ontario. He was a Microsoft Certified Trainer and consultant and taught courses in both New York and Toronto. For five years, he was development lead and architect for Rockwell's flagship Industrial Automation product RSView, an invaluable tool for globally scaled companies such as Kraft and General Motors. Other ventures include the establishment of BoardMaster Software and Motivus Software Ltd. Mr. DeSerranno is considered one of the leading authorities on XML-based graphics technologies and has been designing and developing world-class software products for many years. His current focus is on WinFX by Microsoft.

Bill Ryan is a Microsoft MVP in Windows Embedded Product group. He's currently working as a senior software developer at InfoPro, Inc in Augusta, Georgia. He is a .NET enthusiast and spends a lot of time working with bleeding-edge technologies. His favorite areas in technology are ADO.NET, the Compact Framework, Microsoft Speech Server, Biztalk Server, and Yukon. Outside of technology, his interests include reading, cult movies, techno-music, and cuckoo clocks. You can usually find Bill in one of the Microsoft .NET newsgroups, his blog (`www.msmvps.com/WilliamRyan`) or some of his Web sites (`www.knowdotnet.com`, www.devbuzz.com).

Alexandra Young of Mobiform Software is the team leader for Avalon and XAML education as well as user interface design for Mobiform's XAML Designer for WinFX, Aurora.

With over six years experience in web, multimedia, and database design, Alexandra has acquired necessary skills to program in XAML, ASP, ASP.Net, Visual Basic, VB.Net, T/SQL, and C#. Fully understanding the tools available to designers and developers has led to her passion for, success in, and drive to understand and evangelize new software technologies. These skills have been instrumental in the education of Mobiform's customers.

Experience in various software products has given Alexandra a full understanding of the limitations and benefits of products produced by the likes of Microsoft, Adobe, and Macromedia. This knowledge has fueled her enthusiasm for the universal benefits of Microsoft's "Avalon" API and XAML markup language. She knows that this technology will revolutionize the way we design and build Web and software applications.

For my beautiful wife, Miho, who has patiently stood by me and supported me through the writing of this book. A special thanks goes out to the David family for their ongoing support.

Credits

Senior Acquisitions Editor
Jim Minatel

Development Editors
Marcia Ellett
Sydney Jones

Technical Editors
Derek Comingore
Bill Ryan
Andrew Watt

Production Editor
William A. Barton

Copy Editor
Foxxe Editorial Services

Editorial Manager
Mary Beth Wakefield

Production Manager
Tim Tate

Vice President & Executive Group Publisher
Richard Swadley

Vice President and Publisher
Joseph B. Wikert

Project Coordinator
Bill Ramsey

Graphics and Production Specialists
Jennifer Heleine
Amanda Spagnuolo

Quality Control Technician
Charles Spencer

Proofreading
Publication Services

Indexing
Johnna VanHoose Dinse

Media Development Specialists
Angela Denny
Kit Malone
Travis Silvers

Acknowledgments

First and foremost, I would like to thank my Wrox editors, Jim Minatel and Bob Elliot, for their wisdom, guidance, and patience, and Marcia Ellett and Sydney Jones for their great editing feedback and advice. A very special thanks goes out to my coauthors—Bill Ryan, Ron DeSerranno, and Alexandra Young—for sharing their knowledge and expertise within these pages. I'd also like to thank the Indigo and WinFX product teams for providing fantastic resources and direction—in particular, Steve Swartz, Ami Vora, Erik Weis, Ed Kaim, Ari Bixhorn, Stuart Celarier, Achim Ruopp, Tim Sneath, and Jan Shanahan.
—*Jean-Luc David*

I would like to thank Ron DeSerranno for his leadership and guidance and for giving me the opportunity to coauthor the Avalon chapters. Additionally, I am thankful to my coworkers at Mobiform Software, Gary Fuhr, Jason Wylie, and Glen Sollors, for their technical and proofreading input and support. Mike Swanson and the Avalon team at Microsoft were instrumental in helping me with concepts and markup structure for some of the newer controls. My exceptional editors Maria Ellett and Sydney Jones were paramount to making this book cutting edge by accommodating Avalon updates and changes right up to the moment of going to press. Most important, I would like to thank my mother, Wilma Young, for her unyielding support and patience.
—*Alexandra Young*

Introduction

The Windows Framework Extension (WinFX) is Microsoft's next-generation Windows programming framework. WinFX is based on the .NET Framework 2.0 but incorporates new programming APIs such as "Avalon" (now renamed as Windows Presentation Foundation) and "Indigo" (now known as Windows Communication Foundation). WinFX was first unveiled to the world at the 2003 Professional Developer's Conference (PDC) in Los Angeles and initially was an integral part of what was then code-named Windows "Longhorn" client and is now known as Windows Vista. (Throughout this book, we're still going to refer to the operating system as Longhorn, the codename that included both the client and server versions of the OS. And we'll continue to use the shorter, more convenient Avalon and Indigo nomenclature.) In August 2004, Microsoft made the following decisions:

❑   To remove Windows File System (WinFS)

❑   To port WinFX to downlevel platforms such as Windows XP Service Pack 2 and Windows Server 2003

You may be asking what the core difference between WinFX and Windows Longhorn is. WinFX is a development framework that sits on top of the platform. Windows Longhorn is Microsoft's next-generation operating system. WinFX was intentionally decoupled from the platform to make it portable to other platforms and to minimize the dependencies between the platform and framework. Using WinFX, you can't directly access the shell or the User Experience component (code named Aero).

Microsoft has a history of code naming operating systems after mountains. For example: Windows XP had the code name "Whistler," after a popular ski resort in Vancouver, Canada. Longhorn Server was originally code named Blackcomb (yet another ski resort). The Longhorn Saloon & Grill, a popular bar at the foot of Whistler Mountain, inspired the name Longhorn. I met the saloon's manager on a plane trip a year or so ago—apparently Bill Gates likes to conduct executive meetings in the establishment. Here is the link to the saloon's Web site: `longhornsaloon.ca`.

Why rewrite the .NET Framework? Part of the reason is Moore's law. Hardware technology is developing and innovating by leaps and bounds. In the near future, terabyte drives and ultra-high-resolution displays will be commonplace. Computers are able to handle a greater capacity. Connectivity is at the forefront, along with the need for better security. Standards such as RSS and Web Services are garnering wide adoption and solving integration issues.

For many years, Microsoft had different product divisions working on different solutions for similar problems. For example, in the Win32 API, there are currently over half a dozen ways of generating graphics by using technologies such as the Graphical Device Interface (GDI), DirectX, Direct3D, and others. In developing WinFX, Microsoft took the opportunity to look at the preexisting framework and decided to unify many of the principal APIs, most notably on the presentation and the communication layer. There are several additional reasons why WinFX makes sense:

❑ The Win32 API was designed in the fall of 1992—it's currently over 12 years old. It wasn't originally designed to handle the challenges of Internet and distributed computing environments, especially in terms of security.

❑ DCOM has proven to be overly complicated, lacking the ability to handle asynchronous enterprise-level applications and integrate with multiplatform environments

❑ The Windows visual user interface has not changed much since 1995. All icons and elements are all two-dimensional and can benefit greatly from an upgrade.

Since WinFX is based on the .NET Framework 2.0, you can rest assured that your existing .NET code will continue working. WinFX is primarily designed to provide you with new APIs to leverage the Longhorn platform and new advances in hardware and software. Since the WinFX framework has been downported to Windows XP Service Pack 2 and Windows Server 2003, the code you design will not only work on Windows Longhorn but also on existing systems.

A misconception about WinFX is that it is completely written in managed code. This is largely untrue. Microsoft has written a rich, unmanaged codebase comprising millions of lines of code. It doesn't make sense for them to reinvent the wheel. For example, the Windows threading model works pretty well as is. Using WinFX, Microsoft has provided you with a way to instantiate and control threads in a managed environment. However, behind the scenes WinFX taps into the Win32 API for some of its functionality. The same holds for queuing in Indigo: Why rewrite an entire queuing infrastructure? Indigo leverages the existing Microsoft Message Queue (MSMQ) framework because, frankly, it does the job really well.

Microsoft is currently synchronizing the release of WinFX with the release of the Longhorn betas. For example, Longhorn Beta 2 will be released at the same time as WinFX Beta 2 is released. One of the questions that I've heard many times recently is why would I want to work with these Longhorn-based technologies right now? The short answer is that being an early adopter can give you a competitive advantage. You can gain a better understanding of the technology and gain an early (and larger) market share for new products based on the platform.

Another compelling reason for learning Avalon and Indigo is the simple fact that these technologies are the future of Windows programming. There's no excuse for not being on top of the latest developments on your primary development platform!

Who This Book Is For

This book is designed to provide you with an overview of programming with WinFX, with a special emphasis on Avalon and Indigo. After reading the book, you will be able to:

❑ Upgrade your current Windows .NET applications to take advantage of Longhorn's new programming model, framework, and architecture

❑ Create and deploy Avalon/XAML applications from scratch

This book targets experienced Windows .NET programmers. You'll notice that most of the samples included in this book are written in C#. Programming with WinFX requires the following skill set:

❑ A solid knowledge of fundamental .NET programming concepts in the language of your choice (C# or VB—although the book's examples are in C#, much of this code could be done in VB by experienced VB programmers)

❑ An understanding of the common language runtime (CLR) and managed code

❑ A good handle on XML concepts (such as XML Web Services) and Service Oriented Architecture

❑ Knowledge of the .NET Framework's Base Class API

This book contains plenty of code samples and demonstrations that will help you adapt old applications to take full advantage of the WinFX API and use Longhorn-specific features. Whether you are a .NET developer or an active Longhorn developer, Professional WinFX Beta provides ways to jump easily into this new technology.

If you are an active Longhorn developer, you will feel at ease in these pages. If you are a hobbyist or beginner, Professional WinFX Beta provides a solid entry point to Microsoft's new programming concepts and technologies. The playing field is level in some ways because the technology is new to everyone. If you are starting out, it might be of benefit to read this book from cover to cover.

What This Book Covers

From a big picture perspective, this book delivers an overview of the major APIs and functionality available in WinFX Beta 1. You can fully expect that your code will work on Beta 1 of the framework. Microsoft may decide to make changes to the framework by the time the final version is released. The Object Model (OM) for Avalon and Indigo has matured by leaps and bounds since the 2003 PDC.

In a nutshell, some parts of WinFX will not change between now and the final release; some parts will. If you write code using WinFX Beta 1, expect to be making some changes to it in the future. Depending on what parts of the framework you are using, your mileage may vary. As a rule of thumb, beta code on a beta framework should not be integrated into mission-critical, production environments. For up-to-date guidance (and a release schedule) for WinFX, please consult the Microsoft Longhorn Web site: http://msdn.microsoft.com/longhorn.

We will be talking about familiar concepts such as ADO.NET. As much as possible, we've tried to put it in a "Longhorn" context, tackling issues such as how to bind data to a XAML form.

How This Book Is Structured

The book is divided into the three distinct sections. Each section is composed of chapters that drill down into the particulars of each WinFX technology.

Avalon

Avalon is Longhorn's new presentation subsystem, made accessible through WinFX. Chapters 1 through 4 will provide you with a solid end-to-end overview of the major features of Avalon:

❑ **Chapter 1**—This chapter will provide you with a high-level overview of the important concepts behind Avalon.

❑ **Chapter 2**—This chapter looks at XAML, Microsoft's new Extensible Application Markup Language. You will learn how to create effective forms using XAML for implementations ranging from simple to complex.

❑ **Chapter 3**—Avalon has terrific support for graphics and motion. In this chapter, you learn how to work with shapes, paths, painting, and brushes and find out how to create applications that leverage 2-D animation.

❑ **Chapter 4**—In this chapter, you look at advanced features of Avalon including styling, events, XAML/Windows Forms interoperability, and Avalon 3-D features.

Indigo

Indigo is one of the key pillars of Longhorn, representing the entire communication subsystem. This component comprises an infrastructure based on Web Services and peer-to-peer processing to transmit messages internally and across all types of networks. Indigo's strength lies in facilitating tasks such as creating Web-enabled applications, communicating across application domains, integrating PC-to-PC data transfers, and instant messaging capabilities. Here are the Indigo chapters in the book:

❑ **Chapter 5**—This is an introductory chapter on Indigo. You'll learn the fundamental concepts of Indigo and the Indigo architecture.

❑ **Chapter 6**—This chapter deals with transactions and messaging. You will find out how to send secure, reliable messages and take advantage of Microsoft Message Queuing.

❑ **Chapter 7**—Migration and interoperability are the focus of this chapter. You will learn how to migrate existing communication APIs (such as DCOM, .NET Remoting, Enterprise Services, and many others) to Indigo. You'll also learn how to configure these communication services to interoperate effectively with Indigo.

Data

As with traditional .NET applications, data integration is an important function in any Longhorn-based application. Here is a listing of the data chapters in the book:

❑ **Chapter 8**—This chapter discusses data services, which is the mechanism of setting properties based on values persisted to and retrieved from a data store. It shows you how to bind data to Avalon forms and how to leverage data within the WinFX framework.

❑ **Chapter 9**—This chapter explores ADO.NET and ASP.NET. This chapter will show you how to manipulate data within the WinFX framework.

❑ **Chapter 10**—We will provide an overview of Windows Services. This chapter will explain the new service features in WinFX and how to integrate these services into your Avalon/Indigo applications.

What You Will Not Find in This Book

In this book, you will not find coverage on the Windows File System (WinFS), user experience and shell programming (Aero), or information specific to Beta 2 or the final release of the product. If you are interested in these topics the best place to look is the Longhorn Center on Microsoft's MSDN Web site: `http://msdn.microsoft.com/longhorn`.

What You Need to Use This Book

To write the code and run the samples in this book, you will need the following software:

❑ Windows Longhorn Client Beta 1, Windows XP Service Pack 2, or Windows Server 2003 (you must also install components such as IIS)

❑ Visual Studio 2005 Beta 2

❑ SQL Server 2005

❑ WinFX Beta 1

❑ WinFX Beta 1 Software Developer Kit (SDK)

❑ Optional: Microsoft VirtualPC 2004. (In fact, we strongly recommend that you use this product to install any Beta product. You can download a trial version on the Microsoft Web site.)

Both the WinFX framework and SDK are available in ISO formats. For more detailed information about the system requirements for each of these components, please refer to the appropriate ReadMe files.

XAML Tools

There are many tools available for writing XAML code. Microsoft is currently working on an XAML designer code named *Sparkle*. If you want a designer today, the following third-party tools offer good solutions:

MobiForm Aurora

Aurora is a designer that allows you to produce XAML using the Avalon Object Model. Such a tool is currently missing in the current Visual Studio IDE. With Aurora, you can visually build Avalon documents, graphics, and user interfaces. It enables you not only to draw but also to programmatically create graphic libraries and objects. Finally, Aurora was designed with an extensible plug-in architecture and a well-documented object model. The Avalon chapters in the book were written by experts from MobiForm. To download a trial version of Aurora, visit the following link: `mobiform.com`.

AvPad

Chris Anderson, one of the software architects on the Avalon team, has designed a free, simple XAML designer. Simply plug in your code, and you are able to see the resulting XAML graphics. You can download this tool from `simplegeek.com`.

Indigo Tools

Indigo comes bundled with a bunch of great tools. Pierre Greborio, a solutions architect MVP, has designed many Indigo tools, including an Indigo proxy generator that integrates with Visual Studio 2005 and the Indigo Service Tester to test an Indigo service. You can download these tools on his blog: `http://weblogs.asp.net/pgreborio`.

Languages

XML plays a pivotal role in all facets of WinFX, starting from declarative XAML client user interfaces, MSBuild configuration files, and Indigo support for XML and Simple Object Access Protocol (SOAP) messaging. Most of the nondeclarative logic you'll write using WinFX should primarily be written in C# or VB.NET.

Source Code

As you work through the examples in this book, you may choose to type in all the code manually or to use the source code files that accompany the book. All of the source code used in this book is available for download at www.wrox.com. Once at the site, simply locate the book's title (either by using the Search box or by using one of the title lists), and click the Download Code link on the book's detail page to obtain all the source code for the book.

> *Because many books have similar titles, you may find it easiest to search by ISBN; for this book the ISBN is 0-7645-7874-X (changing to 978-0-7654-7874-8 as the new industry-wide 13-digit numbering system is phased in by January 2007).*

After you download the code, just decompress it with your favorite compression tool. Alternately, you can go to the main Wrox code download page at www.wrox.com/dynamic/books/download.aspx to see the code available for this book and all other Wrox books.

Errata

We make every effort to ensure that there are no errors in the text or in the code. However, no one is perfect, and mistakes do occur. If you find an error in one of our books, such as a spelling mistake or faulty piece of code, we would be very grateful for your feedback. By sending in errata you may save another reader hours of frustration, and at the same time, you will be helping us provide even higher-quality information.

To find the errata page for this book, go to www.wrox.com and locate the title using the Search box or one of the title lists. Then, on the book details page, click the Book Errata link. On this page, you can view all errata that has been submitted for this book and posted by Wrox editors. A complete book list, including links to each book's errata, is also available at www.wrox.com/misc-pages/booklist.shtml.

If you don't spot "your" error on the Book Errata page, go to `www.wrox.com/contact/techsupport.shtml` and complete the form there to send us the error you have found. We'll check the information and, if appropriate, post a message to the book's errata page and fix the problem in subsequent editions of the book.

p2p.wrox.com

For author and peer discussion, join the P2P forums at `p2p.wrox.com`. The forums are a Web-based system for you to post messages relating to Wrox books and related technologies and interact with other readers and technology users. The forums offer a subscription feature to e-mail you topics of interest of your choosing when new posts are made to the forums. Wrox authors, editors, other industry experts, and your fellow readers are present on these forums.

At `p2p.wrox.com`, you will find a number of different forums that will help you, not only as you read this book, but also as you develop your own applications. To join the forums, just follow these steps:

1. Go to `p2p.wrox.com`, and click the Register link.
2. Read the terms of use, and click Agree.
3. Complete the required information to join, provide any optional information you want to, and click Submit.
4. You will receive an e-mail with information describing how to verify your account and complete the joining process.

You can read messages in the forums without joining P2P, but to post your own messages, you must join.

After you join, you can post new messages and respond to messages that other users post. You can read messages at any time on the Web. If you would like to have new messages from a particular forum e-mailed to you, click the Subscribe to this Forum icon by the forum name in the forum listing.

For more information about how to use the Wrox P2P, be sure to read the P2P FAQs for answers to questions about how the forum software works as well as many common questions specific to P2P and Wrox books. To read the FAQs, click the FAQ link on any P2P page.

Contents

Contents

Contents

Contents

Professional WinFX™ Beta: Covers "Avalon" Windows Presentation Foundation and "Indigo" Windows Communication Foundation

Part I
Avalon

1

Avalon

This section of the book provides an introduction to Avalon, a graphics and user interface application programming interface (API) and Extensible Application Markup Language (XAML). These components are a major part of WinFX, the next generation of graphics and communications technologies developed by Microsoft.

The goal of the first four chapters is to equip you with a degree of confidence and expertise in creating and authoring XAML documents and in working with the Avalon API. Avalon is extensive, and covering it in detail could easily span several books. We will be covering key concepts and providing you with the basic skills and knowledge to get great results quickly.

What Is Avalon?

Avalon is the code name for the new presentation API in WinFX. It is revolutionary, not only in its capabilities, but also in how you use it to develop software applications and how you view software and the Web. Avalon is a two-dimensional (2-D) and three-dimensional (3-D) graphics engine with the following characteristics and capabilities:

- ❑ Contains many common user interface components, including buttons, sliders, and edit boxes

- ❑ Does 2-D and 3-D animation

- ❑ Contains hyperlinks (for navigating between documents) and tables

- ❑ Provides various types of grids and panels to assist in layout

- ❑ Has multipage fixed-format and flow-format document layout, styles, storyboards, timelines, effects, data binding, and so on

To get a good mental grip on what documents created in Avalon are capable of, consider a document as a file that has the majority of the features found in a Macromedia Flash document (.SWF) all mixed together, including the following:

❑ HTML page

❑ Cascading Style Sheets (CSS)

❑ Scalable Vector Graphics (SVG)

❑ Microsoft Word document

❑ Virtual Reality Markup Language (VRML)

❑ WinForms controls

Mobiform Software, one of the foremost authorities outside of Microsoft, describes Avalon as "The convergence of documents, media, and applications," where the whole concept of a document, the Internet, and an application begins to blur into something new and more powerful.

This means that within one document you can combine 2-D graphics with 3-D graphics, animate and transform, and apply other effects. Additionally, this API enables you to create applications for either the desktop or the Web with one markup language and, more excitingly, maintains your initial vision of the document structure while maintaining the personal preferences of the users as they interact with the final product.

The Avalon API has been created in .NET 2.0 and can be accessed by any of the .NET languages such as Visual Basic, C#, and managed C++.

At the time of writing this section of the book, the API was still being developed and was not fully complete. All syntax is based on the Beta Release Candidate 2, which was released in June 2005.

Developers have the option of either using C# or VB.NET to code directly against the API. Alternatively, the Avalon objects may be instantiated using the XAML markup, or they can have a mixture of XAML with .NET code behind.

What Is XAML?

XAML is a declarative XML-based language that defines objects and their properties in XML. An XAML parser instantiates and wires up the objects using an appropriate API and sets their properties.

Quite often you will hear XAML and Avalon used interchangeably, but this is incorrect. XAML is simply a form of XML markup. Avalon is the graphics and user interface API. While XAML is used to instantiate Avalon objects, there is nothing that excludes XAML from being used to create objects from other nongraphical APIs. However, at the time of writing, Avalon/XAML runs only on Windows XP or Windows Server 2003 and Longhorn.

When using XAML with Avalon, the procedural code (code behind) is separate from the user interface (UI). The advantage to this approach is that it enables teams to work together at the same time. For example, traditionally designers' and developers' interaction on projects has been negligible; however, with this new API, this barrier has been lowered. A programmer can work on the code behind a document at the same time that a graphics designer works on the UI. This makes for efficient coding practices. Additionally, programmers no longer need to be designers, because the designer's work can be integrated directly into the software. Architects and designers can design and approve their front ends in XAML, which can then be incorporated directly into the software. The developers need to worry only about the back-end logic. Teams of designers can now focus on creating a much richer user interface experience without interrupting the overall development process. Interface skins can be designed; even the localization process of creating applications for different languages gets easier.

Skins are customized interchangeable graphics that enable users to personalize the appearance of their desktop and various applications.

XAML Syntax

XAML is written in XML. The XAML syntax describes objects and properties and their relationship to each other. Properties can be set as attributes. Alternatively, with the use of the period notation, you can specify the object as a property of its parent. The following example shows an object (ListBox) with three children (ListBoxItem one through three). The Content property on the first ListBoxItem object is assigned the value of Item One:

```
<ListBox Name="lbox" Height="127" Width="154">
    <ListBoxItem Name="lBoxItem1" Background="Aqua" Width="100">
        <ContentControl.Content>
            Item One
        </ContentControl.Content>
        <ContentControl.Height>
            30
        </ContentControl.Height>
    </ListBoxItem>
    <ListBoxItem Name="lBoxItem2">
        Item Two
    </ListBoxItem>
    <ListBoxItem Name="lBoxItem3" Content="Item Three" />
</ListBox>
```

For the syntax to be correct, the setting of the Content property on the first ListBoxItem to Item One should be a valid assignment. Therefore, based on that statement, Item One would be considered a subclass of Content. Also note the various manners in which you are able to write the syntax in order to fit your style of coding. Figure 1-1 shows the output produced from either the C# or XAML syntax for creating the parent ListBox, its three children, and their dependent properties.

Figure 1-1

Following is the C# equivalent to the XAML syntax from the previous example:

```
private void WindowLoaded(object sender, EventArgs e) {
        lBox = new ListBox();
        lBox.Width = 154;
        lBox.Height = 127;
        lBoxItem1 = new ListBoxItem();
        lBoxItem1.Content = "Item One";
        lBoxItem1.Background = Brushes.Aqua;
        lBoxItem1.Width = 100;
        lBoxItem1.Height = 30;
        lBox.Items.Add(lBoxItem1);
        lBoxItem2 = new ListBoxItem();
        lBoxItem2.Content = "Item Two";
        lBox.Items.Add(lBoxItem2);
        lBoxItem3 = new ListBoxItem();
        lBoxItem3.Content = "Item Three";
        lBox.Items.Add(lBoxItem3);

        myWindow.Children.Add(lBox);
    }
```

XAML is an example of declarative programming, which describes relationships between variables through the use of functions and logic rules. To come to a solution, the programming is structured as a series of conditions that the application proceeds through to solve the problem presented. XAML is a declarative markup language.

Namespace

A *namespace* is a mechanism used in XML and .NET technologies to group objects together and to prevent naming collisions. A namespace extends the name of an object, much like adding a last name for a person. There might be many Bills in a large group of people, but only one Bill Gates. There might be two or three Node classes in a group of large API's, but when qualified with their namespace prefix, they are unique. Namespaces are also arranged to contain like and related classes. This makes it easier to locate objects and structures while programming. Namespaces can also have child namespaces, which are used for further organization of an API.

The Namespace Hierarchy in Avalon is extensive; it encompasses a large and complex API that includes 2-D and 3-D graphics, user interface type controls, and the animation classes. The API is an addition to the namespaces available in .NET 2.0.

The following list introduces some of the more commonly used namespaces:

❑ System.Windows — This namespace contains the classes and interfaces that are used in creating applications. This namespace defines many common interfaces and structures used throughout the API, such as the Application Class, Window Class, styling, dependency, and the common base classes.

❑ `System.Windows.Controls` — The `Controls` namespace is associated with the application's user interface. This includes menus, hyperlinks, edit boxes (text, check, combo and list boxes), buttons, panels, borders, and sliders for audio and video. The `Viewport3D` (see Chapter 4 to learn more) is also located in this namespace in order to control all 3-D content and interaction.

❑ `System.Windows.Data` — The `Data` namespace controls all the properties for binding properties to data. It is used to specify the source, its classes, and anything specifically associated with implementing the data and its collections.

❑ `System.Windows.Input` — This namespace controls all modes of input, such as a mouse, keyboard, or tablet that a user may interact with when using the application.

❑ `System.Windows.Media` — The `Media` namespace controls all the graphics classes for both 2-D and 3-D. It also defines path segment classes, brushes, colors, image effects, geometry classes, collections, audio, video, enumerations, and structures.

❑ `System.Windows.Media.Animation` — This namespace contains the classes used for 2-D and 3-D animation. This area includes the various `Timelines`, `KeyFrames`, and `Animation` types. (See Chapter 3 to learn more).

❑ `System.Windows.Media.Media3D` — It contains a variety of classes specific to 3-D graphics. These classes are used to further define how the graphics will be presented within an application. Lights, meshes, materials, and 3-D point and vector classes are all included in this namespace.

❑ `System.Windows.Navigation` — This namespace is dedicated to the classes and interfaces used for application navigation, whether it is the navigation between windows, panes, or journaling.

❑ `System.Windows.Shapes` — This is the namespace for all the primitive 2-D shapes used within the API. They are the ellipse, glyphs, line, path, polygon, polyline, and rectangle. These classes are quite similar to those found in Scalable Vector Graphics (SVG).

❑ `System.Windows.Resources` — This namespace contains all the classes that use resources. This is the area of the namespace where you would define properties for styles, animations, and localization that can be accessed by any object, by referencing its name such as `Style="{StaticResource ResourceName}"`, within the application.

❑ `System.Windows.Serialization` — This namespace supports the conversion of the Avalon object model to the XAML declarative language and vice versa.

Important Concepts

This section discusses key Avalon API concepts that are required and used in every application. The next part of the chapter discusses the hierarchical structure of documents and elements and the manner in which properties are passed down from parent to child within the API.

Trees in Avalon

In Avalon there are two important types of trees: Logical Trees and Visual Trees. These trees define aspects of the Avalon API and the object hierarchy.

Logical Tree

Much like an XML document hierarchy, the Logical Tree defines the relationship between objects and their parents. This tree helps determine how properties from one element are inherited from its parent and how event routings occur for the application's events.

You navigate the tree using higher-level classes. For example, `Panel`-derived classes have children, whereas `ListItem`-derived classes have an `Items` property for accessing their children. To navigate the tree without having to worry about the types of objects located in the tree, Avalon has provided the `LogicalTreeHelper` class. This class provides `GetParent`, `GetChildren`, and `FindLogicalNode` methods for traversing the tree. The document's Logical Tree structure is represented on the right side of Figure 1-2.

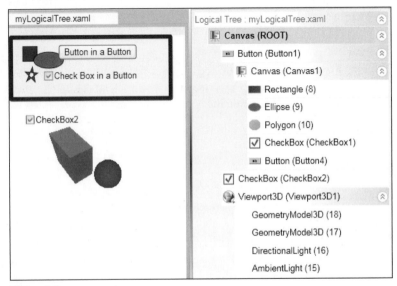

Figure 1-2

Visual Tree

The other tree layer in Avalon defines how an object is rendered. Unlike the Logical Tree, this one is more conceptual. It depicts the structure of visuals and their basic services and properties such as hit-testing and coordinate transformations. For example, a button in Avalon is not rendered simply as a button; it is rendered as a set of visuals. These visuals comprise a structure of primitive drawing objects (brushes, gradients, and primitive objects). The button is rendered as a Visual Tree of drawing primitives. Unlike the Logical Tree, the Visual Tree cannot be navigated through the API. The Visual Tree becomes significant when you look at styles and customization of how objects are rendered. This customization and styling of objects is performed at the level of the Visual Tree.

Dependency Properties

The `FrameworkElement` is the initial class. It forms the baseline that separates the higher framework from the visual presentation of the API. It provides the basic structure implementations for specific methods that are defined in its parent, the `UIElement`. The `UIElement` is the primary base class for frameworks in Avalon; it dictates all basic presentation and rendering characteristics.

The dependency properties for the `FrameworkElement` are properties that are common on most every visible object.

What Is the Dependency Property System?

`DependencyProperties` are registered with the Dependency Property System. These static properties are used as lookup keys to access properties on objects in Avalon. Properties that participate in the Dependency Property System can be styled, animated, used in data binding, and used in expressions.

Regular `DependencyProperties` are used on the objects that are declared. For example, the `Ellipse` class has a `RadiusX` property. It has a corresponding static `DependencyProperty` called `RadiusXProperty`, which is used in animation and other functions. You get the value of a `DependencyProperty` on an object by using the `GetValue()` method and passing in the `DependencyProperty` you are interested in. Another kind of `DependencyProperty` is attached. These properties are not used on the objects that declare them, but are used (inherited) by other classes.

A good example of this is the `DockPanel` in Figure 1-3 where it shows that the button is placed to the right side of the panel. When the property `Dock` is an attached property used by one of the child elements within the `DockPanel` in order to place it, the other two are distributed evenly across the `DockPanel`.

```
<DockPanel Width="300" Height="50" Background="Gray">
    <Button DockPanel.Dock="Right" Width="50" Content="Button"/>
</DockPanel>
```

Figure 1-3

The following code snippet is a gross generalization of what the Dependency Property System looks like:

```
public class DependencyObject
    {

        public static DependencyProperty dependencyProperty1 =
          DependencyProperty.Register("prop1", typeof(String), typeof(Button);

        public static DependencyProperty dependencyProperty2 =
          DependencyProperty.Register("prop2", typeof(String), typeof(Button);

        System.Collections.Hashtable hashTable = new
          System.Collections.Hashtable();

        public object GetValue(DependencyProperty dp)
        {
            return hashTable[dp];
        }

        public void SetValue(DependencyProperty dp, object value)
```

```
    {
            return hashTable.Add(dp, value);
    }
```

Dependency properties are always static variables and are very common within the Avalon API. They are used as a key in locating various properties on an object.

Although Avalon creates dependency properties, they can be created and used by developers, too. In order to create a dependency property, in Avalon, it must be registered. To register the property, you supply the property name, the type associated with the property, and the type of the owner.

Consider the following code, which creates a `Rectangle` and sets its `Height`:

```
Rectangle rect = new Rectangle();
rect.Height = 40;
```

Looking at the `Rectangle` class in the `System.Windows.Shapes` namespace, you will note that it has a `DependencyProperty` for the `RectangleHeight`.

```
public static DependencyProperty HeightProperty;
```

The following code is also valid and equivalent to the preceding code:

```
Rectangle rect = new Rectangle();
rect.SetValue(Rectangle.HeightProperty), 40;
```

While dependency properties are normally used in the class in which they are declared, some can be "attached" to other classes. Consider the following:

```
Button button = new Button();
button.Width = 40;
button.Height = 20;
```

This code creates a button and sets its width and height, but what is the position of the button? The answer to that depends on its parent. If the parent of the button is a `Canvas`, then you set the position by using dependency properties that belong to the `Canvas` class. These properties are then attached to the button.

```
button.SetValue(Canvas.LeftProperty, 40);
button.SetValue(Canvas.TopProperty, 30);
```

However, if the parent of the button is a `DockPanel`, the position is set by using dependency properties that belong to the `DockPanel` class.

```
button.SetValue(DockPanel.DockProperty, Dock.Left);
```

A control located in a table, grid, or panel will use attached dependency properties to determine its position within its parent. Regular and attached dependency properties can also be set in XAML, as in the following example:

```
<Button Name="btnOK" Height="37" Width="80" Canvas.Top="313" Canvas.Left="268"
    BorderBrush="Black" FontSize="12">OK</Button>
```

Here, the button has two dependent properties (`Canvas.Top` and `Canvas.Left`). They inherit their location from their parent, `Canvas`, which could be either the root element or possibly be nested within something larger itself. A period between two properties denotes a dependency property to its parent.

Jump Start

To begin creating an Avalon application, you must already have the WinFX Software Development Kit (SDK) installed. This is available from the MSDN Web site at Microsoft. To follow along with the demos in the next chapters, you must also have a copy of Microsoft Visual Studio 2005 installed to compile and run the applications.

> *Prior to installing and working with this technology, you must be running on the following: Longhorn, Windows XP with Service Pack 2, or Windows Server 2003 with Service Pack 1. Additionally, you must have the latest version of the .NET Framework.*
>
> *Microsoft Visual Studio 2005 and Mobiform Software Aurora are both optional but make constructing much faster and easier.*
>
> *To download the latest version of Avalon go to* http://msdn.microsoft.com/longhorn.
>
> *To download Microsoft Visual Studio 2005 go to* http://lab.msdn.microsoft.com/vs2005. *(XP Home Edition will not work with this program.)*
>
> *To download Mobiform Software Aurora go to* mobiform.com/Eng/aurora.html.

Creating an Application

To create an application, follow these steps:

1. Open Visual Studio and then select New ⇨ Project from the File menu.

2. The program will bring up a dialog window where you can set your coding preference (C# or VB.NET) in the project type frame.

3. In the Visual Studio installed templates frame, select the Avalon Application. Name the project **HelloWorld**, as shown in Figure 1-4, and click OK.

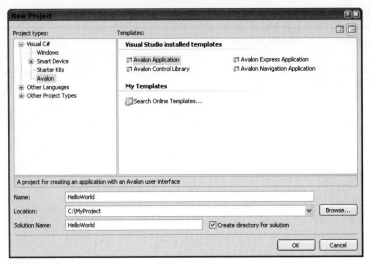

Figure 1-4

4. When the project opens, select `Window1.xaml` in the Solution Explorer panel.

5. Inside the Grid elements insert the following code:

```
<Button>Hello World!</Button>
```

6. Change the run mode from Debug to Release, and then click the Start button, F5, or Build Solution from the Build menu to compile and launch the application.

Once launched, the application appears as if nothing has happened apart from displaying "Hello World!" In fact, the entire window is a giant button, because the button is within a grid. To make it look more like a button, simply add values for the `Width` and `Height` properties (as in the following code) and then rebuild the program.

```
<Button Width="100" Height="50">Hello World!</Button>
```

7. Next, modify the button so that it is housed in a canvas. Use the following code as a guide:

At the time of writing, the schemas were as stated in the sample that follows. However, the schema is dynamically generated by Visual Studio upon opening the document. If you are hand coding, check with the Microsoft Software Development Kit (SDK) to get the current URLs.

```
<Window x:Class="SampleApp.Window1"
    xmlns="http://schemas.microsoft.com/winfx/avalon/2005"
    xmlns:x="http://schemas.microsoft.com/winfx/xaml/2005"
    Text="SampleApp"
    >
    <Canvas Background="Lime">
        <Button Name="btnOK" Width="100" Height="50" Canvas.Top="236"
            Canvas.Left="400" BorderBrush="Red" FontSize="14">OK</Button>
    </Canvas>
</Window>
```

Upon running the application again, notice that the button is now using the attached dependency properties on the `Canvas` to indicate its position. The `Name` property is very significant in the XAML. When Avalon parses the XAML, it will create an object with a name of `btnOK`. This object can be used in the `CodeBehind` as a declared object. Build and run the sample. When you run the application, you will see a purple button with a red border placed in the middle of a lime green window.

8. Next, you add some `CodeBehind`. Open the `Window1.xaml.cs` (located in the Solution Explorer tab) code behind file. In it you will see the `WindowLoaded` method. This method is triggered when the window is loaded. Uncomment the method and follow the instructions above it.

9. In the `Window1.xaml` file, set the `Loaded` property to the value `"WindowLoaded"` as shown in the following code:

```
<Window x:Class="SampleApp.Window1"
    xmlns="http://schemas.microsoft.com/winfx/avalon/2005"
    xmlns:x="http://schemas.microsoft.com/winfx/xaml/2005"
    Text="SampleApp"
    Loaded="WindowLoaded"
    x:CodeBehind="Window.xaml.cs">
```

This indicates to Avalon that when the window is loaded, the `WindowLoaded` method should be called.

10. Return to the `Window1.xaml.cs` code behind file, and add the following code:

```
private void WindowLoaded(object sender, EventArgs e)
{
  btnOK.Background = Brushes.BlueViolet;
}
```

Because the method is called, the background property will be set. You do not need to declare the variable `"btnOK"` because this was already declared in the XAML document.

You may notice that objects morph into variables; this demonstrates the power of Avalon at work. In the XAML, `"btnOk"` is considered an object by the markup. However, when the object is passed back to the logic layer, the C#, in the `CodeBehind`, *recognizes it as a variable because it has a name* `"btnOK"`.

11. Next, hook up an event for the button. This should be very familiar to .NET developers who work with .NET common controls. In the `WindowLoaded` method, hook up a click event to the button. This event will be tripped when the button is clicked.

```
private void WindowLoaded(object sender, EventArgs e)
{
  btnOK.Background = Brushes.BlueViolet;
  btnOK.Click += new RoutedEventHandler(btnOK_Click);
}

void btnOK_Click(object sender, RoutedEventArgs e)
{
  System.Windows.MessageBox.Show("Hello Avalon Developer!");
}
```

12. Press F5 to view the application. You will see that the button has a blue-violet background and a message box pops up when you click the button.

Summary

From this chapter, you should now begin to envision the possibilities of XAML and Avalon for developing better software. You have the option to program the logic using any .NET language, in any manner, including directly against the API; create and use custom controls and integrate them into the API; and so on.

You now know that Avalon is the engine that parses the XAML markup and wires it to objects in the Avalon API. You have a basic understanding of how the objects are placed within the Logical Tree in an application and in parent/child relationships, and how defining the Visual Tree sets the stage for styles and control over the rendering of object content.

The key namespaces present in the Avalon API were introduced. As you move forward through the chapters that follow, these namespaces will be fleshed out in more detail.

With some of the basic concepts behind the structure and hierarchy used in Avalon under your belt, the following chapters will also introduce you to Avalon's most common elements and controls. In addition, you will look at some new user interface concepts and see how your old common controls found in Windows forms are anything but common in Avalon.

2

Avalon Documents in XAML Markup

XAML is the most common method of creating a UI for a WinFX application. As discussed in the first chapter, XAML is derived from XML. Where XML is commonly used as a means to describe data, XAML combined with Avalon does much more.

Understanding XAML

Following is an example of a basic XML file:

```
<?xml version="1.0" encoding="ISO-8859-1"?>
<Window Name="MyWindow">
    <Button Name="MyButton">Hello XML World</Button>
</Window>
```

It is important to note that XAML itself is nothing more than a markup language to create and instantiate an object model, in this case Avalon. It is the power of the Avalon graphics engine that allows you to create rich interfaces, support flow control, and create the UI without any code.

Following is the XAML equivalent to the XML shown previously:

```
<Window xmlns="http://schemas.microsoft.com/winfx/avalon/2005"
Name="MyWindow">
    <Button Name="MyButton">
        Hello XAML World
    </Button>
</Window>
```

When code is required—for example, when events are triggered by users to enhance their experience—a separate file would be created in a .NET procedural code such as C# or VB.NET. This file would then be referenced with the `CodeBehind` attribute. The `xmlns:x`, also present in the code that follows, indicates to the parser which assemblies and namespaces need to be referenced to execute the code.

```
<Window xmlns="http://schemas.microsoft.com/winfx/avalon/2005"
    xmlns:x="http://schemas.microsoft.com/winfx/xaml/2005"
    CodeBehind="myLogic.cs" Name="MyWindow">
```

All XAML documents are saved with a `.xaml` file extension and require the mapping to point to the Avalon and XAML namespaces (see previous sample). As you progress through this chapter, you may note that Avalon has the ability to morph elements; classes will become tags, attributes will turn into properties and events, and even XML namespaces change into common language runtime namespaces. For example, a button written in XAML is an object, but when it is referenced in the C# `CodeBehind`, it is considered a variable because it has a name.

Whereas traditional user interfaces (UI) were written by software developers, the Avalon API now empowers designers to control the layout and presentation of their application regardless of where it will ultimately be viewed. The API provides a selection of standard and specialized panels in which to display a variety of documents a specific way. Instead of a single page that scrolls forever, you can actually navigate through documents like a book. Additionally, the API provides specialized classes that control how the text flows despite the end user's preferences. The API maintains the intended appearance and adapts these settings to the end user's choice of text and screen size. This, in turn, speeds up the development process for testing various screen sizes and localized versions of software products.

To effectively define the various types of layouts available, Microsoft has placed them in three namespaces:

- ❏ `System.Windows.Controls`—This encompasses many of the interactive controls in the application, such as buttons, check boxes, and list boxes.

- ❏ `System.Windows.Controls.Primitives`—These are mainly base classes for the more complex controls used on the interface, such as `BulletPanel`, `RepeatButton`, and `TabPanel`.

- ❏ `System.Windows.Documents`—As its name implies, this is the namespace used to programmatically create documents. It also controls the text object model and editing capabilities.

The Avalon API Hierarchy

Now that you know where the elements are coming from in the API, let's discuss some of the more important base classes.

UIElement

The `UIElement`, from the `System.Windows` namespace, is the base class from which many visual objects are derived. It determines each element's initial appearance, layout, position, and user interaction.

The following table defines the most commonly used dependency properties of the UIElement.

Property	Definition
AllowDrop	Enables the element to have drag-and-drop capabilities.
IsEnabled	A Boolean type valued property that allows you to control whether a control is to work or not. For example, when creating a login interface, the OK button can have the property IsEnabled="False" until the user enters his/her username and password.
IsFocused	A Boolean type valued property that determines whether the control has keyboard focus or not.
IsMouseOver	Also a Boolean type valued property that controls mouse events when over an element as well as its children.
Opacity	A double type valued property that gets or sets the level of opacity an object has. The value range is from 0 (transparent) to 1(opaque).
Visibility	Gets or sets the visibility of an object.

FrameworkElement

Derived from UIElement, the FrameworkElement is also a base class. It is the class from which most visual elements inherit their appearance and features—for example, the width and height of a ToolTip, context menu, or cursor. The first of three key areas that pertain in particular to Visual Studio developers and is found on this element is the Name property. When writing the .NET code, you access an object in the XAML document by referencing its Name property.

Consider the following XAML:

```
<Canvas Name="MyCanvas">
    <Button Name="btnOK" Height="37" Width="80" Canvas.Top="313" Canvas.Left="268"
        BorderBrush="Red" FontSize="14">OK</Button>
</Canvas>
```

To access the button via your CodeBehind, use the Name of the object "btnOK" as a declared variable in your C#. The variable has full IntelliSense and behaves like a regular defined variable. Figure 2-1 illustrates how IntelliSense assists you as you code.

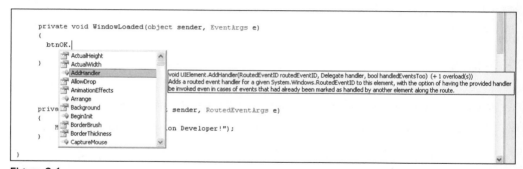

Figure 2-1

When an application is compiled, dynamic code is created in a hidden file. It contains the variable declarations for the object(s) in the XAML file. To see this generated file, select an object in the code behind the file, right-click, and select the Go To Definition option from the context menu. The variable was created in a partial class. The partial class is new syntax in .NET 2.0. It allows a class to be spread over multiple source code files. A partial class is especially effective for large projects where more than one programmer is involved in its development. It is not necessary to add to or modify the partial class because it is dynamically generated and will be overwritten upon compilation.

Following is a sample of generated code for a button:

```
public partial class Window1 : System.Windows.Window,
System.Windows.Serialization.IPageConnector {

    protected internal System.Windows.Controls.Button btnOK;

    private bool _contentLoaded;

    private SampleApp.MyApp MyApplication {
        get {
            return ((SampleApp.MyApp)(System.Windows.Application.Current));
        }
    }
}
```

The second area of note is a class found in the `FrameworkElement` is the `LogicalTreeHelper`, which is used to locate an object in the Logical Tree by its name. It contains static methods for locating an object by its name as well as methods to retrieve the children of that `FrameworkElement` present in the Logical Tree.

The third area is the `TagProperty`, an object that is not actually used by Avalon. Instead, it has been created for developers to use to associate an Avalon object to an object or piece of information in their application.

Following is a table of the common properties used in the `FrameworkElement`.

Property	Definition
Cursor	This is a read/write property that allows you to get or set the cursor. With this property you would set the width and height, the representation of the cursor if it is to change states on mouseEvents, and so on.
FlowDirection	This determines the manner in which all of the panel's elements should flow. The values can be LeftToRightThenTopToBottom, RightToLeftThenTopToBottom, TopToBottomThenLeftToRight, or TopToBottomThenRightToLeft.
Focusable	A Boolean type valued property to determine whether an element may receive focus. By default, elements are not focusable.
Height	A double type valued property that gets or sets the height of an element

Property	Definition
HorizontalAlignment	Determines how the control will be displayed along the horizontal plane. Although the control is ultimately dependent on its parent as to its layout, with this property the values can vary from Left, Center, Right to Stretch. Stretch is the default value for this property, which means that it is evenly laid across the parent element. Note: Explicit height and width values applied on the parent element will take precedence over the alignment properties.
Name	This is used to get or set the identity of an element. Using the Name property is an effective way of referring to a specific element in code in cases of events or styling. Each element must be uniquely identified. Refer to the Style property if you want to affect more than one element.
LogicalTreeHelper	A means of locating an object in the Logical Tree by its Name. The class also has methods to retrieve the children of a `FrameworkElement` present in the Logical Tree.
Margin	The space surrounding an Element. To set the margin requires four double values separated with commas. Instantiate the margin's values as a string in the order `<Element Margin="Left,Top,Right,Bottom" />`.
Resources	Gets or sets the resources required for the immediate use in order to render the elements present within the panel. (See the "Resources" section to learn more.)
Style	This is used to get or set the style of an object(s) from the resource. For example, to make all the buttons appear like gel buttons the syntax would be `<button style="GelButton" />`. (See "Styles" for more information).
Tag	This property is made available for developers to use to associate an Avalon object to an object or piece of information in their own application.
ToolTip	This property is a small pop-up window to enter a label as to the control's purpose. The ToolTip is triggered when the mouse hovers over the control.
VerticalAlignment	Determines how the control will be displayed along the vertical plane. Although the control is ultimately dependent on its parent for its layout, with this property the values can be Top, Center, Bottom, or Stretch. Stretch is the default value for this property, which means it is evenly laid across the parent element. Note: Explicit height and width values applied on the parent element will take precedence over the alignment properties.
Width	A double typed value property that gets or sets the width of an element.

The `UIElement` and the `FrameworkElement` are two of the most important elements in the API. It is these two elements that influence the basic appearance of each and every other element present in the API. For example, `Height` and `Width` are two properties that are inherited from the `FrameworkElement`. Based on the previous table, you know that both properties have double type values; this means that any element in the entire API also has double type value, for this is a property inherited from the `UIElement`. Being aware of the basic structures of the API will make building applications that much easier.

Working with Controls

This next section will discuss the various controls that you can add to your panels to create the layout of your UI. Avalon has a variety of panels for hosting controls. This section will focus on the controls themselves. The subsequent section will go into more depth on the panels and other control hosts.

A control is anything that requires interaction from the user. Avalon has a rich set of controls, including many similar to those available in Win32 and some additional controls. A key difference between the Avalon controls and those previously used in Windows development is that the look and behavior of the control can be modified or changed completely without complex source code. Most of the derived look and feel of a control can be accomplished declaratively in the XAML document.

The functionality of a control in Avalon is actually spread over two base classes: the `FrameworkElement` class and the `Control` class. The `FrameworkElement` has enough of the base implementation that it can be used for what we typically define as a control. Commonly used dependency properties were defined earlier in the chapter. (See the properties table in the "Framework Element" section to review.)

Dependency Properties

The following table shows some of the more commonly used properties found on the `Control` class.

Property	Description
Background	This property gets or sets the brush used to define the control's appearance. This could be a solid color, a linear or radial gradient, an image, or an opacity mask. (See the "Brushes" section to learn more.)
BorderBrush	This also gets or sets the brush to apply; however, it applies only to the brush for the outline of the control.
BorderThickness	Gets or sets the breadth of the outline surrounding the control.
FontFamily	Gets or sets the name of the font to apply on the control.
FontSize	Gets or sets the size of the font to be used on the control's text.
FontStretch	Determines the amount of stretch to apply to the font on the control.
FontStyle	Gets or sets the style that is applied to the font used on the control. (See the "Styles" section to learn more.)

Property	Description
FontWeight	Determines the thickness of the font to be applied to the control's text.
Foreground	Gets or sets the brush used to define the appearance to the control's foreground (usually the text on the control). As with the Background property, one may opt to use a solid color, a linear or radial gradient, an image, or an opacity mask to alter the appearance of the control's foreground. (See the "Brushes" section to learn more.)
HorizontalContentAlignment	Gets or sets how the content will be placed horizontally on the control. It too has values of Left, Center, Right, and Stretch. Stretch is the default value, which stretches it out across the control evenly. However, the stretch value is canceled out when the height and width of the control have been defined.
Padding	Gets or sets the space surrounding the control.
VerticalContentAlignment	Gets or sets how the content will be placed vertically on the control. It too has values of Top, Center, Bottom, and Stretch. Stretch is the default value, which stretches it out across the control evenly. However, the stretch value is canceled out when the height and width of the control have been defined.

The Control class is a public base class derived from FrameworkElement. Elements based on the Control class also inherit all of their properties from both the FrameworkElement and UIElement. The Control base class contains additional properties for Font, Border, and Background.

Control Types

In WinFX controls are separated into 10 groups (patterns). The separation is based on similarities and unique features that distinguish them from the other types of controls. Due to space limitations, this book discusses only the first six.

- ❑ ContentControl
- ❑ DocumentViewer
- ❑ InkCanvas
- ❑ ItemsControl
- ❑ RangeBase
- ❑ Thumb
- ❑ TextBoxBase
- ❑ PasswordBox
- ❑ ResizeGrip
- ❑ Separator

Content Controls

These are controls that can hold content and use the `Content` property in which to contain it. This property acts as an object that is typically set to accept one child (usually a string). But this value can be set to contain other more complex objects such as a panel that can have more than one child. This approach of using a panel as the content within content controls will ultimately change the way that you view and use them. The following is the list of controls grouped under content controls:

- ❑ `ButtonBase`
- ❑ `Frame`
- ❑ `GroupItem`
- ❑ Headered content controls
- ❑ `ListBoxItem`
- ❑ `Label`
- ❑ `ScrollViewer`
- ❑ `StatusBarItem`
- ❑ `ToolTip`
- ❑ `Window`

ButtonBase

In Avalon, the `Button`, `RepeatButton`, and `ToggleButton` are the three types of buttons derived from the `ButtonBase` class. The `RepeatButton` repeats the click event until the user releases the mouse button. The `ToggleButton` is a button that has two states like that of an on/off switch. Their basic syntax is virtually the same. Following is a simple example of each:

```
<StackPanel>
    <Button>Button</Button>
    <ToggleButton>ToggleButton</ToggleButton>
    <RepeatButton>RepeatButton</RepeatButton>
</StackPanel>
```

The following example uses an image as the content within a button:

```
<StackPanel>
    <Button>
        <Image Source="Flower.jpg"/>
    </Button>
</StackPanel>
```

When the window opens up, it will be filled with the image that acts as a button.

Now apply more complex content such as a panel that contains an image and text. Using the same code, define the `Button`'s `Height` and `Width`, wrap a `DockPanel` around the image, and add a `TextBlock`. Figure 2-2 is a simple example of how you can apply complex content to a button.

```
<StackPanel>
    <Button Height="100" Width="375">
        <DockPanel>
            <Image Source="Flower.png"/>
            <TextBlock>Button with an Image and a body of Text</TextBlock>
        </DockPanel>
    </Button>
</StackPanel>
```

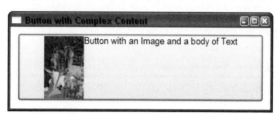

Figure 2-2

The Content of a content control is typically set to a string, but the child of the control can have a more complex object (like panels) that in themselves can have many elements.

Frame

The `Frame` is one of the more interesting content controls because it references contents from another tree. Several `Frames` can be used within a single XAML document. Each `Frame` loads the content with the `Frame`'s `Source` property. Navigation within the `Frame` affects only the content of that `Frame` and not the content of the rest of the document housing the `Frame`.

```
<StackPanel Orientation="Horizontal" Margin="3,3,3,3">
    <Frame Background="LightGray" Width="350" Height="312"
        Source="DocumentOne.xaml"/>
    <Frame Background="Gray" Width="120" Height="100" Source="DocumentTwo.xaml"/>
</StackPanel>
```

Figure 2- 3 illustrates how two different documents can be referenced and viewed independently despite being placed next to one another.

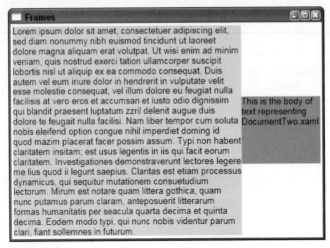

Figure 2-3

Headered Content Controls

The headered content control defines a `Header` property and a `Content` property. The headered content control exists when there is a label or header and a single content item. Unlike the headered items controls, which allow plural content, this control supports only one content item. Currently, there are two types of headered content controls: the `TabItem` and the `Expander`.

`TabItem` is used in conjunction with the `TabControl`. `TabControl` contains the collection of tabs, while `TabItem` controls each individual tab within the group. Figure 2-4 illustrates the output of the following code:

```
<TabControl Height="113" Width="188">
    <ItemsControl.Items>
        <TabItem Name="TabItem1" IsSelected="True">
            <ContentControl.Content>
                Tab Item Content on Tab1
            </ContentControl.Content>
            <HeaderedContentControl.Header>
                TabItem1
            </HeaderedContentControl.Header>
        </TabItem>
        <TabItem Name="TabItem2">
            <ContentControl.Content>
                Tab Item Content on Tab2
            </ContentControl.Content>
            <HeaderedContentControl.Header>
                TabItem2
            </HeaderedContentControl.Header>
        </TabItem>
        <TabItem Name="TabItem3">
            <ContentControl.Content>
                Tab Item Content on Tab3
```

```
                </ContentControl.Content>
                <HeaderedContentControl.Header>
                        TabItem3
                </HeaderedContentControl.Header>
        </TabItem>
        <TabItem Name="TabItem4">
                <ContentControl.Content>
                        Tab Item Content on Tab4
                </ContentControl.Content>
                <HeaderedContentControl.Header>
                        TabItem 4
                </HeaderedContentControl.Header>
        </TabItem>
    </ItemsControl.Items>
</TabControl>
```

Figure 2-4

The `Expander` allows the user to view or collapse additional information attached to the headered content. Figure 2-5 shows you the two states of an `Expander`.

```
<StackPanel Height="50" Width="500" Orientation="Horizontal">
    <Expander Width="150" IsExpanded="True" Background="Red" Header="Headered
        Content 1" Content="Viewed Content"/>
    <Expander Width="150" HorizontalAlignment="Left" IsExpanded="False"
        Background="Red" Header="Headered Content 2" Content="Collapsed Content"/>
</StackPanel>
```

Figure 2-5

ListBoxItem

As the name implies, this controls the individual items within a `ListBox`.

Label

This control allows you to provide information about the application to the user. Additionally, it can be used as a keyboard access to controls in dialog boxes.

```
<StackPanel Orientation="Horizontal">
    <Label Height="40" Width="150">
        This is a label.
    </Label>
    <ListBox Height="20" Width="150">
        <ListBoxItem>Apples</ListBoxItem>
    </ListBox>
</StackPanel>
```

Figure 2-6 shows the result of the preceding code.

Figure 2-6

DocumentViewer

This control enables you to create environments for your fixed or flow documents, while allowing users to customize their viewing experience and maintaining the integrity of your document.

```
<DocumentViewer Zoom="250">
    Document Structure here (see Document section for markup syntax)
</DocumentViewer>
```

InkCanvas

InkCanvas is a new control that allows you to dynamically write on the application with your mouse or digitizer. Figure 2-7 shows the output of the preceding code with dynamically generated script, which occurs when a user passes the mouse over InkCanvas.

```
<InkCanvas Background="Beige" EditingMode="Ink" Width="600" Height="300" />
```

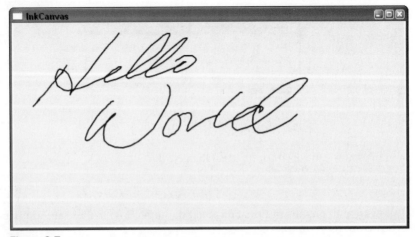

Figure 2-7

Items Controls

Unlike the previous control class, the `Items Control` class does not have the `content` property; instead it holds a series of items within a collection, hence `ItemsCollection`. This collection is generic and accepts objects as valid items. The collection can be one or many items. Typically, the item is text, but it can be other objects including visuals.

The following lists some examples of items controls:

- ❏ `MenuBase`
- ❏ `HeaderedItemsControl`
- ❏ `Selector`
- ❏ `StatusBar`

MenuBase

Within this class there are two types of menus: the `Menu` and the `ContextMenu`. The first one acts as a container for the `MenuItem` control (as mentioned in the next section). The `ContextMenu` allows you to extend the optionability of a control through the enabling the mouse right-click.

The `ContextMenu` is a little different from the other Items controls, for it sits within another control and creates a menu in the form of a pop-up. In the sample that follows, the advantage of adding the `ContextMenu` is that it empowers the `Button` with both left- and right-click functionality; the left mouse key is used to click the button, and the right key is used to view and select from the menu. In Figure 2-8, you can see the `ContextMenu` contained within the button upon right-clicking.

```
<Canvas>
    <Button Width="300" Height="45">A ContextMenu within a Button
        <Button.ContextMenu>
            <ContextMenu>
                <MenuItem Header="File"/>
                <MenuItem Header="New"/>
                <MenuItem Header="SaveAs"/>
                <MenuItem Header="Recent Files">
                    <MenuItem Header="DocumentOne.txt"/>
                    <MenuItem Header="SpreadSheetOne.xls"/>
                </MenuItem>
            </ContextMenu>
        </Button.ContextMenu>
    </Button>
</Canvas>
```

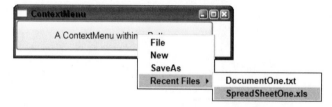

Figure 2-8

HeaderedItem Controls

`HeaderedItem` controls have two components: the header (title/caption) for the control and the items collection holding the children or content. They include:

❑ `MenuItem`

❑ `ToolBar`

The `MenuItem` is an example of this type of control, where the header specifies the label for the `MenuItem` and the `ItemsCollection` contains all the submenu items. The following example shows a `MenuItem` control (see Figure 2-9):

```
<Menu>
    <MenuItem Header="File">
      <MenuItem Header="New"/>
      <MenuItem Header="New2"/>
      <MenuItem Header="submenu">
        <MenuItem Header="submenuitem1"/>
        <MenuItem Header="submenuitem2">
          <MenuItem Header="submenuitem21"/>
        </MenuItem>
        <MenuItem Header="submenuitem3"/>
      </MenuItem>
    </MenuItem>
</Menu>
```

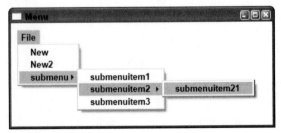

Figure 2-9

The `ToolBar` and `ToolBarTray` are two new controls that work together much as the `Menu` and `MenuItem` controls do. The `ToolBarTray` is the container, and the `ToolBar` displays the item. This control enables you to create your own vector graphic (such as an icon) and have the corresponding text next to it. This particular control ultimately allows you to create your own vector-based graphics that could be 2-D, 3-D, or animated. Figure 2-10 illustrates how the `ToolBar` and `ToolBarTray` work together.

```
<ToolBarTray>
    <ToolBar>
        <Canvas Height="100" Width="100">
            <Rectangle Fill="#FFFF0000" Height="25" Name="Chimney"
                Canvas.Left="59" Stroke="#FF000000"
                Canvas.Top="22.7383333333333" Width="9" />
            <Rectangle Fill="#FF0000FF" Height="38" Name="HouseBase"
```

```
                    Canvas.Left="27" Stroke="#FF000000" Canvas.Top="53.7383333333333"
                    Width="42" />
                <Polygon Fill="#FF008000" Name="Roof" Canvas.Left="0"
                    Points="23,56.7383333333333 48,7.73833333333333
                    74,57.7383333333333" Stroke="#FF000000" Canvas.Top="0" />
                <Rectangle Fill="#FFFFFF00" Height="12" Name="RightWindow"
                    Canvas.Left="55" Stroke="#FF000000" Canvas.Top="62.7383333333333"
                    Width="10" />
                <Rectangle Fill="#FFFFFF00" Height="12" Name="LeftWindow"
                    Canvas.Left="32" Stroke="#FF000000" Canvas.Top="61.7383333333333"
                    Width="10" />
                <Rectangle Fill="#FFFF0000" Height="18" Name="Door"
                    Canvas.Left="43" Stroke="#FF000000" Canvas.Top="73.7383333333333"
                    Width="10" />
            </Canvas>
        </ToolBar>
        <ToolBar>
            <TextBlock HorizontalAlignment="Stretch" VerticalAlignment="Center"
                FontSize="20">Body of Text</TextBlock>
        </ToolBar>
    </ToolBarTray>
```

Figure 2-10

Selector

The `Selector` class includes any control that has multiple children from which a user can select.

Examples of `Selector` controls are:

❑ ListBox

❑ ComboBox

❑ RadioButtonList

❑ TabControl

Typically, you would expect that a `ListBox` would contain `ListItems`:

```
<ListBox>
    <ListItem>Item 1</ListItem>
    <ListItem>Item 2</ListItem>
    <ListItem>Item 3</ListItem>
    <ListItem>Item 4</ListItem>
    <ListItem>Item 5</ListItem>
</ListBox>
```

But part of the power and flexibility of Avalon is that visuals are interchangeable when you are defining content and rendering. This means that you are no longer confined to having only ListItems within a ListBox. The following code and Figure 2-11 illustrate how you can place a variety of controls and have them contained within a ListBox:

```
<ListBox>
      <TextBlock>Item 1</TextBlock>
      <RadioButton>Item 2</RadioButton>
      <TextBox>Item 3</TextBox>
      <Button>Item 4</Button>
      <ListItem>Item 5</ListItem>
</ListBox>
```

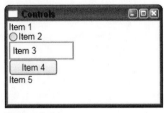

Figure 2-11

The code following shows the syntax for creating a ComboBox and a RadioButtonList. Figure 2-12 illustrates the code that follows; on the left is an example of a ComboBox, and on the right is a RadioButtonList.

```
<StackPanel Orientation="Horizontal">
      <ComboBox Width="100">
            <ComboBoxItem>One</ComboBoxItem>
            <ComboBoxItem>Two</ComboBoxItem>
            <ComboBoxItem>Three</ComboBoxItem>
      </ComboBox>

      <RadioButtonList Width="100">
            <RadioButtonList.Items>
                  <RadioButton>
                        <ContentControl.Content>One</ContentControl.Content>
                  </RadioButton>
                  <RadioButton>
                        <ContentControl.Content>Two</ContentControl.Content>
                  </RadioButton>
                  <RadioButton>
                        <ContentControl.Content>Three</ContentControl.Content>
                  </RadioButton>
            </RadioButtonList.Items>
      </RadioButtonList>
</StackPanel>
```

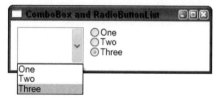

Figure 2-12

The `TabControl` acts as the container for the tabs and determines the overall alignment of all the tabs. (See `TabItem` in the "Headered Content Control" section.)

RangeBase

This class contains elements that have a set value range. The `Sliders` and `ScrollBars` are, in fact, composites (more than one control combined to create a new control).

The `Slider` control enables you to adjust the value based on the range set on the element. This control is commonly used as a volume control. As their names imply, the `HorizontalSlider` controls the horizontal (left and right) plane, while the `VerticalSlider` handles the vertical (up and down) plane. Figure 2-13 illustrates the two sliders as coded here:

```
<StackPanel>
    <HorizontalSlider Width="100" />
    <VerticalSlider Height="100" />
</StackPanel>
```

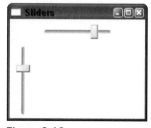

Figure 2-13

The `ScrollBar control` allows a user to scroll through an interface that extends the size of the screen. As their names imply, the `HorizontalScrollBar` controls the horizontal (left and right) plane, while the `VerticalScrollBar` handles the vertical (up and down) plane. Figure 2-14 is a representation of the `ScrollBar` syntax, shown here:

```
<StackPanel>
    <HorizontalScrollBar Width="100"></HorizontalScrollBar>
    <VerticalScrollBar Height="100"></VerticalScrollBar>
</StackPanel>
```

Figure 2-14

Thumb

This class works in conjunction with the RangeBase class. The thumb is the element that enables a user to adjust the value on the Slider or ScrollBar control.

Working with Multimedia

The following sections describe the multimedia classes available to you.

Image

The Image class is used purely for placing an image within a document or application. The image is referenced through the control's Source property, the location of the image must be referenced with either an absolute or relative path. The control will accept any of the following image types: .jpg, .gif, .png, .tiff, .bmp, and .ico.

Create a new Avalon application in Visual Studio and save it as an Image. Inside the Grid tags of Window1.xaml (the default root element in an Avalon application) add the image tag syntax:

```
<Image Source="myImage.jpg" />
```

When adding the name of your own image, it either needs to be an absolute path or in the same folder as Window1.xaml.

When the window opens, the image will fill the dimensions of the window and is automatically resized in relation to the window's resizing. This happens because neither the Height nor Width was defined in the code; therefore, the image is inheriting its height and width values from the Grid. If a value is added to the Width, Image no longer has this resizing feature.

MediaElement

This control is used for adding either Audio or Video to an application with full streaming capabilities:

```
<StackPanel>
    <MediaElement Name="mySound" Source="SoundFile.wma"/>
    <MediaElement Name="myVideo" Source="VideoFile.wpl" Stretch="Fill" />
</StackPanel>
```

Working with Panels

The development of an Avalon document usually starts with the selection of one of the premade panels. The next sections will introduce you to each of the panels that are present in the API and their behaviors.

Properties

`Panel` is a class derived from the `FrameworkElement`, but it also looks to the `UIElement` for inheriting many of its properties. `Panel` is the base class for all the panel-derived classes. The purpose of the `Panel` class is to act as a container and as a means of placing elements within it. The panel can control the object's dimension, position, and overall arrangement. There are five common and two specialized `Panel` classes used in Avalon (listed following the next table). The specialized panels are used for specific tasks and have limitations different from the other more common panels. The following table lists some common properties used for this class.

Property	Description
Background	This property gets or sets the brush used to define the panel's appearance. This could be a solid color, a linear or radial gradient, an image, or an opacity mask. (See the "Brushes" section to learn more.)
Children	Contains the FrameworkElements found below this element in the LogicalTree.
IsItemsHost	A Boolean-valued property to indicate the panel holds items for use by an ItemsControl.

Common Panels

- ❑ Canvas
- ❑ DockPanel
- ❑ Grid
- ❑ StackPanel

Specialized Panels

- ❑ BulletPanel
- ❑ TabPanel
- ❑ ToolBarOverFlowPanel

Canvas

`Canvas` is used to explicitly position things in an exact X, Y position with the (0,0) position in the upper left, increasing to the right and down. It uses a painter's model of rendering similar to that of Scalable Vector Graphics (SVG). Objects that appear first in the markup are rendered first on-screen. As objects are added, they are subsequently layered on top of the initial objects, like layers of paint on a painting. Then effects can be added, such as opacity and animation. The added effects, in turn, give the whole presentation a feeling of depth and structure.

Following is a simple sample of a `Canvas` that contains a `TextBlock` as a child:

```
<Canvas Name="MyCanvas" Background="Red" Width="300" Height="100" >
    <TextBlock Name="MyTextBlock" Canvas.Top="10" Canvas.Left="20">
        Hello World!</TextBlock>
</Canvas>
```

`Canvas` uses a special kind of dependency property (as do many of the other panels) called the *attached dependency property*. This type of property is not normally used by the class that declares it but is used by the elements contained within the panel. For example, you will not see a `Left`, `Top`, `X`, or `Y` property on any of the common controls in Avalon. Instead, the controls use the dependency properties of their parent panel to specify their position. In the previous sample, the `TextBlock` specified its X and Y position by using the dependency properties `Canvas.Left` and `Canvas.Top`. These are, in fact, the `Canvas's` attached dependency properties. If the `TextBlock` was housed in a different panel-derived class, it would use a different attached dependency property to specify its location.

All child elements on a `Canvas` use the attached dependency properties described in the following table to explicitly position themselves.

Property	Type	Description
Top	Double	This determines the distance of the top of the child element in relation to the top of the canvas (which is its parent).
Bottom	Double	This determines the distance of the bottom of the child element in relation to the bottom-right corner of the canvas (which is its parent).
Left	Double	This determines the distance of the left of the child element in relation to the left side of the canvas (which is its parent).
Right	Double	This determines the distance of the right of the child element in relation to the right side of the canvas (which is its parent).

`Panel` classes often have helper functions to set the attached dependency properties. For example, `Canvas.SetLeft` is the static method used in the `Canvas` class. Other static methods are available for each of the panel-derived classes. Dependency properties can also be set on `FrameworkElement`(s) by using the `SetValue` method. `SetValue` is used to apply a regular or attached dependency property to an object. Attached and regular dependency properties can be removed using the `ClearValue` method.

Following is an example of a simple XAML document:

```
<Canvas xmlns="http://schemas.microsoft.com/winfx/avalon/2005" Name="Canvas"
    Background="BlanchedAlmond" Width="400" Height="300">
    <TextBlock Name="TextBlock" Width="300" Height="200" Canvas.Left="50"
        Canvas.Top="10">
        Hello World
    </TextBlock>
</Canvas>
```

Objects don't always have to be created using XAML. Avalon is an API, essentially an extension of .NET, so you can create objects in code just as you do today in the System.Forms namespace. The following code will create a Canvas and a TextBlock like the XAML code you looked at earlier. The sample uses the static Canvas helper methods and the SetValue method for defining the dependency properties. Following is the C# equivalent to the preceding XAML code. Figure 2-15 illustrates the outcome from either method of programming.

```csharp
private void WindowLoaded(object sender, EventArgs e)
    {
        // Create the Canvas.
        Canvas canvas = new Canvas();

        // Set the background using a premade brush.
        canvas.Background = Brushes.BlanchedAlmond;

        // Set the Canvas's width and height.
        canvas.Width = 400;
        canvas.Height = 300;

        // Create a TextBlock.
        TextBlock textBlock = new TextBlock();
        textBlock.Width = 300;
        textBlock.Height = 200;

        // Set the X position of the text block using Canvas helper function.
        Canvas.SetLeft(textBlock, 50);

        // Set the Y position of the text block using the SetValue method.
        textBlock.SetValue(Canvas.TopProperty, (double) 10);

        // Set the content.
        textBlock.TextContent = "Hello world";

        // Add the text block to the Canvas.
        canvas.Children.Add(textBlock);

        // Set the Canvas as the root element for this window.
        Content = canvas;

    }
```

Figure 2-15

Generally, a Canvas has better performance when rendering its children than the DockPanel or StackPanel do because it explicitly places its children, whereas the other panel types use implicit positioning to place controls and UI elements. Apart from the minimal rendering time difference, it is beneficial to use the other panel types if resizing capabilities are desired in your application. The Canvas is best suited for diagrams and printable material, but not suited to creating a dialog box or window in an application.

DockPanel

DockPanel arranges elements horizontally or vertically relative to each other. Elements use the attached dependency property Dock to position themselves in a DockPanel. The Top or Bottom settings pile the elements above or below one another, whereas Left and Right place objects to the left or right of one another. Unless the child elements have values for their Height and Width attributes, they will be evenly sized in order to fill the space of the DockPanel. An additional value, LastChildFill, is the default value. It is a Boolean-valued property that fills the remaining space available within the panel. To override the default, set LastChildFill="False". The purpose of the DockPanel is to place a variety of elements as well as to have resizing capabilities on the window. As previously mentioned, if the dimensions of a child element in a DockPanel are not explicitly written, the child element will inherit the dimensions of the remaining available space in the DockPanel.

To familiarize you with DockPanel, let's add a series of buttons as children:

```
<DockPanel Name="MyDockPanel">
    <Button Name="myButton1">Button 1</Button>
    <Button Name="myButton2">Button 2</Button>
    <Button Name="myButton3">Button 3</Button>
    <Button Name="myButton4">Button 4</Button>
</DockPanel>
```

Once the code is compiled, the application window that comes up will appear as a series of stripes instead of a series of buttons, as shown in Figure 2-16.

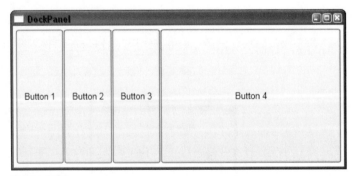

Figure 2-16

Another thing you will notice is that the first three buttons have similar dimensions, and then third is three times the size of the first buttons. The size of the last button is determined by the default value LastChildFill. This means that, as the last element in the panel, it will fill the remaining space not already filled.

With the same code, now add in docking properties to each of the buttons:

```
<Button Name="myButton1" DockPanel.Dock="Left">Button 1</Button>
<Button Name="myButton2" DockPanel.Dock="Right">Button 2</Button>
<Button Name="myButton3" DockPanel.Dock="Top">Button 3</Button>
<Button Name="myButton4" DockPanel.Dock="Bottom">Button 4</Button>
```

The result is shown in Figure 2-17.

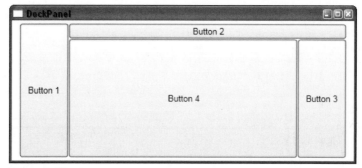

Figure 2-17

Button 4 still appears to be larger than the rest despite being docked to the bottom. This happens because the makeup is always read from top to bottom; therefore, the last child listed in the DockPanel will have the LastChildFill="True". "myButton4", being last, defaults to LastChildFill ="True" whether it is docked or not. The reason for this is that the DockPanel acts as a rubber band around its children and resizes them accordingly with as little null space(s) present as possible. Add another button, label it "LastChildFill", and recompile the application:

```
<Button Name="myButton5">LastChildFill</Button>
```

The result is shown in Figure 2-18.

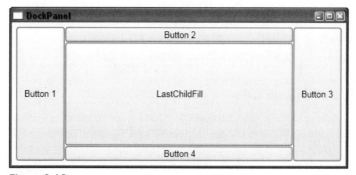

Figure 2-18

The items are docked in the order in which they are placed in the code. For example, if you place the code for Button 3 before the code for Button 2, the docking order will be altered. The placement of previous elements has precedence over the elements that follow. The image in Figure 2-19 shows the button docking order of Left, Top, Right, and Bottom. Figure 2-20 moves the code for Button 3 above the code of Button 2. Now, the docking order is Left, Right, Top, and Bottom.

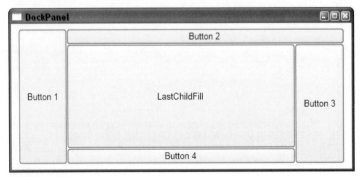

Figure 2-19

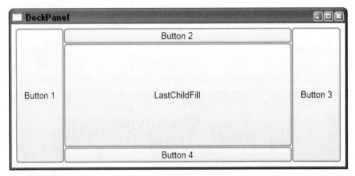

Figure 2-20

When placing elements on a DockPanel is it important to remember precedence (of placement) is given to the elements in the order in which you enter them in the code.

If rendering time is of more concern than the resizing capabilities, specifying the Height and Width properties of the panel (even specifying one) greatly improves its rendering performance. This specification of height and width is applicable to the StackPanel as well.

Grid

The Grid is a series of flexible columns and rows, and you can give the contents of each precise spacing by using the Margin property.

The Grid is a good option for using as the top-level element in a dialog box or for styling component visuals or data when resizing is a constant requirement. The Grid adds elements based on a row and column index. Grids are also more flexible than tables (which will be covered later in the chapter) in that the grid allows layering (more than one element to exist in a single cell). Elements are positioned relative to the upper-left corner of each cell boundary. The positioning is altered by redefining the four margin values.

UI elements added to a grid are placed using the row and column attached dependency properties. These are described in the following table.

Property	Definition
Column	Defines the column and determines the placement of the cell content on the vertical plane.
ColumnSpan	Determines the width of a cell. This allows the developer to set the content to extend across one or more columns without affecting the other content within the Grid.
Row	Defines the row and determines the placement of the cell content on the horizontal plane.
RowSpan	This determines the width of a cell. The RowSpan allows the developer to set the content to extend across the row without affecting the other content within the Grid.

Grid.ColumnSpan and Grid.RowSpan specify the number of cells in which an object may cross in either the X or Y direction.

Following is an example of a simple Grid:

```
<Grid Name="MyGrid" ShowGridLines="True">
    <ColumnDefinition Name="MyColumn1"/>
    <ColumnDefinition Name="MyColumn2"/>
    <ColumnDefinition Name="MyColumn3" Width="*"/>

    <RowDefinition Name="MyRow1" Height="Auto"/>
    <RowDefinition Name="MyRow2" Height="Auto"/>
    <RowDefinition Name="MyRow3" Height="Auto"/>
    <RowDefinition Name="MyRow4" Height="Auto"/>
    <RowDefinition/>

    <!-- Column Headings -->
    <TextBlock Name="MyTextBlock1" Grid.Column="0" Foreground="White"
       FontWeight="Bold">
         Name
    </TextBlock>
    <TextBlock Name="MyTextBlock2" Grid.Column="1" Foreground="White"
       FontWeight="Bold">
         Address
    </TextBlock>
    <TextBlock Name="MyTextBlock3" Grid.Column="2" Foreground="White"
       FontWeight="Bold">
       Home Number
```

```
    </TextBlock>

    <!-- Grid Content-->
    <!-- 1st Row-->
    <TextBlock Name="MyTextBlock4" Grid.Column="0" Grid.Row="1">
        Dick
    </TextBlock>
    <TextBlock Name="MyTextBlock5" Grid.Column="1" Grid.Row="1">
        24 Park Street
    </TextBlock>
    <TextBlock Name="MyTextBlock6" Grid.Column="2" Grid.Row="1">
        555-5555
    </TextBlock>

    <!-- 2nd Row-->
    <TextBlock Name="MyTextBlock7" Grid.Column="0" Grid.Row="2">Jane</TextBlock>
    <TextBlock Name="MyTextBlock8" Grid.Column="1" Grid.Row="2">
        2468 Celebration Ave
    </TextBlock>
    <TextBlock Name="MyTextBlock9" Grid.Column="2" Grid.Row="2">
        775-1234
    </TextBlock>

    <!-- 3rd Row-->
    <TextBlock Name="MyTextBlock10" Grid.Column="0" Grid.Row="3">Spot</TextBlock>
    <TextBlock Name="MyTextBlock11" Grid.Column="1" Grid.Row="3">
        123 Main Street
    </TextBlock>
    <TextBlock Name="MyTextBlock12" Grid.Column="2" Grid.Row="3">
        553-0071
    </TextBlock>

    <!-- 4th Row-->
    <TextBlock Name="MyTextBlock13" Grid.Column="0" Grid.Row="4">
        Fluffy
    </TextBlock>
    <TextBlock Name="MyTextBlock14" Grid.Column="1" Grid.Row="4">
        23 Mockingbird Lane
    </TextBlock>
    <TextBlock Name="MyTextBlock15" Grid.Column="2" Grid.Row="4">
        264-4578
    </TextBlock>
</Grid>
```

Setting the Width="*", as specified in the third ColumnDefinition, acts as a wildcard to say that this column will absorb all the remaining column space available in the Grid. In the RowDefinition section there is an extra, required tag, <RowDefinition />; otherwise, the last two rows will be laid on top of one another.

Unless specifically defined in the ColumnDefinitions or RowDefinitions, the dimensions of each Cell will be set to an equal portion to the rest of the Grid. For example, in Figure 2-21 there appears to be a lot of wasted space in the Name column; however, you will also note that its width is one-third of the entire Grid.

Figure 2-21

StackPanel

The StackPanel is similar to the DockPanel in that they both enable resizing. However, as the name reflects, the StackPanel piles the elements on top of one another. Create a basic StackPanel using the following code:

```
<StackPanel Name="myStackPanel">
    <Button Name="myButton1">Button 1</Button>
    <Button Name="myButton2">Button 2</Button>
    <Button Name="myButton3">Button 3</Button>
    <Button Name="myButton4">Button 4</Button>
</StackPanel>
```

When the application is run with the preceding code, the buttons are all the same dimension and all equally fill the size of the window. The equality continues as the window is resized. This is so because the StackPanel manages the positioning of the content through measuring the size of the object and then flowing it until a break is required (usually the dimension of the panel). Figures 2-22 and 2-23 are two screenshots of the preceding StackPanel sample.

Figure 2-22

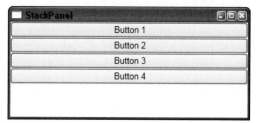

Figure 2-23

The child elements in a StackPanel are resized in relation to the dimensions of resized panel.

Figure 2-23 also shows how the StackPanel can affect the appearance of its children. The buttons have been elongated to the proportion of the StackPanel; however, the height of the buttons does not appear to be affected. The reason for this is that the StackPanel will flow its children only along one plane (Horizontal or Vertical) with its Orientation property; thus, there is an empty space below the buttons.

Now, add the following dimensions to the buttons and recompile the application:

```
<StackPanel Name="myStackPanel">
    <Button Name="myButton1" Width="75" Height="30">Button 1</Button>
    <Button Name="myButton1" Width="75" Height="30">Button 2</Button>
    <Button Name="myButton1" Width="75" Height="30">Button 3</Button>
    <Button Name="myButton1" Width="75" Height="30">Button 4</Button>
</StackPanel>
```

Although the default flow direction is Vertical, the stacking can be done either vertically or horizontally. To override the panel's default alignment value set the attribute Orientation="Horizontal".

In Figure 2-24 the StackPanel is using the default Orientation property, whereas Figure 2-25 has the attribute set to Horizontal.

Figure 2-24

Figure 2-25

To distribute the buttons horizontally, the code on the start tag of the StackPanel element would be as follows:

```
<StackPanel Name="myStackPanel" Orientation="Horizontal">
```

BulletPanel

BulletPanel is one of the two specialized panels within the Avalon API. It is a panel used for controlling layout. Unlike the other panels, the BulletPanel may contain only two children. The most common children found in the BulletPanel are a text string and a glyph.

```
<StackPanel>
    <BulletPanel>
        <RadioButton />
        <TextBlock>First BulletPanel</TextBlock>
    </BulletPanel>
    <BulletPanel>
        <RadioButton />
        <TextBlock>Second BulletPanel</TextBlock>
    </BulletPanel>
    <BulletPanel>
        <RadioButton />
        <TextBlock>Third BulletPanel</TextBlock>
    </BulletPanel>
</StackPanel>
```

The result of the code is shown in Figure 2-26.

Figure 2-26

TabPanel

`TabPanel` is the other specialized panel in Avalon. It acts as host for the `TabItems` used in the `TabControl`. The panel gets and sets the size and positioning, determines the controls for multiple rows, and allows styles to be applied to the child.

```
<TabPanel>
    <TabControl>
        <TabItem>One</TabItem>
        <TabItem>Two</TabItem>
        <TabItem>Three</TabItem>
        <TabItem>Four</TabItem>
    </TabControl>
</TabPanel>
```

Figures 2-27 and 2-28 show the same `TabPanel`, but the tabs are dynamically rearranged by the `Panel` upon the window's resizing in Figure 2-28.

Figure 2-27

Figure 2-28

Figure 2-28 is a resized version of Figure 2-27. It is also a good example of how the `TabPanel` controls the sizing and positioning of its child elements. The `TabPanel` will not let you reduce its width any further, for it would not be able to properly display them without compromising their appearance.

ToolBarOverflowPanel

This is a new tool that allows you to control the overflow of toolbar items. The `ToolBarOverFlowPanel` works like the ones you see in any of the Microsoft Office 2003 products in that there are more toolbar options than there is space on the toolbar. Within this `Panel`, the tools can be hidden or revealed when required.

```
<ToolBarOverflowPanel Name="MyTlBOPanel"Width="250">
    <ToolBarTray Name="MyToolBarTray">
        <ToolBar Name="MyTray">
            <Canvas Name="MyCanvas" Height="100" Width="100">
                <Rectangle Name="Chimney" Fill="#FFFF0000" Height="25"
                    Canvas.Left="59" Stroke="#FF000000"
                    Canvas.Top="22.7383333333333" Width="9" />
                <Rectangle Name="HouseBase" Fill="#FF0000FF" Height="38"
                    Canvas.Left="27" Stroke="#FF000000"
                    Canvas.Top="53.7383333333333" Width="42" />
                <Polygon Name="Roof" Fill="#FF008000" Canvas.Left="0"
                    Points="23,56.7383333333333 48,7.73833333333333
                    74,57.7383333333333" Stroke="#FF000000" Canvas.Top="0"/>
                <Rectangle Name="RightWindow" Fill="#FFFFFF00" Height="12"
                    Canvas.Left="55" Stroke="#FF000000"
                    Canvas.Top="62.7383333333333" Width="10" />
                <Rectangle Name="LeftWindow" Fill="#FFFFFF00" Height="12"
                    Canvas.Left="32" Stroke="#FF000000"
                    Canvas.Top="61.7383333333333" Width="10" />
                <Rectangle Name="Door" Fill="#FFFF0000" Height="18"
                    Canvas.Left="43" Stroke="#FF000000"
                    Canvas.Top="73.7383333333333" Width="10" />
            </Canvas>

            <TextBlock Name="MyTextBlock" HorizontalAlignment="Stretch"
                VerticalAlignment="Center"  FontSize="20">
                Body of Text
            </TextBlock>
        </ToolBar>
    </ToolBarTray>
</ToolBarOverflowPanel>
```

In Figure 2-29, the `TollBarOverFlowPanel` has been repeated twice so that you can see it in its two states.

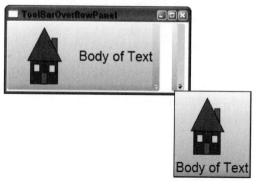

Figure 2-29

Working with Documents

Located in the `System.Windows.Documents` namespace, the goal of the Avalon document services is to provide a better online document-viewing experience and to integrate other capabilities present in the Avalon API and add them into documents. The API has both document-viewing components and document-layout services.

There are two kinds of documents in Avalon: `FixedFormat` documents, which are analogous to PDF (Portable Document Format), and `FlowFormat` documents, which parallel HTML. Both formats allow the reader to specify viewing preferences, while maintaining the overall design concepts as intended by the document's author.

Fixed-Format Documents

Fixed-format documents display content as the author intended regardless of the screen's size, resolution, or available fonts; this makes fixed-format documents ideal for printing and publishing.

The two classes that contribute to a fixed-format document are the `FixedDocument` class and the `FixedPage` class. The `FixedDocument` class provides specialized functionality for managing the `FixedPage`(s). The following sample shows a two-page document that is viewed within the `DocumentViewer`. Figure 2-30 illustrates how the following markup appears when you run it.

```
<Window x:Class="WroxSamples.Window1"
    xmlns="http://schemas.microsoft.com/winfx/avalon/2005"
    xmlns:x="http://schemas.microsoft.com/winfx/xaml/2005"
    Text="WroxSamples"
    >
    <DocumentViewer Name="MyViewer" ZoomPercentage="100">
        <FixedDocument Name="MyFirstDoc">
            <PageContent Name="MyContent">
```

```
                    <FixedPage Name="MyFirstDoc" Width="500" Height="400"
                        Background="White">
                        <TextBlock Name="MyTextBlock1">
                            Images, Glyphs, for Page 1 could go here.
                        </TextBlock>
                    </FixedPage>
                </PageContent>

                <PageContent>
                    <FixedPage Name="MyOtherDoc" Width="500" Height="400"
                        Background="White">
                        <TextBlock Name="MyTextBlock2">
                            Shapes and Drawings for Page 2 could go here!
                        </TextBlock>
                    </FixedPage>
                </PageContent>
            </FixedDocument>
        </DocumentViewer>
    </Window>
```

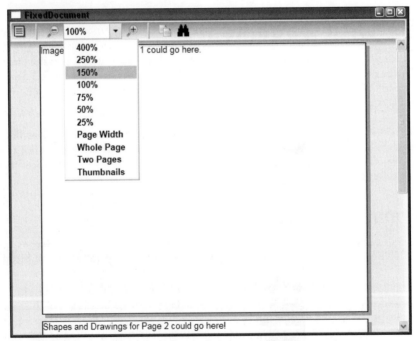

Figure 2-30

Instead of inheriting its `Height` and `Width` properties from the `FrameworkElement`, `FixedDocument` combines the two into one property called `PageSize`. The default value is that of the standard page dimensions 8.5 by 11 and is instantiated as `PageSize="8.5,11"`. When creating your document, `PageContent` is the only type of child you place within `FixedDocument`. The `PageContent` class is significant to a document's structure because it signifies the starting point of the Visual Tree for each page. To fill `PageContent`, use this to reference external XAML files as the source of its content. The only child that `PageContent` may have is a `FixedPage`; therefore, your referenced `.xaml` file must have `FixedPage` as the root element. `FixedPage` automatically sets page breaks at the beginning and end of the document. The content inside a referenced `FixedPage` must be placed inside either a `TextBlock` or `Canvas`.

```
<Window x:Class="AvalonApplication30.Window1"
    xmlns="http://schemas.microsoft.com/winfx/avalon/2005"
    xmlns:x="http://schemas.microsoft.com/winfx/xaml/2005"
    Text="FixedDocument">

    <FixedDocument Name="MyDoc" PageSize="8.5,11"  >
        <PageContent Name="MyFirstPage" Source="Page1.xaml" />
        <PageContent Name="MySecondPage" Source="Page2.xaml" />
    </FixedDocument>
</Window>
```

Following is the syntax to the referenced `FixedPage` file. Figure 2-31 shows the two code documents combined.

```
<FixedPage xmlns="http://schemas.microsoft.com/winfx/avalon/2005"
    xmlns:x="http://schemas.microsoft.com/winfx/xaml/2005" Name="MyFixedPage1">
    <TextBlock Name="MyTextBlock" Background="LightGreen" Foreground="White"
        Height="500" Width="500" TextWrap="Wrap">
        This is the body of a FixedPage document.
    </TextBlock>
</FixedPage>
```

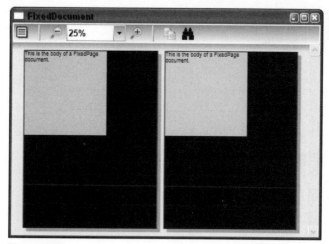

Figure 2-31

Flow Format Documents

Flow format documents are similar to HTML pages. They adjust and resize content based on the user's preferences and the screen size. The `FlowDocument` element is the root for all flow-format documents.

Tables

The table in the Avalon API is better than that of previous technologies because you can easily create rich-document-styled tables. Tables in Avalon are similar to their HTML counterparts in many respects. Tables are still created as a series of columns and rows and have the cell padding, column span, and margins to assign specific placement of the data. However, the structure is slightly different in that all the columns are defined at the top of the table instead of being implied with the cells in each row. This format will ultimately speed up the process of building tables as well as reducing the number of programming errors. One requirement in using a table is that the `Table` must be nested within a `TextFlow` element. This is likely due to several of the inherited properties relating to the strict typographical structure from the `TextElement`. The table has some resizing capabilities; if you specify a width or height for a column or row, or add padding to a cell, the value will be carried through all the contents along that vertical or horizontal plane.

Apart from this rigorous structure involved in the table, it actually has a more efficient rendering time than that of the resizable `Grid`.

The basic structure of a table in Avalon is:

```
<Table>
     <TableColumn />
     <TableColumn />
          <TableHeader />
               <TableBody>
                    <TableRow>
                         <TableCell>Content</TableCell>
                         <TableCell>Content</TableCell>
                    </TableRow>
                    <TableRow>
                         <TableCell>Content</TableCell>
                         <TableCell Text="Content" />
                    </TableRow>
               </TableBody>
          <TableFooter />
   </Table>
```

Content is logically divided by the header, body, and footer, each of which can have its own set of styles applied. The content is added to the table in a `TableCell`. The `TableCell` has `ColumnSpan` and `RowSpan` properties (like HTML), which allow a cell to cross row and column boundaries.

```
<TextFlow Name="MyTextFlow">
     <Table Name="MyTable" TextAlignment="Justify" BorderBrush="Black"
        BorderThickness="3">
          <TableColumn Name="MyColumn1"></TableColumn>
          <TableColumn Name="MyColumn2"></TableColumn>
          <TableColumn Name="MyColumn3"></TableColumn>
```

```
        <TableHeader Name="MyHeader">
            <TableRow Name="MyRow1">
                <TableCell Name="MyCell_1" Background="WhiteSmoke"
                    ColumnSpan="3" TextAlignment="Center"
                    TextElement.FontWeight="Bold">Phone List</TableCell>
            </TableRow>
            <TableRow Name="MyRow2"Background="DimGray"
               TextElement.Foreground="White">
                <TableCell Name="MyCell_2" >Name</TableCell>
                <TableCell Name="MyCell_3" >Address</TableCell>
                <TableCell Name="MyCell_4" >Phone Number</TableCell>
            </TableRow>
        </TableHeader>
        <TableBody>
            <TableRow Name="MyRow3" Background="LightGray">
                <TableCell Name="MyCell_5" BorderThickness="1"
                    Text="Dick"/>
                <TableCell Name="MyCell_6">24 Park Street</TableCell>
                <TableCell Name="MyCell_7">555-5555</TableCell>
            </TableRow>
            <TableRow Name="MyRow4" Background="AliceBlue">
                <TableCell Name="MyCell_8" BorderThickness="1">
                    Jane
                </TableCell>
                <TableCell Name="MyCell_9">
                    2468 Celebration Ave
                </TableCell>
                <TableCell Name="MyCell_10">775-1234</TableCell>
            </TableRow>
            <TableRow Name="MyCell_15" Background="LightGray">
                <TableCell Name="MyCell_11" BorderThickness="1">
                    Spot
                </TableCell>
                <TableCell Name="MyCell_12" >123 Main Street</TableCell>
                <TableCell Name="MyCell_14" >553-0071</TableCell>
            </TableRow>
            <TableRow Name="MyCell16" Background="AliceBlue">
                <TableCell Name="MyCell_15" >Fluffy</TableCell>
                <TableCell Name="MyCell_16" >
                    23 Mockingbird Lane
                </TableCell>
                <TableCell Name="MyCell_17" >264-4578</TableCell>
            </TableRow>
        </TableBody>
    <TableFooter>
        <TableRow Name="MyRow6" >
            <TableCell Name="MyCell18" Background="WhiteSmoke"
                ColumnSpan="3" />
        </TableRow>
    </TableFooter>
    </Table>
</TextFlow>
```

Notice that the cell content can either be written between the opening and closing `TableCell` *tag or as an attribute of* `TableCell`, *as in the first cell in the table's body. This is another example of the flexibility that you have when working with Avalon.*

```
<TableCell BorderThickness="1" Text="Dick"/>
```

Choosing whether to use `Grids` or `Tables` can be confusing. Each has its own advantages and disadvantages. Figure 2-32 illustrates the table based on the preceding code.

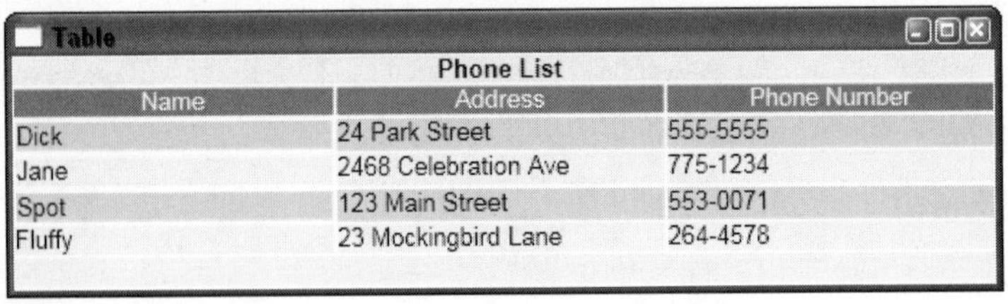

Figure 2-32

Tables are more structured than grids are typographically, with a `TableHeader`, `TableBody`, and `TableFooter`. The table is set into these three areas to separate the data for ease of use and readability. The table header located at the top usually contains the title and column headings. The body contains all the data that fills the cells within the table. The footer usually contains any credits or conclusions related to the table.

Although the two formats (`Table` and `Grid`) can do virtually the same thing, they should be used differently. Tables are suited to laying out tabular type data, where it is preferable to have everything uniform and relatively static. Grids should be used when each cell's content needs to be addressed individually with specific placement within a resizable container.

TextFlow

Unlike other text classes within the `System.Windows.Controls` namespace, `TextFlow` is located in `System.Windows.Document`. This control is designed specifically for use with printed text and multi-page documents. Figure 2-33 illustrates the `TextFlow` code with each paragraph's content present.

```
<TextFlow TextWrap="Wrap" TextAlignment="Justify" Margin="20,15,20,15">
    <Paragraph>
        Lorem ipsum dolor sit ... sollemnes in futurum.
    </Paragraph>
    <Paragraph Margin="0,10,0,0">
        <Bold>This is a second paragraph within the TextFlow Document.</Bold>
        Lorem ipsum dolor sit ... sollemnes in futurum.
    </Paragraph>
</TextFlow>
```

Note: For the purpose of viewing the code, the body of each paragraph has been removed.

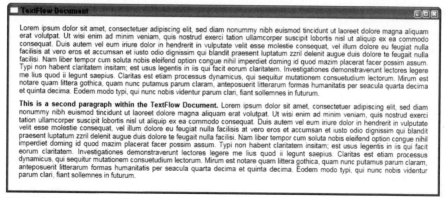

Figure 2-33

TextBlock

TextBlock is meant for creating a simple block of text, commonly used on user interfaces. To create rich documents that require formatting of paragraphs and other features, use FlowDocument, because it can handle formatting a much richer layout. Figure 2-34 shows the rendering of the following XAML syntax:

```
<Canvas>
    <TextBlock>This is a TextBlock of Text</TextBlock>
</Canvas>
```

Figure 2-34

Hyperlinks

In Avalon, the hyperlink has been defined as an inline control that allows you to navigate to either internal or external content. As with Table, Hyperlinks must be nested within a TextFlow element:

```
<TextFlow>
    <Hyperlink NavigateUri="home.xaml" >Home</Hyperlink>
</TextFlow>
```

Application Types in Visual Studio

When you create a new application in Visual Studio, you are presented with four project types.

Avalon Control Library

The Avalon control library project is simply a project for the creation of a reusable .NET library. It sets up references to the Avalon libraries `PresentationCore.dll` and `PresentationFramework.dll` and creates an empty class for your custom control derived from `ContentControl`.

Avalon Application

Selecting a new Avalon application as the project type creates a new Avalon application. The application has two classes: an `Application` class derived from `System.Windows.Application` and a main `Window` class, which is derived from `System.Windows.Window`. Both the `Application` class and the main `Window` class have their own XAML file and code behind file. The XAML files are mostly empty and waiting for content to be added. If you try adding some of the controls discussed instead of coding by hand, you can use a XAML designer like Aurora by Mobiform to create the content faster.

Browser Application and Navigation Application

If you are creating an application that can make use of multiple pages, you may wish to select a browser or navigation application to create your project. `NavigationApplication` is derived from the `Application` class.

When creating a new navigation application, Visual Studio creates an application class as it does in a regular Avalon application, but instead of creating a main `Window` for your project, it creates a main `Page`.

```
<Page x:Class="AvalonApplication2.Page1"
    xmlns="http://schemas.microsoft.com/winfx/avalon/2005"
    xmlns:x="http://schemas.microsoft.com/winfx/xaml/2005"
    >
    <Canvas Background="Red" Width="300" Height="100" >
            <TextBlock Canvas.Top="10" Canvas.Left="20">Hello World!</TextBlock>
    </Canvas>
</Page>
```

This main page is referenced by the XAML for the application in the `StartupURI` property. When the navigation application is launched, it loads and displays this page.

```
<NavigationApplication x:Class="AvalonApplication2.MyApp"
    xmlns="http://schemas.microsoft.com/winfx/avalon/2005"
    xmlns:x="http://schemas.microsoft.com/winfx/xaml/2005"
    StartupUri="Page1.xaml"
    >
    <NavigationApplication.Resources>

    </NavigationApplication.Resources>
</NavigationApplication>
```

A `NavigationApplication` has built-in smarts to remember the pages that you have been viewing; this is accomplished via a journal. As with a Web browser, it too has Back and Forward buttons to return to previously viewed content. The journal keeps track of the content and the pages the user visits.

By getting the NavigationService and calling the Navigate method, you can programmatically change pages within the application. The NavigationService is acquired by calling the static NavigationService.GetNavigationService() method and passing in the root element of the page. The Navigate method is called after the NavigationService is present. The NavigationWindow also uses the Navigate method, and it can be called through the NavigationApplication as an alternative.

```
private void btnGoToAnotherPage(object sender, RoutedEventArgs args)
{
  app = (NavigationApplication) System.Windows.Application.Current;
  navWindow = (NavigationWindow) app.MainWindow;
  navWindow.Navigate(new Uri("NextPage.xaml", UriKind.RelativeOrAbsolute));
}
```

For ease of development and testing, Visual Studio makes the NavigationApplication available to both the navigation and browser applications. They are essentially the same, however; once your application is completed, the NavigationApplication is converted into a BrowserApplication. The conversion occurs when the application's .csproj file is opened and the HostInBrowser setting is set to true. Then you build the program. After it is built, an .application file will be generated in the bin directory. The application can be loaded in a browser by navigating to the application file; this installs the application on your system. If you wish to remove the application after viewing it, go to Add/Remove programs on your computer's Control Panel.

Chapter Exercise: Creating a Calculator

In this project, you create the basic layout of a calculator using the elements discussed in this chapter. In the chapters that follow, you add to the functionality and improve the visual appearance of this project as various subjects are brought up within the context of the book. Figure 2-35 is a representation of the XAML project used in constructing the calculator; use Aurora to quickly build the interface, and then open up the saved file in Visual Studio to write the code.

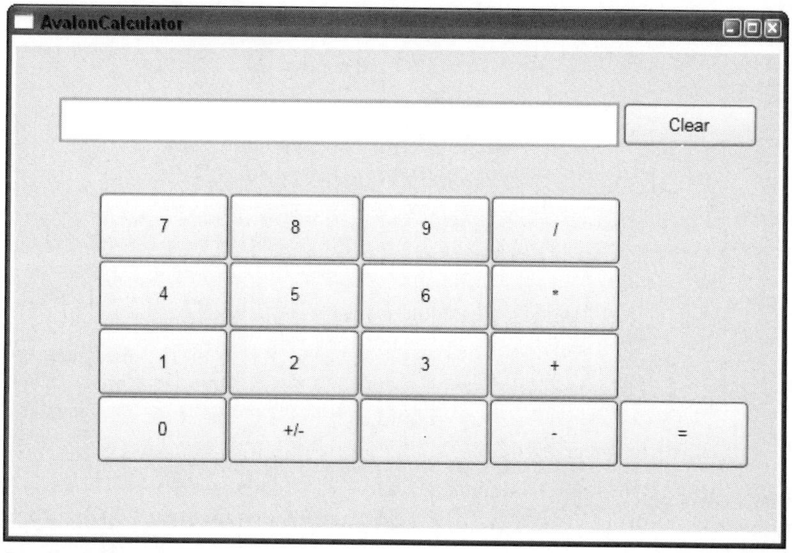

Figure 2-35

Following is the XAML used in constructing the calculator; use Aurora to quickly build the interface, and then open up the saved file in Visual Studio to write the code. A downloadable version of this project is available at www.wrox.com.

```xml
<Window xmlns="http://schemas.microsoft.com/winfx/avalon/2005" Name="ROOT"
    x:Class="AvalonCalculator.Window1"
    xmlns:x="http://schemas.microsoft.com/winfx/xaml/2005" Loaded="WindowLoaded">
        <Window.Text>AvalonCalculator</Window.Text>
            <ContentControl.Content>
                <Canvas Background="#FFECE9D8" Height="355.99331331257372"
                    Canvas.Left="0" Canvas.Top="0" Width="585.79723818560637">
                <Panel.Children>

                    <!-- Notice that the grid is nested within a canvas that also
                        contains the calculator screen and "Clear" button. -->

                    <TextBox FlowDirection="RightToLeftThenTopToBottom" Height="33"
                        HorizontalAlignment="Left" HorizontalContentAlignment="Left"
                        ID="textBoxValue" Canvas.Left="33.9493264988669"
                        Canvas.Top="37.8582880370136" Width="428" />
                    <Button Height="32" Name="btnClear"
                        Canvas.Left="464.949326498867" Canvas.Top="37.8582880370136"
                        Width="103">
                        <ContentControl.Content>Clear</ContentControl.Content>
                    </Button>

                    <!-- top of Grid that holds the buttons -->
                    <Grid Background="#00FFFFFF" Height="201" Name="grid"
                        Canvas.Left="64.9999999999221" Canvas.Top="108.111666666745"
                        Width="598">
                        <Grid.ColumnDefinitions>
                            <ColumnDefinition MinWidth="10" />
                            <ColumnDefinition MinWidth="10" />
                            <ColumnDefinition MinWidth="20" />
                            <ColumnDefinition MinWidth="20" />
                            <ColumnDefinition MinWidth="20" />
                            <ColumnDefinition MinWidth="10" />
                        </Grid.ColumnDefinitions>
                        <Grid.RowDefinitions>
                            <RowDefinition MinHeight="10" />
                            <RowDefinition MinHeight="10" />
                            <RowDefinition MinHeight="20" />
                            <RowDefinition MinHeight="10" />

                        </Grid.RowDefinitions>
                        <Panel.Children>
                        <!-- Buttons on top row of calculator -->
                            <Button Grid.Column="0" Grid.ColumnSpan="1" Name="btn7"
                                Canvas.Left="0" Grid.Row="0" Canvas.Top="0">
                                    <ContentControl.Content>7</ContentControl.Content>
                            </Button>
                            <Button Grid.Column="1" Name="btn8" Canvas.Left="0"
                                Grid.Row="0" Canvas.Top="0">
                                    <ContentControl.Content>8</ContentControl.Content>
```

```xaml
    </Button>
    <Button Grid.Column="2" Name="btn9" Canvas.Left="0"
       Grid.Row="0" Canvas.Top="0">
         <ContentControl.Content>9</ContentControl.Content>
    </Button>

    <!-- Buttons on second row of calculator -->
    <Button Grid.Column="0" Name="btn4" Canvas.Left="0"
       Grid.Row="1" Canvas.Top="0">
         <ContentControl.Content>4</ContentControl.Content>
    </Button>
    <Button Grid.Column="1" Name="btn5" Canvas.Left="0"
       Grid.Row="1" Canvas.Top="0">
         <ContentControl.Content>5</ContentControl.Content>
    </Button>
    <Button Grid.Column="2" Name="btn6" Canvas.Left="0"
       Grid.Row="1" Canvas.Top="0">
         <ContentControl.Content>6</ContentControl.Content>
    </Button>
    <!-- Buttons on 3rd row of calculator -->
    <Button Grid.Column="0" Name="btn1" Canvas.Left="0"
       Grid.Row="2" Canvas.Top="0">
         <ContentControl.Content>1</ContentControl.Content>
    </Button>
    <Button Grid.Column="1" Name="btn2" Canvas.Left="0"
       Grid.Row="2" Canvas.Top="0">
         <ContentControl.Content>2</ContentControl.Content>
    </Button>
    <Button Grid.Column="2" Name="btn3" Canvas.Left="0"
       Grid.Row="2" Canvas.Top="0">
         <ContentControl.Content>3</ContentControl.Content>
    </Button>

    <!-- Logic Buttons in right column of calculator -->
    <Button Grid.Column="3" Name="btnDivide" Canvas.Left="0"
       Grid.Row="0" Canvas.Top="0">
         <ContentControl.Content>/</ContentControl.Content>
    </Button>
    <Button Grid.Column="3" Name="btnMultiply"
       Canvas.Left="0" Grid.Row="1" Canvas.Top="0">
         <ContentControl.Content>*</ContentControl.Content>
    </Button>
    <Button Grid.Column="3" Name="btnAdd" Canvas.Left="0"
       Grid.Row="2" Canvas.Top="0">
         <ContentControl.Content>+</ContentControl.Content>
    </Button>
    <Button Grid.Column="3" Name="btnMinus" Canvas.Left="0"
       Grid.Row="3" Canvas.Top="0">
         <ContentControl.Content>-</ContentControl.Content>

    </Button>
    <Button Grid.Column="2" Name="btnPeriod" Canvas.Left="0"
       Grid.Row="3" Canvas.Top="0">
         <ContentControl.Content>.</ContentControl.Content>
```

```
            </Button>
            <Button Grid.Column="1" Name="btnPlusMinus"
                Canvas.Left="0" Grid.Row="3" Canvas.Top="0">
                    <ContentControl.Content>+/-</ContentControl.Content>
            </Button>

            <!-- Buttons on bottom row of calculator -->
            <Button Grid.Column="0" Name="btn0" Canvas.Left="0"
                Grid.Row="3" Canvas.Top="0">
                        <ContentControl.Content>0</ContentControl.Content>
            </Button>
            <Button Grid.Column="4" Name="btnEquals" Grid.Row="3">
                    <ContentControl.Content>=</ContentControl.Content>
            </Button>
        </Panel.Children>
    </Grid>
        </Panel.Children>
    </Canvas>
    </ContentControl.Content>
</Window>
}
```

Points to note in the code behind are:

❑ This is a partial class because Visual Studio generates another hidden code behind file that adds declarations to the class in this file.

❑ This second file also creates declarations for the objects (variables) found in the XAML file.

❑ XAML object events were wired up in `WindowLoaded`, which was declared in the root section of the file. Therefore, the `WindowLoaded` method is applied to hook up all the events in the code behind in order for the calculator to run once it opens.

Summary

This chapter reviewed a portion of the Avalon hierarchy so that you could understand why elements appear or are laid out in a panel in a particular way. This led to a discussion of the various layout options provided in the Avalon API. You now know that the panel you choose will also determine the properties and functionality that each control will inherit from the panel.

The chapter discussed the more common controls from several of the classes so that you can recognize their differences.

The four types of navigation and each of their strengths were then reviewed, which led you into creating the layout of a calculator to which you will apply styles and functionality over the next chapters.

In the chapters to follow, you learn about adding 2-D and 3-D graphics that are created using the XAML syntax. You will also learn how to apply styles and brushes to make the calculator more visually appealing and reactive to user interaction.

3

Avalon Graphics and Animation

The graphics and animation capabilities in Avalon have marked similarities to those found in SVG. Avalon has graphics classes for regular shapes (lines, polygons, ellipses, and rectangles). It also has complex arcs and Bezier curves. Any dependency property in Avalon can be animated; this includes properties for position, opacity, color, and size. In this chapter, you will be looking at the Shapes subsystem in Avalon and basic animation capabilities.

Working with Shapes

The Shapes class is an abstract base class found in the System.Windows.Shapes namespace of Avalon. In addition to the dependency properties inherited from the FrameworkElement class, the following table lists DependencyProperties common to all of the shape classes.

Dependency Property	Description
Fill	This determines the type of brush that will be applied to illustrate the shape's inner area.
Stroke	The outline that surrounds a shape or in regards to a path; the stroke represents the line between its points.

Table continued on following page

Dependency Property	Description
StrokeDashArray	This property is a list (or collection) of double values. It determines the pattern that a shape's (or path's) outline will take. The output is a combination of spaces and dashes. A minimum of one number is required, and multiple numbers are separated by a space or comma. The first number sets the length of the dash, while the second number sets the length of the gap. The next set of numbers fixes the length of the following dash and gap and so on. When the sequence finishes, it repeats from the beginning, until the stroke has been completed.
StrokeDashCap	This property alters the appearance of each end of the dashes on a shape's stroke. The default value is Flat, but it can also be Round or Triangle.
StrokeDashOffset	A double type valued property that determines how far into the shape's stroke that this property should go into the array of values before applying the pattern. For example, instead of starting the pattern from the beginning, you can start it 45 pixels in, offsetting the original pattern's appearance.
StrokeEndLineCap	Determines the appearance of the end part of the stroke's dashes of a path. The default value is Flat, but it can also be Square, Round, or Triangle.
StrokeLineJoin	Finishes the corner edges of the stroke on a path. The default value is Miter, but the join can also be Bevel or Round.
StrokeMiterLimit	A double type valued property that identifies the limit of proportion applied to the Miter length in relation to the StrokeThickness of the shape.
StrokeStartLineCap	Determines the appearance of the beginning part of the stroke's dashes of a path. The default value is Flat, but it can also be Square, Round, or Triangle.
StrokeThickness	A double type valued property that sets the width of the Stroke surrounding the shape.

All sizing properties such as Height, Width, Top, and bottom are double type valued properties. This means that neither percentages nor relative sizing measurements are accepted. However, it is possible to add units to the double values (cm, in, pt, and px). Avalon then converts it (sizing units used) into pixels based on 96 dpi (dots per square inch).

Ellipse

The ellipse class enables you to create ellipse and circular shapes. Its dimensions are controlled with the RadiusX and RadiusY properties. They indicate how wide the horizontal or vertical arc will be on the ellipse. There are also two properties that control where the center of the ellipse is to be placed on the parent panel: the CenterX for the vertical plane and the CenterY for the horizontal.

```
<Ellipse RadiusX="100" RadiusY="50" Stroke="#000000" StrokeThickness="3">
    <Ellipse.Fill>
        <SolidColorBrush Color="Yellow" Opacity="0.4" />
    </Ellipse.Fill>
</Ellipse>
```

Figure 3-1 shows the result of this code.

Figure 3-1

Line

Lines are the direct connection between two points.

To create a more complex line, see the section on paths.

```
<Line Stroke="Black" X1="450" Y1="50" X2="300" Y2="180" StrokeThickness="9"
    StrokeStartLineCap="Round" StrokeEndLineCap="Triangle" />
```

Figure 3-2 shows the result of executing this code.

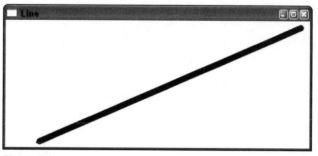

Figure 3-2

Polygon

A polygon is a series of lines arranged to form a multisided closed shape.

```
<Polygon Stroke="#FF000000" Fill="#FF008000"  Points="99.5,298.238333333333
    199.5,101.238333333333 299.5,302.238333333333 99.5,147.238333333333
    299.5,150.238333333333" />
```

Figure 3-3 shows the result of the preceding code.

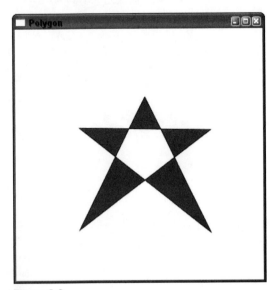

Figure 3-3

Polyline

`Polyline` is similar to the polygon, but it does not need to be closed. Another difference is that the area inside the `Polyline` cannot be filled. To illustrate the differences, the same points have been used in the following sample. In this sample, the star appears to be unfinished. For it to be closed, the start point would need to be added.

```
<Polyline Stroke="#FF000000" Points="99.5,298.238333333333 199.5,101.238333333333
    299.5,302.238333333333 99.5,147.238333333333 299.5,150.238333333333"    />
```

Figure 3-4 shows the result of this code.

Figure 3-4

Rectangle

This is the class that enables you to create a four-sided shape, such as a rectangle or square.

MaxHeight and MaxWidth control how much of the rectangle will be filled. For example, if you have a rectangle with a Width greater than its MaxWidth, the rectangle will take the dimension of the Width property but will only display the rectangle filled to the MaxWidth. This example is best viewed using the Aurora XAML Designer.

```
<Rectangle Fill="#FF0000FF" Stroke="#FF000000" Height="125" Width="214"
    MaxHeight="500" MaxWidth="100" MinHeight="0" MinWidth="0" />
```

Figure 3-5 shows the result of the preceding code.

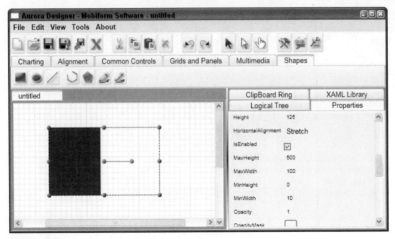

Figure 3-5

The `MinWidth` and `MinHeight` properties do the opposite of their `Max` counterparts.

The rectangles built in XAML by default have square corners; however, if you want rounded corners, you can implement the `RadiusX` and `RadiusY` properties. As discussed in the "Ellipse" section, the radius properties control the curvature of arc on the rectangle's corners. The higher the value, the rounder the corner will be, based on the plane on which it has been placed.

```
<-- First Rectangle with equal RadiusX and RadiusY values -->
<Rectangle Height="100" Width="100" Fill="Red" Opacity="0.4" RadiusX="20"
    RadiusY="20" />

<-- Second Rectangle with the RadiusX value to be greater than the RadiusY -->
<Rectangle Fill="Red" Stroke="Black" StrokeThickness="10" Height="85"
    Width="160" RadiusX="50" RadiusY="10" />
```

Figure 3-6 shows the preceding code's result when executed.

Figure 3-6

Glyphs

Glyphs are shapes that take on the appearance of fonts. For the code to work, the Uniform Resource Identifier (URI) for the font must have either an absolute or relative path to the file's location. (if you want to try this syntax with your system's fonts, the font folder is most likely located at `C:\WINDOWS\Fonts`). Glyphs are often applied in fixed-format documents intended for print.

```
<Glyphs FontUri="CURLZ___.ttf" FontRenderingEmSize="48" OriginX="85"
    OriginY="60" Fill="Red" UnicodeString="Hello World!" />
```

Figure 3-7 shows the result of executing the preceding code.

Figure 3-7

Using Paths

`Paths` are also derived from the `Shape` base class and are found in the `System.Windows.Shapes` namespace of Avalon. Paths are composed of geometries, which are located in the `System.Windows.Media` namespace.

`Paths` are more complex than the shapes previously discussed (`Line`, `Polygon`, and `Polyline`) because they are a combination of many connected lines and curves that make up a two-dimensional (2-D) graphic. `Paths` can vary from simple to complex. Examples of more intricate paths include elaborate images, linear maps, and computer-aided design (CAD drawings).

`Paths` have a data property that is a type of geometry. Geometry is a series of connected mathematical points, lines arcs, and surfaces that can be combined to create 2-D graphics (path).

In the Avalon API, the `Path` is defined as a class of objects that have clipping, hit-testing (the ability to select with a mouse), and rendering capabilities. Therefore, the geometry of a path is the instructions defining how it will be rendered.

Geometries are categorized into the classes listed in the following table.

Geometry Class	Definition
EllipseGeometry	Represents the geometry of a circle or ellipse.
GeometryCollection	Represents a collection of Geometry objects. Note that a GeometryCollection is derived from Geometry and represents a composite shape of the Geometry objects it contains.
LineGeometry	Represents the geometry of a line.
PathGeometry	Represents a complex shape comprising a variety of segments. The segments may be composed of arcs, curves, ellipses, lines, and rectangles.
RectangleGeometry	Represents the geometry of a rectangle.

Simple Geometries

A simple geometry, as the name implies, is a basic shape created using the path syntax. `EllipseGeometry`, `LineGeometry`, and `RectangleGeometry` are relatively simple formats for creating a `Path` in relation to some of the other geometries covered next.

```
<!-- Beginning of an EllipseGeometry -->
<Path Fill="Blue" Stroke="Black">
    <Path.Data>
        <EllipseGeometry Center="440, 100" RadiusX="40" RadiusY="75"/>
    </Path.Data>
</Path>

<!-- Beginning of a LineGeometry -->
<Path Fill="Blue" Stroke="Black">
    <Path.Data>
        <LineGeometry StartPoint="50,50" EndPoint="300,50"/>
    </Path.Data>
</Path>

<!-- Beginning of a RectangleGeometry -->
<Path Fill="Blue" Stroke="Black">
    <Path.Data>
        <RectangleGeometry >
            <RectangleGeometry.Rect>
                <Rect X="200" Y="25" Width="100" Height="50"/>
            </RectangleGeometry.Rect>
        </RectangleGeometry>
    </Path.Data>
</Path>
```

Figure 3-8 shows the results of the preceding code.

Figure 3-8

This is an example of how to create a path using each of the simple geometries.

To control the placement of an `EllipseGeometry`, another property named `Center` is added. The two numbers on the `Center` property are X,Y values. This same X,Y format is used when creating `LineGeometry`; however, the coordinates are placed on the `StartPoint` and `EndPoint` to indicate where the beginning and ending points of the line are located. The `RectangleGeometry` is a little more obvious where it uses X and Y as a means of placing the rectangle on the document and subsequently is filled out based on its `Height` and `Width` values. However, if the amount of code is an issue, `RectangleGeometry` can be written in an abbreviated fashion. Following is the syntax for creating the same rectangle two different ways; the top part is written in the abbreviated fashion, whereas the bottom part has each property name and value written out separately:

```
<!-- The abbreviated version -->
<Path Fill="Pink" Stroke="Black">
    <Path.Data>
        <RectangleGeometry Rect="50,25 100,50" />
    </Path.Data>
</Path>

<!-- The same rectangle but naming each of the properties -->
<Path Fill="Blue" Stroke="Black">
    <Path.Data>
        <RectangleGeometry >
            <RectangleGeometry.Rect>
                <Rect X="50" Y="25" Width="100" Height="50"/>
            </RectangleGeometry.Rect>
        </RectangleGeometry>
    </Path.Data>
</Path>
```

A `TranslateTransform` was applied to the rectangle on the right to show two geometries side by side. (See the "Transforms" section, later in this chapter to learn more about `TranslateTransforms`.)

Figure 3-9 shows the results of the preceding code.

Figure 3-9

GeometryCollection

Derived from the Geometry abstract base class, the GeometryCollection can have several geometries, grouped together or nested, within the GeometryGroup. Collectively, they can be interconnected to create one image.

```
<Path Stroke="LinearGradient 1,0 0,1 Red DimGray" StrokeThickness="3"
    Fill="RadialGradient LightGray Red">
      <Path.Data>
          <GeometryGroup>
              <RectangleGeometry Rect="20,125 100 60" />
              <LineGeometry StartPoint="20,10" EndPoint="50,220" />
              <EllipseGeometry Center="40,150" RadiusX="30" RadiusY="80" />
          </GeometryGroup>
      </Path.Data>
</Path>
```

Figure 3-10 shows the result of this code.

Figure 3-10

In the preceding image there is a white space where the rectangle and ellipse geometries intersect. The Path class has a property called the FillRule. It has two values: nonzero and evenodd. This property creates cutout effects to the GeometryCollection. To override the default value (evenodd), set FillRule="nonzero".

PathGeometry

PathGeometry is an intricate combination of arcs, curves, and shape geometries. The
PathFigureCollection is used within PathGeometry to hold more than one subpath (PathFigure).
The PathFigure itself can be composed of a combination of PathSegment, ArcSegment, and
BezierSegments.

When there is more than one of the segments present, they would be placed within a
PathSegmentCollection. The segments further define the final outcome to the subpath's appearance.
Following is the syntax structure used to encompass multiple the paths:

```
<Path Stroke="Black" StrokeThickness="1">
    <Path.Data>
        <PathGeometry>
            <PathGeometry.Figures>
                <PathFigureCollection>

                    //collection of figures goes here

                </PathFigureCollection>
            </PathGeometry.Figures>
        </PathGeometry>
    </Path.Data>
</Path>
```

Within each PathSegmentCollection there must be a StartSegment. This indicates where the path is
to be started. The CloseSegment property ends the segment and is also a useful indicator in more complex paths when one path ends and another begins.

```
<Path Stroke="Black" StrokeThickness="3">
    <Path.Data>
        <PathGeometry>
            <PathGeometry.Figures>
                <PathFigureCollection>
                    <!-- Start of triangle (first subpath)-->
                    <PathFigure>
                        <PathFigure.Segments>
                            <PathSegmentCollection>
                                <StartSegment Point="10,10" />
                                <LineSegment Point="30,50"/>
                                <LineSegment Point="50,20"/>
                                <CloseSegment />
                            </PathSegmentCollection>
                        </PathFigure.Segments>
                    </PathFigure>

                    <!-- Start of diamond shape (second subpath) -->
                    <PathFigure>
                        <PathFigure.Segments>
                            <PathSegmentCollection>
                                <StartSegment Point="50,20" />
                                <LineSegment Point="75,50"/>
                                <LineSegment Point="100,20"/>
```

```
                            <LineSegment Point="75,3"/>
                            <CloseSegment />
                        </PathSegmentCollection>
                    </PathFigure.Segments>
                </PathFigure>
            </PathFigureCollection>
        </PathGeometry.Figures>
    </PathGeometry>
  </Path.Data>
</Path>
```

Figure 3-11 shows the result of the preceding code.

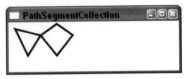

Figure 3-11

ArcSegment

ArcSegment represents an elliptical arc between two points. The Size property represents the X,Y coordinates of the arc's radius. The X,Y values of Point define the endpoint of the arc. Another property is the XRotation. It determines the amount of rotation to apply in relation to the other coordinates.

```
<Path Stroke="Black" StrokeThickness="1">
    <Path.Data>
        <PathGeometry>
            <PathGeometry.Figures>
                <PathFigureCollection>
                    <PathFigure>
                        <PathFigure.Segments>
                            <PathSegmentCollection>
                                <StartSegment Point="10,30" />
                                <ArcSegment Size="10,50" XRotation="130"
                                    LargeArc="True" SweepFlag="False"
                                    Point="100,10"/>
                            </PathSegmentCollection>
                        </PathFigure.Segments>
                    </PathFigure>
                </PathFigureCollection>
            </PathGeometry.Figures>
        </PathGeometry>
    </Path.Data>
</Path>
```

Figure 3-12 shows the ArcSegment defined in the preceding code.

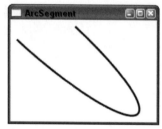

Figure 3-12

BezierSegment

This represents a cubic Bezier curve (a curve that is mathematically created from three points).

For most segments, the current point is a point used in calculations and is significant. The Bezier for example is constructed from four points: the current point, Point1, Point2, Point3. In the following sample, the start segment is defining the current point:

```
<Path Stroke="Black" StrokeThickness="1">
    <Path.Data>
        <PathGeometry>
            <PathGeometry.Figures>
                <PathFigureCollection>
                    <PathFigure>
                        <PathFigure.Segments>
                            <PathSegmentCollection>
                                <StartSegment Point="10,100" />
                                <BezierSegment Point1="100,0"
                                    Point2="200,200" Point3="300,100"/>
                            </PathSegmentCollection>
                        </PathFigure.Segments>
                    </PathFigure>
                </PathFigureCollection>
            </PathGeometry.Figures>
        </PathGeometry>
    </Path.Data>
</Path>
```

Avalon divides the curve into thirds and controls them with Point1, Point2, and Point3. Each point controls the X,Y coordinates of the curve.

LineSegment

This represents a line between two points. Point A (or the starting point) is represented by the StartSegment of the line, while the LineSegment represents point B.

```
<Path Stroke="Black" StrokeThickness="1">
    <Path.Data>
        <PathGeometry>
            <PathGeometry.Figures>
                <PathFigureCollection>
                    <PathFigure>
                        <PathFigure.Segments>
                            <PathSegmentCollection>
                                <StartSegment Point="10,50" />
                                <LineSegment Point="200,70"/>
                            </PathSegmentCollection>
                        </PathFigure.Segments>
                    </PathFigure>
                </PathFigureCollection>
            </PathGeometry.Figures>
        </PathGeometry>
    </Path.Data>
</Path>
```

QuadraticBezierSegment

This class creates a quadratic Bezier segment (a curve based on three anchor points: 0, 1, and 2). As with all other curves, the StartSegment is the starting point, Point0. Point2 is the ending point, and Point1 controls the curvature of the arc.

```
<Path Stroke="Black" StrokeThickness="1">
    <Path.Data>
        <PathGeometry>
            <PathGeometry.Figures>
                <PathFigureCollection>
                    <PathFigure>
                        <PathFigure.Segments>
                            <PathSegmentCollection>
                                <StartSegment Point="50,100" />
                                <QuadraticBezierSegment Point1="250,300"
                                    Point2="500,100"/>
                            </PathSegmentCollection>
                        </PathFigure.Segments>
                    </PathFigure>
                </PathFigureCollection>
            </PathGeometry.Figures>
        </PathGeometry>
    </Path.Data>
</Path>
```

Figure 3-13 shows the QuadraticBezierSegment result defined in the preceding code.

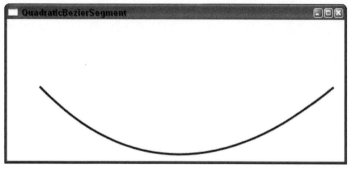

Figure 3-13

Poly Segments

There are three types of poly segments: `PolyBezierSegment`, `PolyLineSegment`, and `PolyQuadraticBezierSegment`. They each enable one or more segments of their type to be created and connected. Because the syntax is similar in each, they have been listed together in the following code:

```
<Path Stroke="Black" StrokeThickness="1">
    <Path.Data>
        <PathGeometry>
            <PathGeometry.Figures>
                <PathFigureCollection>
                    <!-- Beginning of PolyBezierSegment-->
                    <PathFigure>
                        <PathFigure.Segments>
                            <PathSegmentCollection>
                                <StartSegment Point="10,50" />
                                <PolyBezierSegment Points="100,0 200,200
                                    300,100 400,0 500,200 600,100"/>
                            </PathSegmentCollection>
                        </PathFigure.Segments>
                    </PathFigure>
                    <!-- Beginning of PolyLineSegment-->
                    <PathFigure>
                        <PathFigure.Segments>
                            <PathSegmentCollection>
                                <StartSegment Point="10,150" />
                                <PolyLineSegment Points="200,250 400,180"/>
                            </PathSegmentCollection>
                        </PathFigure.Segments>
                    </PathFigure>
                    <!-- Beginning of PolyQuadraticSegment-->
                    <PathFigure>
                        <PathFigure.Segments>
                            <PathSegmentCollection>
                                <StartSegment Point="50,200" />
                                <PolyQuadraticBezierSegment Points="250,400
                                    500,200 750,400 900,200" />
```

```
                                    </PathSegmentCollection>
                                </PathFigure.Segments>
                            </PathFigure>
                        </PathFigureCollection>
                    </PathGeometry.Figures>
                </PathGeometry>
            </Path.Data>
        </Path>
```

Figure 3-14 shows the result.

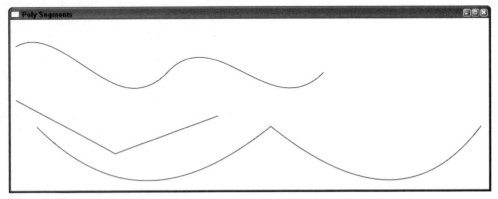

Figure 3-14

Abbreviated Path Syntax

Abbreviated syntax is used to help create smaller documents. Paths can also be created in this manner. This concept was adopted from the SVG abbreviated syntax. Following is the syntax for the same line written in two different manners: The top section of code is written in full syntax; the bottom part is in the abbreviated format. If you wish to test the syntax, remember to nest the paths within a StackPanel; otherwise, the lines will be on top of one another.

```
<StackPanel>
    <Path Stroke="Black" StrokeThickness="3">
        <Path.Data>
            <PathGeometry>
                <PathGeometry.Figures>
                    <PathFigureCollection>
                        <PathFigure>
                            <PathFigure.Segments>
                                <PathSegmentCollection>
                                    <StartSegment Point="10,50" />
                                    <LineSegment Point="200,70"/>
                                </PathSegmentCollection>
                            </PathFigure.Segments>
                        </PathFigure>
                    </PathFigureCollection>
```

```
            </PathGeometry.Figures>
         </PathGeometry>
      </Path.Data>
   </Path>

   <!-- Same line as above but in abbreviated version-->
   <Path Stroke="Black" StrokeThickness="3" Data="M 10,50 L 200,70" />
</StackPanel>
```

Figure 3-15 shows the resulting lines.

Figure 3-15

Data is the property that holds the string of commands and points in which the path will proceed to render the graphic. The M (for Move) represents the starting (or current) point from which it will proceed to the ending point of the segment, which is defined by the L (Line) coordinates. This syntax produces a much smaller document size for large drawings. Multiple subpaths can also be specified with the abbreviated path syntax. Each subpath contains its own move, draw, and optional close statements. The following example demonstrates a simple path, which is drawn using abbreviated syntax:

```
<Path Stroke="#000000" StrokeThickness="3" Data="M 250 20 L 150 50 L 350 150 z" />
```

Figure 3-16 illustrates the resulting shape.

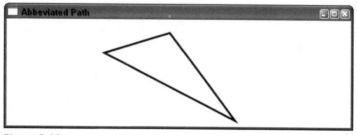

Figure 3-16

Chapter 3

In addition to lines, a draw command can create other lines and curves, including the following:

- ❏ Horizontal line
- ❏ Vertical line
- ❏ Cubic Bezier curve
- ❏ Quadratic Bezier curve
- ❏ Smooth cubic Bezier curve
- ❏ Elliptical arc

The command letter can be entered as either uppercase or lowercase. However, there is a difference between the two because the uppercase commands denote absolute values, whereas the lowercase ones indicate relative values. When entering more than one command of the same type (such as a series of lines) sequentially, it is not necessary to repeat the L command for each point. For example, both fragments define the same shape, However, the second is more efficient in its syntax size, which could ultimately improve the performance of the final product. This efficiency would be more prevalent when creating more complex graphics.

```
L 100,200 L 300,400.
L 100,200 300,400
```

Following is a table listing all the abbreviated commands available, with the most commonly used commands first. Either a space or comma may be used after each coordinate. To illustrate this format, the Abbreviated Syntax column shows the commas in the pseudocode and spaces in the sample fragment.

Command	Abbreviated Syntax	Description
Move	M x,y or m x,y M 100 200 or m 100 200	Denotes the beginning point (StartSegment) for the path (or subpath). As with all paths it requires a StartSegment; however, in abbreviated syntax, it is defined as Move (M).
Line	L x,y or l x,y L 200 300 or l 200 300	This creates a line from the last coordinate of the X,Y values specified in the Line command.
Horizontal Line	H x or h x H 100 or h 100	A command to create a horizontal line from the previous point to the X value of this command.
Vertical Line	V y or v y V 200 or v 200	A command to create a vertical line from the previous point to the Y value of this command.

Command	Abbreviated Syntax	Description
Close Path	Z or z	This represents the CloseSegment of the path. A straight line from the current point to the initial point of the current subpath. If there is a command other than a move command (to indicate a new subpath) following the close, the Z point will become the starting point for the new subpath. For example: `Data="M 250 20 L 150 50 L 350 150 z L 30 250"`.
Cubic Bezier Curve	C x1,y1 x2,y2 x3,y3 or c x1,y1 x2,y2 x3,y3 C 100 300 200 300 300 100 or c 100 300 200 300 300 100	This signifies a cubic Bezier curve. The arc starts at the current position or the last point drawn in the previous segment. x1,y1, and x2,y2 control the curvature of the arc. x3,y3 specify the endpoint of the curve and becomes the start point for the next segment of the path.
Smooth Cubic Bezier Curve	S x1,y1 x2,y2 or s x1,y1 x2,y2 S 100 200 200 300 or s 100 200 200 300	This command also creates a cubic Bezier curve; while the second point completes the curve, the first point reflects the curve with the ending point of the previous command. For example, if the syntax fragment of this curve followed the cubic Bezier curve's fragment, it would look like an upside-down loop. If it followed a Z, it would look like a cup.
Quadratic Bezier Curve	Q x1,y1 x2,y2 or q x1,y1 x2,y2 Q 50 150 200 150 or q 50 150 200 150	This creates a quadratic Bezier curve. The second point completes the curve, while the first point controls the arc of the curve.

Table continued on following page

Command	Abbreviated Syntax	Description
Elliptical Arc	A xr,yr rx flag1 flag2 x,y or a xr,yr rx flag1 flag2 x,y A 300 50 180 1 0 50 50 a 300 50 180 1 0 50 50	This creates an elliptical arc. The first coordinates control the radius for both the X and Y plane. The next value (which is a degree value) controls the overall dimension and placement of the ellipse. The center point is not defined because it is calculated in from the other values. The next two values are the flags and have a value of 0 or 1. Flag1 controls which of the arc sweeps to apply. Within an elliptical arc there are actually four candidate arc sweeps; two represent large arcs with sweeps of 180 degrees or greater, and two represent smaller arcs with sweeps 180 degrees or less. Therefore, if Flag1 has a value of 1, the larger sweep will be applied. Flag2 indicates if the arc will be drawn in a positive or negative angled direction. Therefore, if Flag2 has a value of 1, the arc will be drawn as a positive angle.

Following is the syntax of an abbreviated path using all the values displayed from the preceding table:

```
<Path Stroke="#000000" StrokeThickness="3" Data="M 100 200 L 200 300 H 100 V 200 Z
C 100 300 200 300 300 100 S 100,200 200,300 Q 50 150 200 150 A 300 50 180 1 0 50 50
z " />
```

Figure 3-17 shows the result.

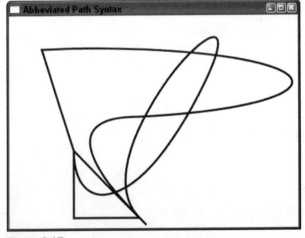

Figure 3-17

Painting and Brushes

Brushes are used for specifying how color will be applied (painted) on the `Stroke` and `Fill` of 2-D graphics. They are used to specify the painting of the `Background`, `Foreground`, and `Borders` for `Controls` and `Material` on 3-D objects.

Some of the concepts for painting and filling 2-D graphics in Avalon are very similar to those in SVG. To illustrate the outline of a graphic, you use the shape's `Stroke` property, and you use the `Fill` property to color the shape's interior. For controls and 3-D objects, the properties are `BorderBrush` (for the outline) and `Background` or `Material` for their interior areas. Controls also have a `Foreground` property that controls the visual appearance of the content (usually text) in the control.

```
<Rectangle Height="74" Width="144" Fill="Red" Stroke="Black" />

<Button Height="74" Width="144" Background="Blue" BorderBrush="Black"
    Foreground="White" >Button</Button>
```

Figure 3-18 shows the result of executing this code.

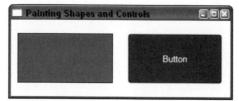

Figure 3-18

This XAML fragment creates two objects. The first is a red rectangle with a black outline, and the second is a blue button with a black border and white text. This sample leads into how to specify colors in an Avalon document. As with much of the API, you have options in the area of color; both common color names and hexadecimal conventions are valid formats to use.

Common color names, such as red and black, are valid. The property's value is not case-sensitive. Hexadecimal RGB (Red, Green, Blue) is the other option for specifying a brush's color. At the time of printing, system color names, such as `ActiveCaption`, are not a valid naming convention. Instead, use the equivalent in the hexadecimal format (#FF0054E3) or the RGB format (#0054E3).

In both Avalon and SVG, `Transparent` is considered a valid color name; however, in Avalon the color must be specified like `Fill="Transparent"` not `Fill= ""` or it will be considered an empty string. Opacity can also be set for the stroke (or fill) by using the ARGB format (#AARRGGBB), where `AA` represents the opacity value. In addition to specifying the opacity, using the alpha channel in the color, brushes also have an `Opacity` property to control the transparency.

The following fragments are all equivalent and valid formats:

- ❏ **Named format** — `Fill="Red" Stroke="Black"`
- ❏ **Abbreviated format** — `Fill="#F00" Stroke="#000"`

❑ **Standard format** — `Fill="#FF0000" Stroke="#000000"`

❑ **Extended format** — `Fill="#FFFF0000" Stroke="#FF000000"`

Solid Color Brush

`SolidColorBrush` uniformly applies a single solid color to an element. The `System.Windows.Media` namespace in Avalon also defines some premade `SolidColorBrushes`. They are static system brushes accessible from the `Brush` class.

`SolidColorBrush` can be specified by simply assigning a color value to a property expecting a brush, such as `Fill="Green"`. The *Internal Type Converters* convert the color to a `SolidColorBrush`. Alternatively, `SolidColorBrush` itself may be explicitly set and assigned in XAML. Both formats are provided in the following sample:

```
<!-- Applying a color value -->
<Ellipse CenterX="120" CenterY="120" RadiusX="100" RadiusY="50" Fill="Yellow"
    Opacity="0.4"/>



<!-- Format used to specify the brush  which is to apply the color -->
<Ellipse CenterX="120" CenterY="120" RadiusX="100" RadiusY="50">
    <Ellipse.Fill>
            <SolidColorBrush Color="Yellow" Opacity="0.4"/>
    </Ellipse.Fill>
</Ellipse>
```

Gradient Brushes

Both gradients (`LinearGradientBrush` and `RadialGradientBrush`) represent multicolored brushes that blend the colors on an axis. As their names imply, the linear gradient flows across a linear plane, whereas the radial radiates the colors out from its center. There is no limit to the number of colors that either brush can have, but they must have a minimum of two colors or the result will look as if `SolidColorBrush` was applied.

`GradientStop` controls the gradation from one color to the next, and both brushes share this property.

Each stop controls an individual color in the gradient and its position or offset. `Offset` is a double type valued property with a range from 0 to 1. The purpose of the offset is to interpolate the color at various positions in relation to the offset values of the other colors present in the gradient. Colors where a large gap between offset values is present result in a gradual gradation, whereas colors with a small separation have a sharper color change, as illustrated in Figure 3-19.

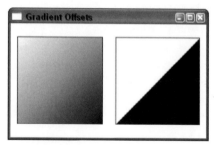

Figure 3-19

The rectangle on the left shows a large offset value difference; the rectangle on the right has no difference.

```
<!-- Large value difference between offsets -->
<Rectangle Height="130" Stroke="#FF000000" Width="130">
    <Shape.Fill>
        <LinearGradientBrush EndPoint="1,1" Opacity="1">
            <GradientBrush.GradientStops>
                <GradientStopCollection>
                    <GradientStop Color="White" Offset="0" />
                    <GradientStop Color="Black" Offset="1" />
                </GradientStopCollection>
            </GradientBrush.GradientStops>
        </LinearGradientBrush>
    </Shape.Fill>
</Rectangle>

<!-- No gap in value between offsets -->
<Rectangle Height="130" Stroke="#FF000000" Width="130">
    <Shape.Fill>
        <LinearGradientBrush EndPoint="1,1" Opacity="1">
            <GradientBrush.GradientStops>
                <GradientStopCollection>
                    <GradientStop Color="White" Offset="0.5" />
                    <GradientStop Color="Black" Offset="0.5" />
                </GradientStopCollection>
            </GradientBrush.GradientStops>
        </LinearGradientBrush>
    </Shape.Fill>
</Rectangle>
```

Linear Gradient Brush

LinearGradientBrush represents a multicolored brush, and the colors flow along a linear axis. To further define the appearance, it has two other properties, the StartPoint and the EndPoint. Together they orient the flow in which the gradient is to travel. To further explain this concept, the following example (see Figure 3-20) displays how the colors are interpolated along the diagonal created between the start- and endpoints:

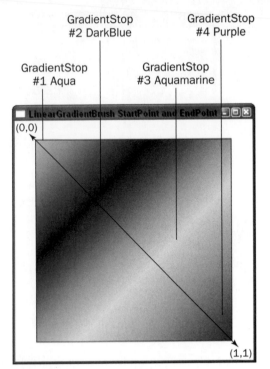

Figure 3-20

```
<Rectangle Height="300" Stroke="#FF000000" Width="300">
    <Shape.Fill>
        <LinearGradientBrush EndPoint="1,1" Opacity="1" StartPoint="0,0">
            <GradientBrush.GradientStops>
                <GradientStopCollection>
                    <GradientStop Color="Aqua" Offset="0" />
                    <GradientStop Color="DarkBlue"
                        Offset="0.29652605459057074" />
                    <GradientStop Color="Aquamarine"
                        Offset="0.60607940446650121" />
                    <GradientStop Color="Purple" Offset="1" />
                </GradientStopCollection>
            </GradientBrush.GradientStops>
        </LinearGradientBrush>
    </Shape.Fill>
</Rectangle>
```

Radial Gradient Brush

RadialGradientBrush is similar to LinearGradientBrush except that the axis used for interpolation of the colors is defined from the center of an ellipse outwards.

RadialGradientBrush has four properties (GradientOrigin, Center, RadiusX, and RadiusY) to further the exact positioning and appearance of the gradient. The GradientOrigin determines where the gradient will begin. The `Center` property controls where the gradient will radiate out from. The two radius properties control the vertical and horizontal arc that will be applied to the gradient.

```
<Ellipse StrokeThickness="25px" RadiusX="100px" RadiusY="50px">
    <Shape.Fill>
        <RadialGradientBrush Center="0.653846153846154,0.730769230769231"
            RadiusX="0.77149321266968374" RadiusY="0.77149321266968374"
            GradientOrigin="0.144796380090498,0.30316742081448" >
            <GradientBrush.GradientStops>
                <GradientStopCollection>
                    <GradientStop Color="Aqua" Offset="0.28054298642533937" />
                    <GradientStop Color="DarkBlue"
                        Offset="0.50904977375565619" />
                    <GradientStop Color="Magenta"
                        Offset="0.59162895927601811" />
                    <GradientStop Color="AquaMarine"
                        Offset="0.71662895927601822" />
                </GradientStopCollection>
            </GradientBrush.GradientStops>
        </RadialGradientBrush>
    </Shape.Fill>
</Ellipse>
```

Figure 3-21 shows the results.

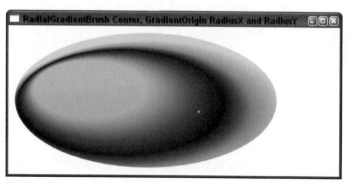

Figure 3-21

Abbreviated XAML Gradient Syntax

As you can see from the previous examples, the syntax for specifying a gradient brush can be verbose. To shorten the lengthy syntax, the Avalon type converters can translate it into a simpler string representation. Unfortunately, it can have only two colors.

```
<!-- LinearGradientBrush full syntax -->
<Rectangle Margin="10,10,10,10" Width="150" Height="100"  Stroke="#FF000000" >
    <Shape.Fill>
        <LinearGradientBrush EndPoint="0.5,0.5" Opacity="1"
            StartPoint="0.1,0.1">
```

```
                        <GradientBrush.GradientStops>
                            <GradientStopCollection>
                                <GradientStop Color="Red" Offset="0.0" />
                                <GradientStop Color="AliceBlue" Offset="1.0" />
                            </GradientStopCollection>
                        </GradientBrush.GradientStops>
                </LinearGradientBrush>
            </Shape.Fill>
</Rectangle>

<!-- LinearGradientBrush in abbreviated syntax -->
<Rectangle Width="150" Height="100"
    Fill="LinearGradient 0.1,0.1 0.5,0.5 Red AliceBlue"/>


<!-- RadialGradientBrush full syntax -->
<Rectangle Margin="10,10,10,10" Width="150" Height="100" Stroke="#FF000000" >
    <Shape.Fill>
            <RadialGradientBrush Opacity="1" GradientOrigin="0.5,0.5"
                Center="0.5,0.5"  RadiusX="0.5" RadiusY="0.5">
                <GradientBrush.GradientStops>
                    <GradientStopCollection>
                        <GradientStop Color="Red" Offset="0.0" />
                        <GradientStop Color="AliceBlue" Offset="1.0" />
                    </GradientStopCollection>
                </GradientBrush.GradientStops>
            </RadialGradientBrush>
        </Shape.Fill>
</Rectangle>


<!-- RadialGradientBrush abreviated syntax -->
<Rectangle Fill="RadialGradient Red AliceBlue" Width="150" Height="100" />
```

Figure 3-22 shows results for both the full and abbreviated syntax.

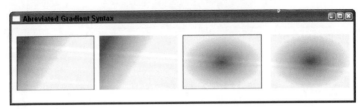

Figure 3-22

The two outlined shapes were created with the full syntax, whereas the shapes without a Stroke *were written with the abbreviated syntax.*

Brushes that Paint with Graphics

The next three brushes are a little different in that instead of a color they illustrate elements with graphics. Graphics can be images, drawings, patterns, 3-D images or video. Before discussing each one individually, the common layout properties of each of them are reviewed.

To control the appearance of the graphics there are four formatting properties available:

- ❑ VerticalAlignment
- ❑ HorzontalAlignment
- ❑ ImageStretch
- ❑ TileMode

The alignment of the image is set using HorizontalAlignment or VerticalAlignment with one of the following values: Left, Right, or Center.

To have the graphic fill the element, apply the brush to the ImageStretch property. This property has four values: Fill, None, Uniform, and UniformToFill. Because the values are fairly self-explanatory, see the sample shown in Figure 2-23 to identify their differences.

Figure 3-23

This figure illustrates the four ImageStretch properties (from left to right: None, Fill, Uniform, and UniformToFill).

Another common property is the TileMode property. It allows you to reverse or invert the graphic to create a tiled pattern. The values available are FlipX, FlipY, FlipXY, Tile, or None. Tile repeats the initial pattern without any flipping; the value None means that no tile effects are implemented.

Image Brush

As its name implies, this brush paints an object with an image. An image can be any of the following formats: .jpg, .gif, .png, .tiff, .bmp, and .ico.

```
<Button FontSize="26px" FontWeight="ExtraBold" Foreground="#FF000000" Height="149"
    Name="myButton" Canvas.Left="47" Canvas.Top="25" Width="216">
    <Control.Background>
        <ImageBrush AlignmentX="Right" AlignmentY="Top"
            ImageSource="MyFlower.png" Opacity="0.5" Stretch="None"
            TileMode="None" />
    </Control.Background>
    <ContentControl.Content>Button1</ContentControl.Content>
</Button>
```

Figure 3-24 shows the results of the preceding code.

Figure 3-24

Drawing Brush

The drawing brush is similar to the image brush, but it fills the interior area of an element with a drawing. The benefit of this brush is that it can fill an area with vector or bitmap images as well as video and drawings. In addition, it's smaller and has a faster rendering time than other FrameworkElements, which makes this brush an ideal option for creating clipart and backgrounds.

DrawingBrush displays the drawing's elements in proportion to the area it is to fill. Because DrawingBrush is independent from the element, it is able to fill the area of one or more differently shaped elements consistently with its tiling property. Nesting within the DrawingGroup enables you to apply multiple drawings to elements.

The size of the elements can be controlled by setting the output proportions with double values between 0 and 1. Therefore, if you set the proportion size to 0.5, the drawing element will fill 50 percent of the area. To prevent any distortion set Stretch="None".

DrawingBrush has two other properties to control the horizontal and vertical layout. AlignmentX controls the horizontal plane and has three values to choose from: Left, Center, and Right. AlignmentY controls the vertical plane and has three values to choose from: Top, Center, and Bottom. This tool is an effective means for creating and repeating intricate patterns, as shown in the following:

```
<Rectangle Width="200" Height="200"
    Stroke="LinearGradient 0.0,0.5 0.1,0.7 Silver Black" StrokeThickness="3">
    <Rectangle.Fill>
        <DrawingBrush>
            <DrawingBrush.Drawing>
                <GeometryDrawing Brush="RadialGradient Blue Red">
                    <GeometryDrawing.Geometry>
                        <GeometryGroup>
                            <EllipseGeometry RadiusX="0.3" RadiusY="0.45"
                                Center="0.5,0.5" />
                            <EllipseGeometry RadiusX="0.45" RadiusY="0.2"
                                Center="0.5,0.5" />
                            <EllipseGeometry RadiusX="0.2" RadiusY="0.3"
                                Center="0.5,0.5" />
                            <EllipseGeometry RadiusX="0.45"
                                RadiusY="0.45" Center="0.5,0.5" />
                        </GeometryGroup>
                    </GeometryDrawing.Geometry>
                    <GeometryDrawing.Pen>
                        <Pen Thickness="0.026"
                            Brush="RadialGradient Black Transparent" />
                    </GeometryDrawing.Pen>
                </GeometryDrawing>
            </DrawingBrush.Drawing>
        </DrawingBrush>
    </Rectangle.Fill>
</Rectangle>
```

Figure 3-25 shows the result of the preceding code.

Figure 3-25

VisualBrush

VisualBrush is similar to DrawingBrush except that it maintains the layout. The most interesting thing about this tool is that it empowers you to add something from another part of the Visual Tree. VisualBrush enables you to create side-by-side views of an item, where one is a zoomed-in version of the original. Also this brush empowers you to paint the surface of 3-D objects with visuals. To illustrate the power of this brush, Figure 3-26 uses the 3-D syntax. (The actual syntax follows the figure.)

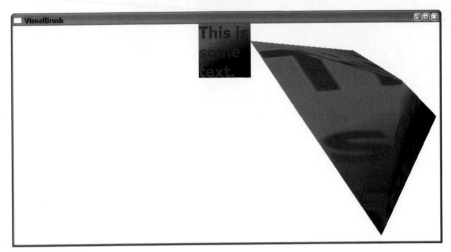

Figure 3-26

```
<StackPanel >
    <StackPanel.Resources>
        <VisualBrush x:Key="visualBrush" Viewbox="0,0,1,1">
            <VisualBrush.Visual>
                <StackPanel Background="LinearGradient 0.3,0.3 0.55,0.78  Red
                    Black">
                    <TextBlock Height="100" Width="100" FontSize="30"
                        FontWeight="Bold" FontFamily="times" Foreground="Blue"
                        TextWrap="Wrap" >
                            This is some text. That can wrap around the corners
                                of a 3D Object!
                    </TextBlock>
                </StackPanel>
            </VisualBrush.Visual>
        </VisualBrush>
    </StackPanel.Resources>

    <!-- Please note, the Canvas tag on the next line is a workaround for Beta
        Release Candidate 2 and will likely be unnecessary in later releases. -->
    <Canvas Background="{StaticResource visualBrush}" Height="100" Width="100" >
        <Viewport3D Canvas.Left="60" ClipToBounds="True" Height="480"
            Width="640">
            <Viewport3D.Camera>
                <PerspectiveCamera NearPlaneDistance="1" FarPlaneDistance="100"
                    LookAtPoint="0,-1,0" Position="-8, 0, 8" Up="1, 1, 0"
                    FieldOfView="30"/>
            </Viewport3D.Camera>
            <Viewport3D.Models>
                <Model3DGroup>
                    <Model3DGroup.Children>
                        <!--Lights-->
                        <DirectionalLight Color="#FFFFFFFF"
                            Direction="3,-1,-3" />
```

```
                                    <AmbientLight Color="#66666666" />

                                    <!--Pyramid-->
                                    <GeometryModel3D>
                                        <GeometryModel3D.Geometry>
                                            <MeshGeometry3D Positions="-1 -2 -0.5 2 -1
                                                -0.5 -1 2 -0.5 1 1 -0.5 0 0 1"
                                                Normals="-1 -1 0 0 -1 0 -1 0 1 0 0.5
                                                0 0 0 1" TextureCoordinates="0 1 1 1 0
                                                0 1 0 0.25 0.25" TriangleIndices="0 4 2
                                                2 4 3 4 1 3 0 1 4" />
                                        </GeometryModel3D.Geometry>
                                        <GeometryModel3D.Material>
                                            <DiffuseMaterial
                                                Brush="{StaticResource visualBrush}" />
                                        </GeometryModel3D.Material>
                                    </GeometryModel3D>
                                </Model3DGroup.Children>
                            </Model3DGroup>
                        </Viewport3D.Models>
                    </Viewport3D>
                </Canvas>
            </StackPanel>
```

To learn more about 3-D, go to Chapter 4, "Advanced Features."

Opacity Mask

An opacity mask enables you to combine one object with other objects. You can then define areas on the combined objects with transparencies. In Avalon, the opacity is a little different from the brushes in that it is actually a property to which you apply a brush to alter the appearance of an element. It seems to work like a combination of the image brush and the gradient brush; however, instead of a gradation of colors, it is a gradation of opacity. With the use of alpha channels it blocks out areas, enabling you to create visual effects or cutouts to an image. The opacity value is a double-valued range between 0 and 1, where 0 is transparent and 1 is opaque.

Figure 3-27 shows different ways of creating a mask. The first is without any mask; the second is with a radial gradient; next is the image that has been applied as a mask to the button on the far right. The code to recreate them follows.

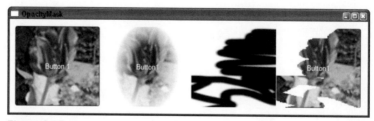

Figure 3-27

```
<StackPanel Orientation="Horizontal">

    <!-- Button with an image applied without an opacity mask applied -->
        <Button Height="149" Width="165" Foreground="White" Content="Button 1">
            <Control.Background>
                <ImageBrush BitmapSource="MyFlower.png" Stretch="UniformToFill" />
            </Control.Background>
        </Button>

    <!-- Button with an image applied with a radial gradient opacity mask applied --
>
        <Button Height="149" Width="165" Foreground="White" Content="Button1">
            <Control.Background>
                <ImageBrush BitmapSource="MyFlower.png" Stretch="UniformToFill" />
            </Control.Background>
            <UIElement.OpacityMask>
                <RadialGradientBrush Center="0.490074441687345,0.508684863523573"
                    GradientOrigin="0.5,0.46029776674938" Opacity="1"
                    RadiusX="0.37593052109181158" RadiusY="0.5496277915632749">
                    <GradientBrush.GradientStops>
                        <GradientStopCollection>
                            <GradientStop Color="#FF000000"
                                Offset="0.42718446601941745" />
                            <GradientStop Color="#00FFFFFF" Offset="1" />
                        </GradientStopCollection>
                    </GradientBrush.GradientStops>
                </RadialGradientBrush>
            </UIElement.OpacityMask>
        </Button>

    <!-- Image that is applied as a mask the last button -->
        <Image Height="149" Width="165" Source="ImageMask.gif" />

    <!-- Button with the image above that is applied as a mask -->
        <Button Height="149" Width="165" Content="Button1" Foreground="White">
            <Control.Background>
                <ImageBrush BitmapSource="MyFlower.png" Stretch="UniformToFill" />
            </Control.Background>
            <UIElement.OpacityMask>
                <ImageBrush BitmapSource="ImageMask.gif" Opacity="1"
                    Stretch="UniformToFill />
            </UIElement.OpacityMask>
        </Button>
</StackPanel>
```

Transforms

Transforms enable you to alter the location, size, appearance, and rotation of an object. Transforms affect any visual element, including controls (both visually and through animation). There are six types of transforms:

- TransformGroup
- TranslateTransform
- RotateTransform
- ScaleTransform
- SkewTransform
- MatrixTransform

Each transform is defined by a 3×3 matrix, which is applied as a Matrix property on each Transform class. Transforms are set on an individual object using the RenderTransform.

TransformGroup

TransformGroup acts as a container when more than one transform is present. Without using the TransformGroup, a transform can have only one child. However, as with the elements discussed earlier, the child can be a complex object such as a Canvas. This can come in handy if you have laid out an intricate table and you then want to scale it down to fit within the formatting of another XAML document.

```
<Canvas>
    <Canvas.RenderTransform>
        <TransformGroup>
            <SkewTransform AngleX="10" AngleY="10" />
            <RotateTransform Center="0 0" Angle="-30" />
            <TranslateTransform X="100" Y="50" />
            <ScaleTransform ScaleX="1.5" ScaleY="1.5" />
        </TransformGroup>
    </Canvas.RenderTransform>
    <Polygon Fill="Pink" Stroke="#FF000000" StrokeThickness="3"
        Points="65,150.238333333333 10,64.2383333333333 61,9.23833333333332
        149,62.2383333333333 67,35.2383333333333 38,67.2383333333333"/>

    <Ellipse CenterX="245" CenterY="101.23833333333332" Fill="#FFFF0000"
        RadiusX="88" RadiusY="44" Stroke="#FF000000"/>

    <Button Width="100" Height="30">Translated Button</Button>
</Canvas>
```

Figure 3-28 shows the result of the preceding code, where each element has been transformed with all of the transforms in the TransformGroup.

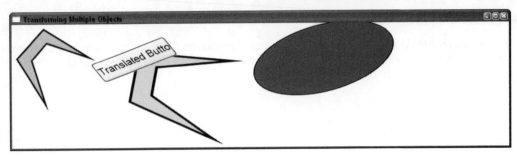

Figure 3-28

TranslateTransform

`TranslateTransform` changes the object's horizontal and/or vertical location.

The gold polygon in Figures 3-29 through 3-32 denotes the polygon before the transform has been applied.

```
<Polygon Fill="Pink" Stroke="#FF000000" StrokeThickness="3"
    Points="65,150.238333333333 10,64.2383333333333 61,9.23833333333332
    149,62.2383333333333 67,35.2383333333333 38,67.2383333333333" >
    <Polygon.RenderTransform>
        <TranslateTransform X="350" Y="55" />
    </Polygon.RenderTransform>
</Polygon>
```

Figure 3-29 shows how the polygon has been relocated to the new coordinates stated in the preceding code.

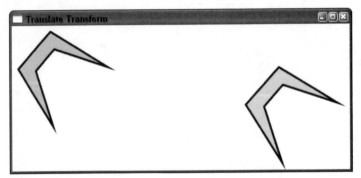

Figure 3-29

RotateTransform

RotateTransform rotates an object around a specific point (Center) by the specified angle.

```
<TransformDecorator AffectsLayout="false">
    <TransformDecorator.Transform>
        <RotateTransform Center="80,80" Angle="20"/>
    </TransformDecorator.Transform>

<Polygon Fill="Pink" Stroke="#FF000000" StrokeThickness="3"
    Points="65,150.238333333333 10,64.2383333333333 61,9.23833333333332
    149,62.2383333333333 67,35.2383333333333 38,67.2383333333333" >
    <Polygon.RenderTransform>
        <RotateTransform Center="80,80" Angle="-40" />
    </Polygon.RenderTransform>
</Polygon>
</TransformDecorator>
```

Figure 3-30 shows how the polygon has been rotated to the new coordinates stated in the preceding code.

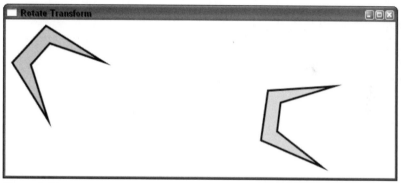

Figure 3-30

ScaleTransform

This property scales a child by the specified values in ScaleX and ScaleY, as shown in the following code and Figure 3-31:

```
<TransformDecorator AffectsLayout="false">
    <TransformDecorator.Transform>
        <ScaleTransform ScaleX="1.5" ScaleY="0.5" />
    </TransformDecorator.Transform>

<Polygon Fill="Pink" Stroke="#FF000000" StrokeThickness="3"
    Points="65,150.238333333333 10,64.2383333333333 61,9.23833333333332
    149,62.2383333333333 67,35.2383333333333 38,67.2383333333333" >
    <Polygon.RenderTransform>

</TransformDecorator>
```

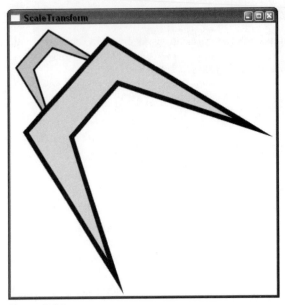

Figure 3-31

SkewTransform

SkewTransform enables you to distort the original shape of an element by an angle on either the X-axis, the Y-axis, or both. This is demonstrated in the following code and Figure 3-32:

```
<Polygon Fill="Pink" Stroke="#FF000000" StrokeThickness="3"
    Points="65,150.238333333333 10,64.2383333333333 61,9.23833333333332
    149,62.2383333333333 67,35.2383333333333 38,67.2383333333333">
    <Polygon.RenderTransform>
        <SkewTransform AngleX="25" AngleY="30"/>
    </Polygon.RenderTransform>
</Polygon>
```

Figure 3-32

MatrixTransform

The MatrixTransform is for creating custom transforms that cannot be accomplished with the previous transform classes. It is a 3 × 3 matrix that performs the transform over a two-dimensional X, Y plane. The structure of the markup is:

```
MatrixTransform="(M11,M12,M21,M22,OffsetX,OffsetY)"
```

Implementing 2-D Animation

The animation subsystem in Avalon relies heavily on DependencyProperties for its functionality. Generally speaking, any dependency property that represents a property of a type can be organized into one of the four animation class types listed in the following table.

Property	Animation	Definition
Color	ColorAnimation	Animates the color on a Brush or GradientStop.
Double	DoubleAnimation	Animates the Opacity, Angle, or Length properties.
Point	PointAnimation	Animates a specific spot on the X,Y plane in a linear fashion. PointAnimation is commonly used for lines and paths.
String	None	Animates the TextContent of a TextBlock or the Content of a Button.

For each of these classes, there are three common key properties used to determine how an animation is executed:

❑ By — Acts as a measurement in that it determines how much of an animation will occur.

❑ From — Determines the initial stage for which the transition will begin. The double type valued range is from 0 to 1.

❑ To — Determines the final stage of the transition. The double type valued range is from 0 to 1.

Timelines

Before going into each of the animation types, it is best to review some of the key timeline properties. Many of the animations properties come from the Timeline class located in the System.Windows.Media.Animation namespace.

Timeline is a public base class that determines a period of time. It is at this level of the hierarchy that when, where, and how animations will be executed based on the element's properties are defined. The following table lists properties that are common to most animations.

Common Timeline Terms	Definition
AccelerationRatio	A double type valued property that determines the percentage of rate increase that will occur over the duration of the animation.
AutoReverse	A Boolean type valued property that determines the assigned time that a Timeline should be initiated in relation to its parent's Begin-Time.
BeginTime	Determines the assigned time that a Timeline should be initiated.
CutOffTime	Determines when an animation is to end in relation to its parent's BeginTime.
DecelerationRatio	The opposite of the AccelerationRatio, this determines the percentage rate decrease that will occur over the duration of the animation.
Duration	The time it will take for the animation to complete. The format for the time must be H:M:S (Hours:Minutes:Seconds)
FillBehavior	Determines the behavior of a Timeline when it is inactive despite its parent being in an active or hold state.
Name	Determines the Name of the Timeline
RepeatBehavior	This is the looping behavior in Avalon. It determines the number of times the animation will occur. For example, if it is to animate twice, the syntax would be `RepeatBehavior="2x"`, whereas if it were to be infinite the value would be `"Forever"`.
SpeedRatio	A double type valued property that determines the time ratio the animation will progress over the Timeline. If either the AccelerationRatio or DecelerationRatio properties is set, the default value of this property is "1.0".

Stemming from the `Timeline` class is the `TimelineGroup`, which is a base class that holds multiple timelines together. Within this class is determined the `ParallelTimeline`. The `ParallelTimeline` is based on its children's beginning times instead of the order in which they are placed in the group. This control enables multiple and overlapping animations to occur simultaneously.

The third and final time line is the `SetterTimeline`. Inherited from the `ParallelTimeline`, the `SetterTimeline` class determines the value and (its duration) of a property at the point(s) in time. The `SetterTimeline` has three properties (`Path`, `Value`, and `TargetName`) that further establish the manner in which an element will be animated. These properties are described in the following table.

SetterTimeline Properties	Definition
Path	This determines the property of the target element that will be animated. The basic syntax for a path value is (`ClassName.PropertyName`). The syntax to animate the opacity of a shape's fill is: `Path="(Rectangle.Fill).(SolidColorBrush.Opacity)"`.
TargetName	This enables an animation to be triggered based on an Element's Name. If the TargetName is not specified, the animation will animate the base element within the SetterTimeline.
Value	This determines the starting value of the animation.

Storyboard

To create an animation, you must have a Storyboard present. Located on the root element of the application, the Storyboard enables you to manage multiple timelines and objects within a single tree as well as control all the timing behaviors for each, which can vary from simple to the complex. Another benefit is that amount of markup is greatly reduced.

Following is the basic structure for creating an animation in an XAML document.

```
<RootElement>
    <RootElement.Storyboard>
        <ParallelTimeline Name="TimelineOne" BeginTime="00:00:00">
            <SetterTimeline TargetName="Element1">
                <AnimationType />
            </SetterTimeline>
        </ParallelTimeline>

        <ParallelTimeline Name="TimelineTwo" BeginTime="00:00:05">
            <SetterTimeline TargetName="Element2">
                <AnimationType />
            </SetterTimeline>

            <SetterTimeline TargetName="Element2">
                <AnimationType />
            </SetterTimeline>
            <SetterTimeline TargetName= "Element1">
                <AnimationType />
            </SetterTimeline>
        </ParallelTimeline>
    </RootElement.Storyboard>
    <Element Name="Element1"/>
    <Element Name="Element2"/>
</RootElement>
```

Because animation can get quite involved, following are examples of all of the common animation properties to all of the animation types.

In the following sample, the property `DoubleAnimation` property is used to animate the endpoints. The behaviors of the `From`, `To`, and `By` properties are the same for all the animation classes.

This example increases the line's value from 50 to 500 over 20 seconds. The `DoubleAnimation` overrides the line's initial value to the new values stated in the `DoubleAnimation`. The `Duration` property is the measure in time that the animation will take to execute the transition from the beginning value to the target value.

```
<StackPanel xmlns="http://schemas.microsoft.com/winfx/avalon/2005">
    <StackPanel.Storyboards>
        <SetterTimeline TargetName="myLine" Path="(Line.X2)">
            <DoubleAnimation From="50" To="500" Duration="0:0:20"
                RepeatBehavior="Forever"/>
        </SetterTimeline>
    </StackPanel.Storyboards>

    <Line Name="myLine" X1="10" Y1="10" X2="100" Y2="10" Stroke="Green"
        StrokeThickness="10" Opacity="0.5"/>
</StackPanel>
```

In the next example, only the `To` property is set. This means the `From` value will be the base value of the property it is animating or the ending value of a previous animation. This animation uses the base value of the line's `X2` property, 100, as its starting value. This animation will only occur three times because the `RepeatBehavior="3x"`.

This value is case-sensitive and must have a lowercase x to work.

```
<StackPanel xmlns="http://schemas.microsoft.com/winfx/avalon/2005">
    <StackPanel.Storyboards>
        <SetterTimeline TargetName="myLine" Path="(Line.X2)">
            <DoubleAnimation To="300" Duration="0:0:20" RepeatBehavior="3x"/>
        </SetterTimeline>
    </StackPanel.Storyboards>

    <Line Name="myLine" X1="10" Y1="10" X2="100" Y2="10" Stroke="Green"
        StrokeThickness="10" Opacity="0.5"/>
</StackPanel>
```

The `By` property determines "by how much" the animation changes an element's value over a period of time. As stated earlier, the animation uses the base value (or ending value from a previous animation) to build the new animation from its starting value. It then adds 500 to that value over a time period of 20 seconds. Setting the `By` value instead of the `To` value is effective when exact dimensions are more pertinent than layout, as with blueprint drawings.

```
<StackPanel xmlns="http://schemas.microsoft.com/winfx/avalon/2005">
    <StackPanel.Storyboards>
        <SetterTimeline TargetName="myLine" Path="(Line.X2)">
            <DoubleAnimation By="500" Duration="0:0:20"
                RepeatBehavior="Forever"/>
        </SetterTimeline>
```

```
    </StackPanel.Storyboards>

    <Line Name="myLine" X1="10" Y1="10" X2="100" Y2="10" Stroke="Green"
        StrokeThickness="10" Opacity="0.5"/>
</StackPanel>
```

This next sample is the same as the preceding, except that both the By and From properties have set values. Even though the line is defined to be 90 px long the animation From value changes the beginning dimension to 1 px long. This means that the line length will first appear to be 1 px long and then lengthen to 510 px over the next 20 seconds.

```
<StackPanel xmlns="http://schemas.microsoft.com/winfx/avalon/2005">
    <StackPanel.Storyboards>
        <SetterTimeline TargetName="myLine" Path="(Line.X2)">
            <!-- Animate the Line's length from 1  by 510 -->
            <DoubleAnimation From="1" By="500" Duration="0:0:20"
                RepeatBehavior="Forever"/>
        </SetterTimeline>
    </StackPanel.Storyboards>
    <Line Name="myLine" X1="10" Y1="10" X2="100" Y2="10" Stroke="Green"
        StrokeThickness="10" Opacity="0.5"/>
</StackPanel>
```

The base value of the property is used as the destination value when no destination value has been set. In the following syntax, the line will first appear 50 px long and then grow to 100 px long over a period of 5 seconds:

```
<StackPanel xmlns="http://schemas.microsoft.com/winfx/avalon/2005">
    <StackPanel.Storyboards>
        <SetterTimeline TargetName="myLine" Path="(Line.X2)">
            <!-- Animate the Line's length from 50  to 100. -->
            <DoubleAnimation From="50" Duration="0:0:2"
                RepeatBehavior="3x" AutoReverse="True" />
        </SetterTimeline>
    </StackPanel.Storyboards>

    <Line Name="myLine" X1="10" Y1="10" X2="100" Y2="10" Stroke="Pink"
        StrokeThickness="10" Opacity="0.5" />
</StackPanel>
```

Color Animation

The following XAML will animate the color of a SolidColorBrush from red to blue and reverse the colors three times:

```
<StackPanel xmlns="http://schemas.microsoft.com/winfx/avalon/2005">
    <StackPanel.Storyboards>
        <SetterTimeline TargetName="myEllipse"
            Path="(Ellipse.Fill).(SolidColorBrush.Color)">
        <!-- Animate from Red to Blue. -->
            <ColorAnimation From="Red" To="Blue" Duration="0:0:001"
```

```
                    RepeatBehavior="3x" AutoReverse="True" />
         </SetterTimeline>
      </StackPanel.Storyboards>
      <Ellipse Name="myEllipse" Fill="Pink" CenterX="200" CenterY="200"/>
</StackPanel>
```

Double Animation

This XAML sample animates the Opacity of a rectangle five times:

```
<StackPanel xmlns="http://schemas.microsoft.com/winfx/avalon/2005">
    <StackPanel.Storyboards>
        <SetterTimeline TargetName="myRectangle" Path="(Rectangle.Opacity)">
            <DoubleAnimation From="1" To="0" Duration="0:0:3"
                RepeatBehavior="5x" AutoReverse="False"/>
        </SetterTimeline>
    </StackPanel.Storyboards>

    <Rectangle Name="myRectangle" Height="50px" Width="50px" Fill="Red"
        Opacity="1"/>
</StackPanel>
```

The DoubleAnimation class is also used to animate an element's Height or Width properties. The next animation example will repeat the animation 10 times. If the AutoReverse property were set to False, the user would experience a degree of flashing. Instead of growing and shrinking, the element would grow and then immediately jump back to its original size on each of the repeat loops.

```
<StackPanel xmlns="http://schemas.microsoft.com/winfx/avalon/2005">
    <StackPanel.Storyboards>
        <SetterTimeline TargetName="myRectangle" Path="(Rectangle.Width)">
            <DoubleAnimation To="600" Duration="0:0:4" RepeatBehavior="10x"
                AutoReverse="True"/>
        </SetterTimeline>
    </StackPanel.Storyboards>

    <Rectangle Name="myRectangle" Width="200" Height="150" Stroke="Red"
        StrokeThickness="5"/>
</StackPanel>
```

Point Animation

The following XAML animates the StartPoint and EndPoint of a LineGeometry segment in a Path element. The animation makes the line appear to grow as it gets closer to you.

```
<StackPanel xmlns="http://schemas.microsoft.com/winfx/avalon/2005">
    <StackPanel.Storyboards>

        <-- Controls the StartPoint Animation-->
        <SetterTimeline TargetName="myPath"
            Path="(Path.Data).(LineGeometry.StartPoint)">
            <PointAnimation From="20,50" To="100,250" Duration="0:0:3"
```

```
                    RepeatBehavior="Forever" AutoReverse="True"/>
            </SetterTimeline>

            <-- Controls the EndPoint Animation-->
            <SetterTimeline TargetName="myPath"
                Path="(Path.Data).(LineGeometry.EndPoint)">
                    <PointAnimation From="30,50" To="300,350" Duration="0:0:3"
                        RepeatBehavior="Forever" AutoReverse="True"/>
            </SetterTimeline>
        </StackPanel.Storyboards>

        <Path Name="myPath" Stroke="Black" StrokeThickness="5">
            <Path.Data>
                <LineGeometry StartPoint="20,50" EndPoint="30,50"/>
            </Path.Data>
        </Path>
    </StackPanel>
```

Following is markup of a Storyboard that incorporates each of the samples used in this section. To add more complexity to the Storyboard, the `ParallelTimeline` and the `AccelerationRatio` have been introduced. The `ParallelTimeline` enables you to control the time as to when an animation is to begin and end or overlap over other timelines simultaneously. The `AccelerationRatio` (used in the "myRotationAnimation" `ParallelTimeline`) is a double type valued property that makes the animation appear to speed up during the animation's Duration from 0 to the maximum set.

```
<Window x:Class="AnimationStoryBoard.Window1"
    xmlns="http://schemas.microsoft.com/winfx/avalon/2005"
    xmlns:x="http://schemas.microsoft.com/winfx/xaml/2005"
    Text="AnimationStoryBoard" >
    <Window.Storyboards>
        <ParallelTimeline Name="myColorAnimation" BeginTime="00:00:05" >
            <!--Color Animation-->
            <SetterTimeline TargetName="myEllipse"
                Path="(Ellipse.Fill).(SolidColorBrush.Color)">
                    <ColorAnimation From="Red" To="Blue" Duration="0:0:5"
                        RepeatBehavior="3x" AutoReverse="True" />
            </SetterTimeline>
        </ParallelTimeline>

        <ParallelTimeline Name="myOpacityAnimation" BeginTime="00:00:10" >
            <!--Double Animation-->
            <SetterTimeline TargetName="myRectangle" Path="(Rectangle.Opacity)">
                    <DoubleAnimation From="1" To="0" Duration="0:0:3"
                        RepeatBehavior="5x" AutoReverse="True"/>
            </SetterTimeline>
        </ParallelTimeline>

        <ParallelTimeline Name="myRotationAnimation" BeginTime="00:00:20" >
            <!--Double Animation with a Rotate Transform-->
            <SetterTimeline TargetName="myRectangle"
                Path="(Rectangle.RenderTransform).(RotateTransform.Angle)">
                    <DoubleAnimation From="0" To="720" AccelerationRatio="0.5"
                        Duration="0:0:01" RepeatBehavior="Forever"
```

```
                        AutoReverse="True" />
        </SetterTimeline>

        <SetterTimeline TargetName="myRectangle"
            Path="(Rectangle.Fill).(SolidColorBrush.Color)">
                <ColorAnimation From="DarkGreen" To="LightGreen"
                    Duration="0:0:03" RepeatBehavior="Forever"
                    AutoReverse="True" />
        </SetterTimeline>
</ParallelTimeline>

<ParallelTimeline Name="myWidthAnimation" BeginTime="00:00:15" >
        <SetterTimeline TargetName="myRect" Path="(Rectangle.Width)">
                <DoubleAnimation To="600" Duration="0:0:4" AutoReverse="True"
                    RepeatBehavior="10x" />
        </SetterTimeline>
</ParallelTimeline>

<ParallelTimeline Name="myPointAnimationPart1" BeginTime="00:00:20" >
        <!--Point Animation -->
        <SetterTimeline TargetName="myPath"
            Path="(Path.Data).(LineGeometry.StartPoint)">
                <PointAnimation From="20,50" To="100,250" Duration="0:0:3"
                    RepeatBehavior="Forever"/>
        </SetterTimeline>
</ParallelTimeline>

<ParallelTimeline Name="myPointAnimationPart2" BeginTime="00:00:25" >
        <SetterTimeline TargetName="myPath"
            Path="(Path.Data).(LineGeometry.EndPoint)">
                <PointAnimation From="30,50" To="300,350" Duration="0:0:3"
                    RepeatBehavior="Forever"/>
        </SetterTimeline>
</ParallelTimeline>

<ParallelTimeline Name="myTransformAnimation" BeginTime="00:00:00" >
        <!--Animating with a transform-->
        <SetterTimeline TargetName="myPolyline"
            Path="(Polyline.RenderTransform).(RotateTransform.Angle)">
                <DoubleAnimation From="0" To="360" Duration="0:0:01"
                    RepeatBehavior="Forever" />
        </SetterTimeline>
        <SetterTimeline TargetName="myPolyline"
            Path="(Polyline.StrokeThickness)">
                <DoubleAnimation From="0.2" To="20" Duration="0:0:3"
                    RepeatBehavior="Forever" AutoReverse="True" />
        </SetterTimeline>
        <SetterTimeline TargetName="myPolyline"
            Path="(Polyline.Stroke).(SolidColorBrush.Color)" >
                <ColorAnimation From="Red" To="Cyan" Duration="0:0:7"
                    AutoReverse="True" RepeatBehavior="Forever" />
        </SetterTimeline>
</ParallelTimeline>
```

```
        </Window.Storyboards>

        <StackPanel Margin="30" Orientation="Horizontal">

            <!-- Path appears to come closer -->
            <Ellipse Name="myEllipse" CenterX="200" CenterY="200" Fill="Red" />

            <!-- Rectangle fades in and out -->
            <Rectangle Name="myRectangle" Height="50px" Width="50px" Fill="Green"
                Opacity="1" >
                <Rectangle.RenderTransform>
                    <RotateTransform Center="25,25" Angle="0" />
                </Rectangle.RenderTransform>
            </Rectangle>

            <!-- Rectangle resizes its width -->
            <Rectangle Name="myRect" Width="200" Height="150" Stroke="Red"
                StrokeThickness="5" />

            <!-- Path appears to come closer -->
            <Path Name="myPath" Fill="Blue" Stroke="Black" StrokeThickness="5">
                <Path.Data>
                    <LineGeometry StartPoint="20,50" EndPoint="30,50" />
                </Path.Data>
            </Path>

            <!-- Path where its StrokeThickness increases and decreases,
                changes color and rotates  Also note how it is pushed to the right
                as the rectangle with the animating width property grows. -->
            <Polyline Name="myPolyline" Opacity="1" Stroke="Red" StrokeThickness="2"
                StrokeMiterLimit="10" Points="300 180 300.9976 179.9302 301.9805
179.7216 302.9344 179.3763 303.845 178.8974 304.6985 178.2899 305.4813 177.5596
306.1806 176.7137 306.7844 175.7607 307.2812 174.7099 307.6604 173.5721 307.9128
172.3588 308.0296 171.0823 308.0036 169.7559 307.8287 168.3935 307.5 167.0096
307.0139 165.6193 306.3683 164.2379 305.5623 162.881 304.5965 161.5644 303.473
160.3038 302.1951 159.115 300.7678 158.0134 299.1973 157.014 297.4913 156.1315
295.6588 155.3798 293.71 154.7723 291.6566 154.3215 289.511 154.0388 287.2872
153.935 285 154.0192 282.665 154.2998 280.2988 154.7837 277.9187 155.4762 275.5424
156.3816 273.1884 157.5024 270.8754 158.8397 268.6222 160.393 266.448 162.1601
264.3717 164.1373 262.4123 166.3192 260.5883 168.6989 258.9178 171.2677 257.4185
174.0156 256.1072 176.9307 255 180 254.1121 183.2088 253.4574 186.5411 253.0489
189.9798 252.8982 193.5062 253.0154 197.101 253.4092 200.7436 254.0867 204.4125
255.0535 208.0857 256.3131 211.7404 257.8676 215.3533 259.717 218.9009 261.8596
222.3593 264.2916 225.7046 267.0076 228.9132 270 231.9615 273.2594 234.8264
276.7744 237.4854 280.5319 239.9166 284.517 242.0989 288.7129 244.0125 293.1011
245.6384 297.6617 246.9592 302.3732 247.9586 307.2125 248.622 312.1554 248.9365
317.1765 248.891 322.2492 248.4761 327.3463 247.6844 332.4395 246.5108 337.5
244.9519 342.4987 243.0069 347.4059 240.6768 352.1922 237.9653 356.8279 234.878
361.2836 231.423 365.5304 227.6106 369.5399 223.4534 373.2846 218.9661 376.7378
214.1659 379.8739 209.0717 382.6685 203.7048 385.0988 198.0883 387.1436 192.2472
388.7832 186.2083 390 180 390.7783 173.6522 391.1047 167.1961 390.9677 160.6642
390.3586 154.0901 389.2708 147.5081 387.7004 140.9533 385.6459 134.4613 383.1087
128.0679 380.0927 121.8093 376.6044 115.7212 372.6533 109.8395 368.2513 104.1992
```

```
363.4131 98.83489 358.1561 93.7801 352.5 89.06734 346.4673 84.72783 340.0829
80.79133 333.3738 77.2859 326.3695 74.23776 319.1013 71.67115 311.6027 69.60807
303.9088 68.06822 296.0564 67.06883 288.0837 66.6245 280.0305 66.74711 271.9371
67.44569 263.845 68.72639 255.7964 70.5923 247.8338 73.04351 240 76.07695 232.3377
79.68645 224.8893 83.86269 217.6969 88.59319 210.8019 93.86236 204.2444 99.65154
198.0639 105.9391 192.2979 112.7003 186.9827 119.9076 182.1526 127.531 177.84
135.5374 174.0747 143.8915 170.8845 152.5557 168.2943 161.49 166.3264 170.6526 165
180 164.3313 189.4869 164.3333 199.0667 165.0156 208.6918 166.3846 218.3136 168.443
227.8828 171.1901 237.3499 174.6214 246.665 178.7291 255.7785 183.5016 264.6411
188.9236 273.2042 194.9764 281.4201 201.6378 289.2423 208.8821 296.6256 216.6803
303.5266 225 309.9038 233.806 315.7179 243.0598 320.9319 252.7204 325.5117 262.744
329.4255 273.0845 332.6452 283.6936 335.1454 294.5208 336.9044 305.5141 337.9037
316.62 338.129 327.7837 337.5692 338.9494 336.2176 350.0608 334.0712 361.0609
331.131 371.8929 327.4022 382.5 322.8942 392.826 317.6202 402.8155 311.5978
412.4139 304.8483 421.5684 297.3973 430.2275 289.2739 438.3419 280.5113 445.8643
271.1461 452.7499 261.2186 458.9569 250.7722 464.4462 239.8535 469.1821 228.5122
473.1321 216.8004 476.2677 204.7728 478.564 192.4864 480 180 480.5591 167.3741
480.2288 154.6705 479.001 141.9522 476.8721 129.2827 473.8431 116.7263 469.9194
104.347 465.1112 92.20882 459.433 80.37518 452.9042 68.90859 445.5485 57.87035
437.3939 47.32025 428.4731 37.31619 418.8227 27.91393 408.4834 19.16672 397.5
11.12505 385.9207 3.836365 373.7975 -2.655228 361.1854 -8.309189 348.1425 -13.08885
334.7296 -16.96155 321.0102 -19.89891 307.0497 -21.87695 292.9154 -22.87634
278.6762 -22.88248 264.4021 -21.88559 250.1641 -19.88092 236.0335 -16.8687 222.0818
-12.85425 208.3804 -7.847961 195 -1.865326 182.0103 5.073074 169.4798 12.94171
157.4752 21.71016 146.0613 31.34311 135.3004 41.80066 125.2523 53.03839 115.9736
65.00752 107.5174 77.6552 99.93355 90.92467 93.26762 104.7556 87.56117 119.0841
82.85123 133.8436 79.17023 148.9644 76.54565 164.3746 75 180 74.55052 195.765
75.20915 211.5923 76.98235 227.4039 79.87108 243.121 83.8707 258.6646 88.97101
273.9562 95.15616 288.9174 102.4048 303.4712 110.69 317.5417 119.9796 331.0551
130.2358 343.9394 141.416 356.1253 153.4726 367.5466 166.3529 378.14 180 387.8461
194.3526 396.6094 209.3452 404.3785 224.9089 411.1068 240.9711 416.7521 257.4562
421.2779 274.286 424.6524 291.3798 426.8495 308.6551 427.8489 326.0276 427.636
343.412 426.2019 360.7224 423.5442 377.8723 419.6663 394.7755 414.5775 411.3463
408.2937 427.5 400.8365 443.1534 392.2336 458.225 382.5188 472.6357 371.7314
486.309 359.9165 499.1716 347.1248 511.1534 333.4119 522.1886 318.8389 532.2152
303.471" >
                <Polyline.RenderTransform>
                    <RotateTransform Angle="45" Center="300,180" />
                </Polyline.RenderTransform>
            </Polyline>
        </StackPanel>
    </Window>
```

Summary

In this chapter, you learned about the 2-D graphics available in the Avalon API. The chapter also included a discussion of each of the brushes that can be applied to any element within the API as well as the various masks that can be applied to elements with the OpacityMask property.

In the "Transitions" section, you learned how to alter the layout of elements through the use of the five transforms and that a transform can only have one child, but that child can be a complex child (such as a panel with many children of its own).

The last area covered was animation. In this area, you learned that animation is applied to one of the four property types (`color`, `double`, `point`, and `string`). You learned that most of the Avalon animation properties are inherited from the Timeline class such as `Duration`, `RepeatBehavior`, `AutoReverse`, and `BeginTime`.

The chapter concluded by putting all the animations together in a Storyboard. You learned that the Storyboard controls all that occurs in the window as well as how it greatly reduces the amount of markup required.

By the end of the next chapter, you will see how powerful Avalon is and the limitless possibilities with which it empowers both programmers and designers when they are developing future applications.

Advanced Techniques

Styling is a tool that allows you to create dynamic user interfaces and customize the appearance of data. It is one of the most compelling aspects of Avalon.

Styling allows you to separate the presentation layer of an element from the logic. The styling techniques in this chapter can be applied to each individual document, and for the purpose of streamlining and application uniformity, the styles can be placed in a central location for ease of access and subsequent updates.

Types of Styling

Styles are defined in the Resources section of an element or application.

Implicit Styling

Implicit styling is a blanket form of styling that will affect all like elements with the same style. Therefore, if the style of a button is unnamed, the style will be applied to all buttons present. The following XAML creates a style that sets the background color of all buttons in the `DockPanel` to red:

```
<Window x:Class="Styles.Window1"
    xmlns="http://schemas.microsoft.com/winfx/avalon/2005"
    xmlns:x="http://schemas.microsoft.com/winfx/xaml/2005"
    Text="Implicit Styling">
  <Window.Resources>
      <Style TargetType="{x:Type Button}">
          <Setter Property="Control.Background" Value="Red" />
      </Style>
  </Window.Resources>
  <StackPanel>
```

```
            <Button Name="Button1" Height="30">This button is Red.</Button>
            <Button Name="Button2" Height="30">This button is also Red.</Button>
            <Button Name="Button3" Height="30">This button is Red too.</Button>

    </StackPanel>
</Window>
```

Figure 4-1 illustrates the implicit styling from the previous code.

Figure 4-1

Named Styles

Another alternative is to reference the style by name from visual elements with the `Style` property. Styles that are explicitly set override the implicit ones. The following XAML shows a red button with its style set implicitly and a blue button with its style set explicitly (named):

```
<Window x:Class="Styles.Window1"
    xmlns="http://schemas.microsoft.com/winfx/avalon/2005"
    xmlns:x="http://schemas.microsoft.com/winfx/xaml/2005"
    Text="Named Styling">
    <Window.Resources>
        <!-- Implicit Style from earlier sample-->
        <Style TargetType="{x:Type Button}">
            <Setter Property="Control.Background" Value="Red"/>
            <Setter Property="Control.Height" Value="30"/>
        </Style>

        <!-- Named Style-->
        <Style x:Key="BlueButton" TargetType="{x:Type Button}">
            <Setter Property="Control.Background" Value="Blue"/>
            <Setter Property="Control.Foreground" Value="White"/>
            <Setter Property="Control.Height" Value="30"/>
        </Style>

    </Window.Resources>

        <Button Name="Button1">This button is Red.</Button>
        <Button Name="Button2" Style="{StaticResource BlueButton}">
            This button is Blue.
        </Button>

    </StackPanel>
</Window>
```

Figure 4-2 shows the result of the preceding code.

Figure 4-2

Derived Styles

The third and final format to apply a style is *derived*. This means it is a style that is based on (using the BasedOn property) another style. In the following situation, the property values are defined by the new style, which takes precedence over the properties set by the base style:

```
<Window x:Class="Styles.Window1"
    xmlns="http://schemas.microsoft.com/winfx/avalon/2005"
    xmlns:x="http://schemas.microsoft.com/winfx/xaml/2005"
    Text="Named Styling">
    <Window.Resources>
        <!-- Named style which the derived style below is referencing-->
        <Style x:Key="BlueButton">
            <Setter Property="Control.Background" Value="Blue"/>
        </Style>
        <!-- This style is derived from the BlueButton style above -->
        <Style x:Key="BlueButtonWhiteText" BasedOn="{StaticResource BlueButton}">
            <Setter Property="Control.Foreground" Value="White" />
            <Setter Property="Control.FontWeight" Value="Bold" />
            <Setter Property="Control.FontFamily" Value="Bradley Hand ITC" />
            <Setter Property="Control.FontSize" Value="25" />
        </Style>
    </Window.Resources>
    <StackPanel Orientation="Horizontal">
        <Button Name="Button2" Height="30" Style="{StaticResource BlueButton}">
            This button is Blue.
        </Button>
        <Button Name="Button3" Height="30"
            Style="{ StaticResource BlueButtonWhiteText}">
            This button has White Text.
        </Button>
    </StackPanel>
</Window>
```

Figure 4-3 shows the result of the preceding code.

Figure 4-3

Triggers

The Style class contains a collection of Trigger(s). They define style properties that are set condition-ally (usually mouse events or events common to the control). The following XAML sets the background color of the button to orange on mouse over. Triggers can also inherit properties through derived styles with the BasedOn property.

```
<Window x:Class="Styles.Window1"
    xmlns="http://schemas.microsoft.com/winfx/avalon/2005"
    xmlns:x="http://schemas.microsoft.com/winfx/xaml/2005"
    Text="Visual Triggers">
    <Window.Resources>
        <!-- Style with Visual Trigger that changes the button Background
            onMouseOver -->
        <Style x:Key="BlueButton">
            <Setter Property="Control.Background" Value="Blue"/>
            <Style.Triggers>
                <Trigger Property="Button.IsMouseOver" Value="True">
                    <Setter Property="Control.Background" Value="Orange" />
                </Trigger>
            </Style.Triggers>
        </Style>
        <!-- Derived Style-->
        <Style x:Key="BlueButtonWhiteText" BasedOn="{StaticResource BlueButton}">
            <Setter Property="Control.Foreground" Value="White" />
            <Setter Property="Control.FontWeight" Value="Bold" />
            <Setter Property="Control.FontFamily" Value="Bradley Hand ITC"/>
            <Setter Property="Control.FontSize" Value="25"/>
        </Style>

    </Window.Resources>
    <StackPanel Orientation="Horizontal">
        <Button Name="Button2" Height="30"
            Style="{StaticResource BlueButton}">
            This button is Blue.
        </Button>
        <Button Name="Button3" Height="30"
            Style="{StaticResource BlueButtonWhiteText}">
            This button has White Text.
        </Button>
    </StackPanel>
</Window>
```

Figure 4-4 shows the result of the preceding code.

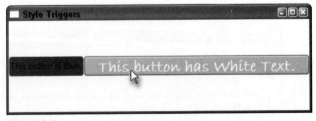

Figure 4-4

Overriding the Visual Tree

Overriding the Visual Tree of an object completely redefines how the object is rendered. The following XAML creates a new button style that supersedes the Visual Tree normally used to draw the button. The `Trigger` property acts on the new content defined in the `Style`. This means that instead of showing a standard button you can personalize its appearance. The code that follows gives the button rounded corners:

```
<Window x:Class="Styles.Window1"
    xmlns="http://schemas.microsoft.com/winfx/avalon/2005"
    xmlns:x="http://schemas.microsoft.com/winfx/xaml/2005"
    Text="Overriding the VisualTree">
  <Window.Resources>
      <Style x:Key="MyButton" TargetType="{x:Type Button}">
          <Setter Property="Template">
              <Setter.Value>
                  <ControlTemplate>
                      <Canvas>
                          <!-- Rectangles that alter button's default
                              appearance-->
                          <!-- Alters the Background property of the
                              Button-->
                          <Rectangle x:Name="MouseOverBack" RadiusX="20"
                              RadiusY="20" Fill="LightGray" Stroke="Blue"
                              Width="75" Height="35" StrokeThickness="2"/>
                          <!-- Alters the Foreground property of the
                              Button-->
                          <Rectangle x:Name="MouseOverFront" Width="60"
                              Height="25" Margin="8,5,0,0" RadiusX="20"
                              RadiusY="23" Fill="LightGray" />

                          <Rectangle x:Name="PressedBase" Width="60"
                              Height="25" Margin="8,5,0,0" RadiusX="20"
                              RadiusY="23" Opacity="0">
                              <Rectangle.Fill>
                                  <ImageBrush ImageSource="myFlower.png"
                                      Stretch="Fill" />
                              </Rectangle.Fill>
                          </Rectangle>
                          <ContentPresenter Content="{TemplateBinding
                              ContentControl.Content}" Margin="15,11,0,0"/>
                      </Canvas>
                      <ControlTemplate.Triggers>
                          <!-- MouseOver Button Events-->
                          <Trigger Property="IsMouseOver" Value="true">
                              <Setter Property="Fill" Value="Red"
                                  TargetName="MouseOverBack"/>
                              <Setter Property="Fill"
                                  Value="RadialGradient Indigo Red"
                                  TargetName="MouseOverFront"/>
                          </Trigger>
                          <!-- Button Pressed Events-->
                          <Trigger Property="ButtonBase.IsPressed"
                              Value="true">
                              <Setter Property="Control.Opacity"
```

```
                                        Value="1" TargetName="PressedBase"/>
                                <Setter Property="Fill" Value="Green"
                                    TargetName="MouseOverBack"/>
                                <Setter Property="Control.Opacity"
                                    Value="0.25"
                                    TargetName="MouseOverBack"/>
                            </Trigger>
                        </ControlTemplate.Triggers>
                    </ControlTemplate>
                </Setter.Value>
            </Setter>
        </Style>
    </Window.Resources>
    <StackPanel Orientation="Horizontal">
        <Button Name="Button1" Style="{StaticResource MyButton}">
            Button 1
        </Button>
        <Button Name="Button2" Style="{StaticResource MyButton}">
            Button 2
        </Button>
        <Button Name="Button3">No Style</Button>
    </StackPanel>
</Window>
```

Figure 4-5 shows the results of the preceding code.

Figure 4-5

The preceding sample also demonstrates the use of property aliasing to expose content. The benefit of `TemplateBinding` is that it allows you to have the overall style set (and stored in a library) that can then be applied to elements that may require specific styling—for example, the Send and Reset buttons on a form.

```
<ContentPresenter Content="{TemplateBinding ContentControl.Content}"
    Margin="15,11,0,0" />
```

`ContentPresenter` is used when applying a style to a control. The objective of this class is to define where the content is placed within the control's Visual Tree.

Events

Events are the action and response from the user's interaction with the application. Connecting mouse and keyboard events in Avalon is accomplished in a way similar to that used for WinForms. Event routing is the term used to describe when one control involved in an event directs one of its child elements to carry out the task. In Avalon there are three approaches to routing events:

- ❑ **Direct**—This is the basic type of event handling where only the element that was accessed is executed. Windows Forms and .NET libraries use this method.

- ❑ **Tunneling**—The event begins from the root and proceeds down the tree to the target element that will perform the rest of the event.

- ❑ **Bubbling**—The opposite of tunneling, this type of event first alerts the target element and reports up the tree to the root via its parent element(s).

Bubbling and Tunneling

Bubbling and tunneling describe the manner in which a procedure navigates through the tree structure, either rising up (bubbling) or digging down (tunneling) the tree. For every bubble event, there is a tunnel to counterbalance it. Using the most common event, the mouse click, the MouseDown (portion of the mouse click caused by the user) is the bubble and PreviewMouseDown is the tunnel event.

The diagram shown in Figure 4-6 is a representation of the bubble/tunnel process of an event. For example, if the target child were a ListItem, a bubble handler would go up the tree to notify all the parent elements (ListBox, DockPanel, and Canvas) that a MouseDown event has been triggered. This would then trigger the PreviewMouseDown event handler to tunnel from the Canvas (Root Parent) down the tree back to the ListItem (target element) to inform it of the actions to execute for this case.

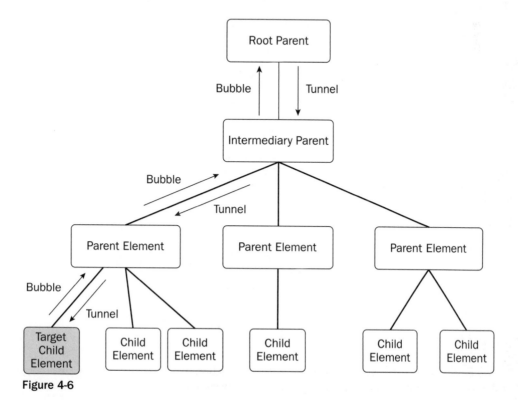

Figure 4-6

Resources

The `Resource` property is found on the `FrameworkElement`. It acts like an encyclopedia and holds data about the defined elements of the application. The data may either be located within the resource or can be referenced from a `Locators` collection that specifies where the objects reside within the application. As the application runs through its procedures, it refers to the `ResourceDictionary` for the manner in which elements are to be displayed or computed. The `ResourceDictionary` is a hash table tool containing the named styles and reusable resources accessible from within the XAML document. It can be placed anywhere in the document, but it is most commonly located at the top of the document on the root element.

```
<DockPanel Background="white" Name="root"
    xmlns="http://schemas.microsoft.com/winfx/avalon/2005"
    xmlns:x="http://schemas.microsoft.com/winfx/xaml/2005">
    <!-- The resource is controlling the color and opacity of each element's
        property that has the named resource notated.-->
    <DockPanel.Resources>
        <SolidColorBrush x:Key="MyBrush" Color="LightGreen" Opacity="0.75"/>
        <SolidColorBrush x:Key="MyOtherBrush" Color="Red" />
        <LinearGradientBrush x:Key="myTextBrush" EndPoint="0.875930521091811,1"
            Opacity="0.57" StartPoint="0.575,0.2">
            <GradientBrush.GradientStops>
                <GradientStopCollection>
                    <GradientStop Color="#FF0000FF" Offset="0" />
                    <GradientStop Color="#FFDC143C" Offset="0.69" />
                </GradientStopCollection>
            </GradientBrush.GradientStops>
        </LinearGradientBrush>
    </DockPanel.Resources>
    <TextBlock FontSize="48" FontWeight="Bold"
        Foreground="{StaticResource myTextBrush}" TextContent="Text" />
    <Button Height="30" Background="{StaticResource  MyBrush}" FontWeight="Bold"
        Foreground="{StaticResource  MyOtherBrush}" >
        Button
    </Button>
    <Ellipse RadiusX="50" RadiusY="50" Fill="{StaticResource  MyOtherBrush}"
        Stroke="{StaticResource myTextBrush}" StrokeThickness="5" />
    <Rectangle RadiusX="5" RadiusY="5" Height="50" Width="100"
        Fill="{StaticResource myTextBrush}" />
</DockPanel>
```

Figure 4-7 shows the results of the preceding code.

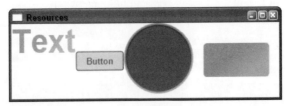

Figure 4-7

As shown in the XAML for the preceding example, all the elements have at least one property that refers to a value in the Resource section.

```
<TextBlock FontSize="48" FontWeight="Bold"
    Foreground="{StaticResource MyTextBrush}" TextContent="Text" />
```

If the Foreground *reference (in the previous sample fragment) were to be removed, the text would default to black.*

To apply styles to the calculator created in Chapter 2, the first step is to define the Resources section. Following is the markup that needs to be placed in the Window.xaml document just before the <ContentControl.Content> opening tag. This section defines how the button's appearance will be overridden. Go to www.wrox.com to download a copy of the code to view the syntax.

```
<Window xmlns="http://schemas.microsoft.com/winfx/avalon/2005" Name="ROOT"
    x:Class="AvalonCalculator.Window1"
    xmlns:x="http://schemas.microsoft.com/winfx/xaml/2005" Loaded="WindowLoaded">
      <Window.Text>AvalonCalculator</Window.Text>
      <FrameworkElement.Resources>
          <ResourceDictionary>
              <Style x:Key="ClearButton" TargetType="{x:Type Button}">
                  <Setter Property="Button.Background" Value="Transparent" />
                  <Setter Property="Button.Height" Value="50" />
                  <Setter Property="Button.Width" Value="100" />
                  <Setter Property="Button.HorizontalAlignment" Value="Left" />
                  <Setter Property="Button.Cursor" Value="Hand" />

                  <Style.Storyboards>
                      <ParallelTimeline>
                          <!-- Animation to make the Clear button pulsate-->
                          <SetterTimeline Path="(Button.Width)">
                              <DoubleAnimation From="100" To="110"
                                  Duration="0:0:1" RepeatBehavior="5x"
                                  AutoReverse="True"/>
                          </SetterTimeline>
                          <SetterTimeline Path="(Button.Height)">
                              <DoubleAnimation From="50" To="60"
                                  Duration="0:0:1" RepeatBehavior="5x"
                                  AutoReverse="True"/>
                          </SetterTimeline>
                          <SetterTimeline
                            Path="(Button.Background).(SolidColorBrush.Color)">
                              <ColorAnimation From="Blue" To="Red"
                                  Duration="0:0:1" RepeatBehavior="5x"
                                  AutoReverse="True"/>
                          </SetterTimeline>
                      </ParallelTimeline>
                  </Style.Storyboards>
```

```
<Setter Property="Template">
    <Setter.Value>
        <ControlTemplate>
            <Canvas>
                <Rectangle
                    Fill="LinearGradient 0,0 0,1 #00FFFFFF
                    #FF000000"
                    Height="{TemplateBinding
                    Control.Height}" Canvas.Left="1"
                    Margin="6,4,6,0" Opacity="0.15"
                    RadiusX="15" RadiusY="15"
                    Stroke="#00FFFFFF" Canvas.Top="1"
                    Width="{TemplateBinding Control.Width}"
                    />
                <DockPanel x:Name="MainDockPanel"
                    Height="{TemplateBinding
                    Control.Height}"
                    Width="{TemplateBinding Control.Width}">
                    <Rectangle Fill="{TemplateBinding
                        Control.Background}" RadiusX="15"
                        RadiusY="15"
                        Stroke="LinearGradient 0,0 0,1
                        #00FFFFFF #CC000000"
                        StrokeThickness="1"/>
                </DockPanel>
                <DockPanel
                    x:Name="RadialGradientShineDockPanel"
                    Height="{TemplateBinding
                    Control.Height}" Width="{TemplateBinding
                    Control.Width}">
                    <Rectangle
                        x:Name="RadialGradientShine"
                        Fill="RadialGradient #99FFFFFF
                        #00FFFFFF" Opacity="0.75"
                        RadiusX="15" RadiusY="15"
                        Stroke="#00FFFFFF"
                        StrokeThickness="2" />
                </DockPanel>
                <DockPanel x:Name="HighLightDockPanel"
                    Height="{TemplateBinding
                    Control.Height}" Width="{TemplateBinding
                    Control.Width}">
                    <Rectangle Fill="LinearGradient 0,0
                        0,1 #99FFFFFF #00FFFFFF"
                        Margin="7,4,6,0" RadiusX="12"
                        RadiusY="12" Stroke="#00FFFFFF" />
                </DockPanel>
```

```
            <StackPanel x:Name="GelButtonTextBlack" >
                <Label x:Name="Content"
                    Foreground="{TemplateBinding
                    ContentControl.Foreground}"
                    Content="{TemplateBinding
                    ContentControl.Content}"
                    Width="{TemplateBinding
                    ContentControl.Width}"
                    Height="{TemplateBinding
                    ContentControl.Height}"
                    VerticalContentAlignment=
                    "{TemplateBinding
                    ContentControl.
                    VerticalContentAlignment}"
                    HorizontalContentAlignment=
                    "{TemplateBinding ContentControl.
                    HorizontalContentAlignment}" />
            </StackPanel>
    </Canvas>
    <ControlTemplate.Triggers>
        <!-- MouseOver events-->
        <Trigger Property="IsMouseOver"
            Value="True">
            <Setter
                TargetName="RadialGradientShine"
                Property="Opacity" Value="1" />
        </Trigger>

        <!-- Button Pressed Events-->
        <Trigger Property="Button.IsPressed"
            Value="True">
            <Setter
                TargetName="RadialGradientShine"
                Property="Opacity" Value="0" />
            <Setter
                TargetName="RadialGradientShine
                DockPanel" Property="Canvas.Top"
                Value="2" />
            <Setter
                TargetName="GelButtonTextBlack"
                Property="Canvas.Top" Value="2"
                />
            <Setter
                TargetName="HighLightDockPanel"
                Property="Canvas.Top" Value="2"
                />
            <Setter TargetName="MainDockPanel"
                Property="Canvas.Top" Value="2"
                />
```

```
                                </Trigger>
                            </ControlTemplate.Triggers>
                        </ControlTemplate>
                    </Setter.Value>
                </Setter>
            </Style>

            <!-- Since all the buttons are Gel type buttons notice, how the next
                two styles use the BasedOn property in order to reduce the
                amount of repetitious code.-->

            <Style x:Key="NumberButton" BasedOn="{StaticResource ClearButton}"
                TargetType="{x:Type Button}">
                    <Setter Property="Button.Width" Value="95" />
                    <Setter Property="Button.Background" Value="LightSteelBlue" />
                    <Setter Property="Button.Foreground" Value="MediumBlue" />
                    <Setter Property="Button.Opacity" Value="75" />
                    <Setter Property="Button.Margin" Value="3,3,3,3" />
            </Style>

            <Style x:Key="LogicButton" BasedOn="{StaticResource ClearButton}"
                TargetType="{x:Type Button}">
                    <Setter Property="Button.Width" Value="100" />
                    <Setter Property="Button.Height" Value="30" />
                    <Setter Property="Button.Background" Value="DodgerBlue" />
                    <Setter Property="Button.Opacity" Value="75" />
                    <Setter Property="Button.Margin" Value="5,0,0,0" />
            </Style>
        </ResourceDictionary>
    </FrameworkElement.Resources>

    <ContentControl.Content>
            <!--Layout of Buttons go here-->
    </ContentControl.Content>
</Window>
```

Because all the buttons were made to have a gel button appearance, the two secondary styles use the `BasedOn` property. This property then refers to the earlier style with the same name. This helps stream-line the size of the file and reduces code redundancy.

```
<Style x:Key="NumberButton" BasedOn="{StaticResource ClearButton}"
    TargetType="{x:Type Button}">
```

Before running the application, a `Style` property needs to be placed on each of the controls that have a style attached. In the project there are three styles (`ClearButton`, `NumberButton`, and `LogicButton`).

```
<Button Style="{StaticResource NumberButton}" Grid.Column="0" Grid.ColumnSpan="1"
    Name="btn7" Grid.Row="0">
        <ContentControl.Content>7</ContentControl.Content>
</Button>
```

Once it is complete, run the calculator. It should look like the example shown in Figure 4-8.

Figure 4-8

Binding

Binding is the combining of user interface properties with custom common language runtime (CLR) objects such as XML, SQL, or other data sources. These objects can then be connected with data, Web Services, or Web properties.

Typically, data binding integrates server or local configuration data into forms or other controls on the interface. In Avalon, binding can also be applied to other properties, including colors, positioning, and more.

Binding in Avalon requires the following:

❑   Source object

❑   Source property

❑   Target element — the control where the data binding is based from on the interface

❑   Target property — the interface

The source object (data item) separates the interface from the data to be displayed. The data can be displayed as a spreadsheet or as any desired visual graph type layout (such as pie and bar charts).

In Avalon three directional flags allow interaction with the source object:

❑   In **One Way Binding,** the data is updated from the source and the changes are reflected in the target. Alterations from the target will not be able to access the source data because the bound control has been rendered as read-only.

❑   In **Two Way Binding,** changes in the source are updated in the target and vice versa.

❑   In **One Time Binding,** the target is updated with the current value of the source once.

The syntax is declared as a string and then assigned as a value. This enables the binding source to be declared and appropriate transforms to be applied to the data and any other characteristics specific to it. The syntax comprises clauses. Each clause is placed within its own parenthesis; clauses are separated with semicolons when more than one clause is present.

The following example declares the string as a bind declaration with a One Time Binding property, `{Bind declaration}`:

```
<TextBlock TextContent="{Bind Path=SimpleProperty, Mode=OneTime}"/>
```

The following table lists all the possible clauses for a bind with their corresponding property and the syntax to declare the binding.

Property	Syntax	Definition
Culture	Culture="en-US"	Determines the information's format, such as calendar and date formats, specific to the country specified.
ElementName	ElementName="MyDataSourceID"	The name of the source element.
Mode	Mode="OneWay"	Determines the type of binding to be performed. The values can be OneWay, TwoWay, or OneTime.
NotifyOnSource Updated	NotifyOnSourceUpdated="NotifyOnTransfer"	Reports when data has been transferred from the target to its source.
NotifyOnTarget Updated	NotifyOnTargetUpdated="NotifyOnTransfer"	Reports when data has been transferred from the source to its target.
Path	Path="MyDataProperty"	Determines the name or description of the source data property to be bound. If the data source is XML, use XPath as the property instead.
Source	Source={StaticResource myObjectDataSource}	Determines the original data source based on the object. When used in XAML, this must be written in compound property syntax, which declares both the Source and Mode. Property="{Bind Path=Bound-Property, BindType=OneWay}".
UpdateSource Trigger	UpdateSourceTrigger="Explicit"	Determines how changes to the target get transmitted back to the source.
XPath	XPath="MyXMLData Property"	Determines the name or description of the XML data source property to be bound.

When bindings are referenced or a transformer is set, the `Compound`-property syntax must be used. Instead of a single string of data, as in a simple declaration, the data becomes an attribute of the element. Therefore, it requires the property to be exposed as a compound, and the binding is within it.

```
<TextBlock Name="myconvertedtext">
    <TextBlock.TextContent>
        <Bind DataSource="{StaticResource MyConverterReference}"/>
    </TextBlock.TextContent>
</TextBlock>
```

Following is a sample where the data is bound to another element's property. As the slider moves, the data in the text box is updated along with the X and Y coordinates of the rectangle.

```
<Canvas>
    <HorizontalSlider Name="HSlider1" Height="25" Width="200" Canvas.Top="20"
        Canvas.Left="50" Foreground="LightGray" Value="500" Minimum="100"
        Maximum="500" SmallChange="1" LargeChange="10" />

    <TextBox Name="TextBox1" Height="25" Width="120" Canvas.Top="20"
        Canvas.Left="270"
        Text="{Binding ElementName=HSlider1,Path=Value,Mode=TwoWay}" />

    <HorizontalSlider Name="HSlider2" Height="25" Width="200" Canvas.Top="55"
        Canvas.Left="50" Foreground="LightGray" Value="300" Minimum="100"
        Maximum="300" SmallChange="1" LargeChange="10" />

    <TextBox Name="TextBox2" Height="25" Width="120" Canvas.Top="55"
        Canvas.Left="270"
        Text="{Binding ElementName=HSlider2, Path=Value, Mode=TwoWay}"/>

    <Rectangle Name="Rectangle1" Fill="#80ff80" Stroke="Black" StrokeThickness="2"
        Opacity="100" Canvas.Left="{Binding ElementName=TextBox1, Path=Text}"
        Canvas.Top="{Binding ElementName=TextBox2, Path=Text}"
        Width="100" Height="100" RadiusX="0" RadiusY="0" />

    <Line Name="Line1" Stroke="Black" StrokeThickness="2"
        X1="{Binding ElementName= TextBox1, Path=Text}"
        Y1="{Binding ElementName= TextBox2, Path=Text}" X2="400" Y2="200" />
</Canvas>
```

Figure 4-9 shows the result of the preceding code.

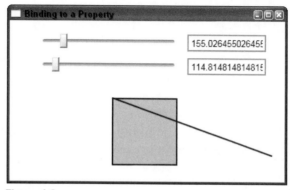

Figure 4-9

Interoperation Capabilities

Avalon provides excellent functionality for bringing your existing .NET controls into an Avalon document, or vice versa.

Hosting a Regular .NET Control in an Avalon Document

The WindowsFormsHost class in System.Windows.Forms.Integration hosts the existing .NET user control. To apply this class in an XAML document, the namespace mapping must first be declared:

```
<?Mapping XmlNamespace="wfi" ClrNamespace="System.Windows.Forms.Integration"
       Assembly="WindowsFormsIntegration"?>
```

The .NET user control can then be added to the XAML document. To specify the assembly and class to be applied, the control also requires a namespace mapping:

```
<?Mapping XmlNamespace="mcl" ClrNamespace="MyControls" Assembly="MyControls"?>
```

Next, add the XML to the XAML document to represent the WindowsFormsHost control:

```
<wfi:WindowsFormsHost Name="WindowsFormsHost" DockPanel.Dock="Left" Height="Auto"
     GotFocus="Form_GotFocus">


</wfi:WindowsFormsHost>
```

The namespace prefix matches that in the namespace mapping declaration. WindowsFormsHost is derived from a FrameworkElement and behaves like a regular Avalon control with respect to positioning and use of DependencyProperties.

The .NET user control can then be added to the XAML document. To specify the assembly and class to be applied, the control also requires a namespace mapping:

```
<?Mapping XmlNamespace="mcl" ClrNamespace="MyCustomControl" Assembly="MyControl"?>
```

Once referenced, the assembly is added to the WindowsFormsHost controls collection:

```
<wfi:WindowsFormsHost Name="windowsFormsHost" DockPanel.Dock="Top" Height="Auto"
     GotFocus="Form_GotFocus">

     <wfi:WindowsFormsHost.Controls>
          <mcl:MyCustomControl Name="myCustomControl"/>
     </wfi:WindowsFormsHost.Controls>

</wfi:WindowsFormsHost>
```

To view a sample application of a .NET user control being hosted by Avalon, you can download a copy of the project from www.wrox.com. The sample in Figure 4-10 displays a .NET control that is placed within an Avalon canvas.

Figure 4-10

Hosting an Avalon Document in a Regular .NET WinForm

Using an Avalon object in a System.Windows.Forms form requires the use of the ElementHost class. The class is derived from System.Windows.Forms.Control and is a new feature in .NET 2.0. It can be added to a form using the standard methods for adding objects to a System.Windows form.

The ElementHost is added to the form in the same manner as any control.

```
private void Form1_Load(object sender, EventArgs e)
{
    ctrlHost = new ElementHost();
    this.Controls.Add(ctrlHost);
}
```

Once the ElementHost is added to the form, the Avalon object can be created and added as a child to the ElementHost. In the following sample, a grid is being instantiated from the Avalon control library. This control is then added as a child of the ElementHost. Note that the Avalon control must be initialized before use. ElementHost objects should have only one child element.

```
private void Form1_Load(object sender, EventArgs e)
    {
        // Create the ElementHost and add it to the Form.
        ctrlHost = new ElementHost();
        this.Controls.Add(ctrlHost);

        // Create and initialize the Grid from an Avalon class library.
        gridCtrl = new MyControls.MyGrid();
        gridCtrl.InitializeComponent();

        // Add the Grid as a child of ElementHost.
        ctrlHost.AddChild(gridCtrl);
    }
```

Serialization

The purpose of serialization is to change the object's state into one that can be stored (persisted) or used elsewhere (transported). Objects are serialized using the `System.Windows.Serialization` namespace. Within the namespace are two modes of serialization: binary XML (BAML) and regular XML (XAML). Binary XAML would be used when an object is to be used in more than one application. XML serialization is purely for data procedures (create/consume). XML serialization maintains the data's platform independence and, by serializing the data separately from the application, eliminates the restriction on the type of data that may be processed by the application.

When you want to save or load an Avalon object, you use the `Parser` class. This class has static methods for saving and loading.

Saving Avalon Objects

The `Parser SaveAsXml` method saves an Avalon object and any children in the Logical Tree to a stream:

```
System.IO.FileStream stream = System.IO.File.Create(@"c:\text.xaml");

System.Windows.Serialization.Parser.SaveAsXml(rootObject, stream);

stream.Close();
```

Loading Avalon Objects

To load an Avalon object, use the `Parser LoadXml` method. This method takes a stream and returns the root Avalon object in the Logical Tree or objects defined in the stream:

```
System.IO.FileStream stream = System.IO.File.Open(@"c:\text.xaml",

System.IO.FileMode.Open);

Object obj = System.Windows.Serialization.Parser.LoadXml(stream);

stream.Close();
```

Avalon 3D

The three-dimensional (3-D) elements are derived from the `System.Windows.Media.Media3D` namespace. The 3-D objects created in Avalon can be primitive or models. They can be manipulated with transforms, animation, and hit testing (the ability to mouse click 3-D objects) as well as be made to appear to be on the same plane as other 2-D objects. A 3-D scene comprises a viewing plane, camera, lights, and objects. To view the objects in the scene, you must apply materials and textures to their surfaces so that the lights can be cast across them. Because the 3-D syntax can quickly get involved, the code samples in this section of the chapter will be fragments focusing on that particular element.

Viewport3D

Before you can create a 3-D environment, you need a viewing plane. The API has two options, the `RetainedVisual3D`, which creates an environment suitable for 3-D graphs, and the `Viewport3D`. The latter option is a base class of the `System.Windows.Controls` namespace and is the rendering plane for 3-D objects. Because `Viewport3D` is more commonly used in 3-D scenes, all subsequent samples will be based on `Viewport3D`.

The basic markup for this control is as follows:

```
<Viewport3D Canvas.Top="50" Canvas.Left="50" Width="300" Height="300"
    ClipToBounds="true">

    #Scene definition of lights, camera, and objects

</Viewport3D>
```

Cameras

The `Camera` is the manner is which a 3-D environment is viewed, or simply put, it serves as your eye. There are two types of camera classes available: `ProjectionCamera` and the `MatrixCamera`. The `MatrixCamera` class is used for applications with built-in matrix calculation devices.

The `ProjectionCamera` is the base class that depicts the viewer's point of view (POV) and determines how the scene will appear to the user on the viewing surface. Because of the constraints of this book, the focus will be on the `ProjectionCamera` class of cameras. The following table lists commonly used properties for the cameras derived from this class.

Property	Syntax	Description
FarPlaneDistance	FarPlaneDistance="*double*"	A double type valued property that determines how far the camera is from the scene's horizon line. This property is used with the `NearPlaneDistance` to define the camera's near and far viewing range (limits).
LookAtPoint	LookAtPoint="*x,y,z*"	Determines the camera's direction: The camera will face this point from its position. The format requires values for its X, Y, Z coordinates.
NearPlaneDistance	NearPlaneDistance="*double*"	A double type valued property that determines how close the camera is to the scene. This property is used with `FarPlaneDistance` to define the camera's near and far viewing range (limits).
Position	Position="*x, y, z*"	This property determines the location of the camera within the scene. The format requires values for its X, Y, Z coordinates.
Up	Up="*x,y,z*"	Determines the amount of tilt (or roll) to apply to the camera to set the scene (like tilting your head).

Perspective Camera

The `PerspectiveCamera` and `OrthographicCamera` are both derived from the `ProjectionCamera` base class. The `PerspectiveCamera` is the most versatile and the most commonly used of the two. As its name implies, it uses perspective and foreshortening to make objects appear near to or far from the camera.

```
<Viewport3D.Camera>
    <PerspectiveCamera Position="-250,250,200" LookAtPoint="0,0,0" Up="0,1,0"
        FieldOfView="40" NearPlaneDistance="1" FarPlaneDistance="500" />
</Viewport3D.Camera>
```

Based on the definitions in the table, the preceding sample code is fairly straightforward. The position of the camera is in the scene and slightly to the left of center with a slight downward tilt. The focal point of the scene is absolute center and the depth of the scene is quite vast because the camera can view from 1 to 500, as determined by `NearPlaneDistance` and `FarPlaneDistance`, before objects disappear. Any object outside of this range will not be visible. When setting the range, you have to consider the size of the range because a degree of distortion can occur based on the depth buffer. It has limited accuracy on larger areas, which can cause flickering, jumping, and other anomalies. A property exclusive to the perspective camera is the `FieldOfView` property. It determines how much of the scene will be seen through the camera along the horizontal plane. (This is similar to using a standard lens versus a wide-angle lens to create the shot.)

Orthographic Camera

`OrthographicCamera` is similar to perspective camera, except it flattens everything out (no perspective is apparent). This camera is good for portraying blueprints or data visualization in graphs, because there is no distortion to the object's sizing properties. This camera uses the `Width` property instead of the `FieldOfView` property that the `PerspectiveCamera` uses. `Width` determines how much of the scene is in view. Although the scene is a 3-D environment, it has a 2-D boxlike appearance in comparison to the `PerspectiveCamera`. This means that although all the objects in the scene are 3-D, they are flattened out. This particular camera is commonly used for displaying 3-D graphs and charts.

```
<Viewport3D.Camera>
    <OrthographicCamera Position="-250,250,200" LookAtPoint="0,0,0" Up="0,1,0"
        Width="150" NearPlaneDistance="1" FarPlaneDistance="500"/>
</Viewport3D.Camera>
```

Model3DGroup

`Model3DGroup` is the class that contains all the children (both the objects and lights) in the scene.

```
<Viewport3D>
    <!--Camera defined here-->
    <Viewport3D.Models>

        <Model3DGroup >
            <Model3DGroup.Children>

                <!-- Insert models and Lights here -->

            </Model3DGroup.Children>
```

```
            </Model3DGroup>

        </Viewport3D.Models>
    </Viewport3D>
```

Lights

Located in the `System.Windows.Media.Media3D` namespace, these classes provide the illumination to a 3-D environment. There are three base classes that are derived from the `Light` class: `AmbientLight`, `DirectionalLight`, and `PointLight`. Lighting in a 3-D scene is required to render the scene. In general, the lights shine across objects with a material and texture. If an object is without either, it will not be seen.

Ambient Light

The first and easiest to use of all the base classes is the `AmbientLight`. It is a universal light (like daylight) that affects the entire scene equally despite the size or shape of the objects; therefore, this light does not have a positioning property.

```
<AmbientLight Color="#C0C0C0" />
```

Directional Light

Another ever-present light that lights all the objects in a scene is the `DirectionalLight`. It differs from the ambient because the light is cast from a specified direction (X, Y, Z format) as opposed to the universality of the `AmbientLight`. Therefore, an object's surface that is directly facing into the light source will be illuminated. Any surface not facing into the source will be cast in shadows. This light is effective in portraying the rays of light from the sun.

```
<DirectionalLight Color="#C0C0C0" Direction="-0.5,-0.25,-0.25"/>
```

Point Light

The `PointLight` is a single point light source that casts its light in a uniform fashion throughout the 3-D scene. This light is more involved than the other two because it requires specification to each of its properties, a position, color, range, and attenuation values. The following table lists properties exclusive to this light class.

Property	Description
ConstantAttenuation	This property determines the intensity of the light as it travels through space toward the object it is to illuminate. Logically speaking, as the distance from the light to the object increases, the intensity will decrease. This is a double type valued property with a range between 0 and 1.
LinearAttenuation	Determines the intensity of light multiplied with the distance from the source to the object. This property has an exponential double value range beginning from 0.001, and the light gets more intense as the number gets smaller.

Table continued on following page

Property	Description
Position	Determines the exact position of the light in the scene. The placement is determined by an X, Y, Z format.
QuadraticAttenuation	Determines the intensity of light multiplied with the square of the distance from the source to the object. This property has an exponential double value range beginning from 0.0001, and the light gets more intense as the number gets smaller.
Range	A double type valued property that determines the distance the light will travel. If an object is outside of the range of the light it will not be seen.

The PointLight is the 3-D equivalent of a light bulb. This light is optimal for illuminating objects that require precision lighting to create a sense of drama to the scene, because it has many definable properties.

```
<PointLight Position="0,100,0" Color="#C0C0C0" Range="100" LinearAttenuation="1" />
```

Spot Light

SpotLight is an additional light that is derived from the PointLight class. This produces the most intense of all the lights. Listed in the following table are additional properties present that further pinpoint the light SpotLight casts on objects.

Property	Description
Direction	Defines the direction the light is to travel from the light source to the object.
InnerConeAngle	Determines the angle of the most intense part (hot spot) of the light in relation to the rest of the light. In other words, as an object gets closer to the InnerConeAngle, the more washed out it will appear.
OuterConeAngle	Defines the angle of the cone-shaped projection from the light. This light is so exact that objects or other areas of the object immediately outside the scope of the OuterConeAngle will appear in shadow.

```
<SpotLight Position="0,100,0" Direction="0,-1,0" Color="#C0C0C0" Range="100"
    ConstantAttenuation="1" InnerConeAngle="20" OuterConeAngle="35"/>
```

3-D Objects

A 3-D object is composed of a mesh, texture, and material. They are located in the System.Windows.Media.Media3d namespace, and all objects in a scene are contained in the MeshGeometry3D base class. The purpose of this base class is to determine how the shape is to be shown, whether it will be created with lines, points, or triangles.

The Positions property is used in conjunction with TriangleIndices to define the collection of points that make up the object. The format of the Positions property is a collection of three double typed values to represent the X, Y, Z coordinates to create the shape. TriangleIndices is also in this format; however, its numbers act as a guide to place the triangle on the point created by the Positions property. Normals, also fashioned in this manner, are values that act as an indicator to the light source, to dictate how light will be cast over each point on the surface of the object. Each value in the Normals collection directly corresponds to a point in the Positions collection. The values in this property are commonly standardized to a length of 1 but can also be 0 or -1. If the values are the same, this indicates a flat surface.

Because you know a normalized vector has a length of 1, to determine the normalization of each component you would use the Pythagoras theorem ($x_ + y_ + z_ = length_$) and then multiply each by $1/length_$.

The TextureCoordinates property directs how the brush is applied to the mesh surface. As with the properties previously mentioned, this property also maps to a point in the Positions collection. The values in this collection are a set of two floats with a double value range between 0 and 1.

Following is a section of code showing each of the object's properties:

```
<GeometryModel3D >
    <GeometryModel3D.Geometry>
        <MeshGeometry3D Normals="0,0,1 0,0,1 0,0,1 0,0,1"
            Positions="-10,-10,30 10,-10,30 -10,10,30 10,10,30"
            TextureCoordinates="0,1 1,1 0,0 1,0"
            TriangleIndices="0 2 1 1 2 3" />
    </GeometryModel3D.Geometry>
    <GeometryModel3D.Material>
        <BrushMaterial Brush="#FF008000" />
    </GeometryModel3D.Material>
</GeometryModel3D>
```

Figure 4-11 shows the result of this code.

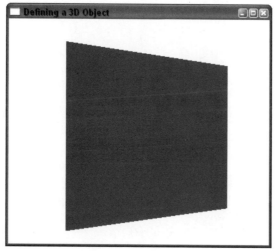

Figure 4-11

Referencing a Mesh

The benefit of referencing a mesh is that it can be defined globally and reused anywhere within the application. Reusable definitions are defined in the `Canvas.Resources` section of the application and can be applied to any `Mesh3D` in the application. To define a referenceable object in 3-D, you use the same format you learned in the styles section, `x:Key="Name of Object"`. The following code adds a second object to the shape discussed in the earlier section:

```
<Canvas xmlns="http://schemas.microsoft.com/winfx/avalon/2005"
    Background="#FFFFFFFF" Height="400" Name="ROOT" Width="500"
    xmlns:x="http://schemas.microsoft.com/winfx/xaml/2005">

    <Canvas.Resources>
        <MeshGeometry3D x:Key="SmallerBox"
            Positions="-10,-10,80  10,-10,80  -10,10,80  10,10,80"
            Normals="0,0,1  0,0,1  0,0,1  0,0,1"
            TextureCoordinates="0,1  1,1  0,0  1,0"
            TriangleIndices="0,2,1  1,2,3" />
    </Canvas.Resources>

    <Panel.Children>
        <Viewport3D Height="137" Canvas.Left="143" Canvas.Top="109" Width="202">
            <Viewport3D.Camera>
                <PerspectiveCamera FarPlaneDistance="5000" FieldOfView="45"
                    LookAtPoint="0,0,1" NearPlaneDistance="1"
                    Position="25,0,-15" Up="0,1,0" />
            </Viewport3D.Camera>
            <Viewport3D.Models>
                <Model3DGroup>
                    <Model3DGroup.Children>
                        <Model3DCollection>

                            <!--Green sample from earlier syntax sample -->
                            <GeometryModel3D>
                                <GeometryModel3D.Geometry>
                                    <MeshGeometry3D
                                        Normals="0,0,1 0,0,1 0,0,1 0,0,1"
                                        Positions="-10,-10,30 10,-10,30
                                        -10,10,30 10,10,30"
                                        TextureCoordinates="0,1 1,1 0,0
                                        1,0"
                                        TriangleIndices="0 2 1 1 2 3" />
                                </GeometryModel3D.Geometry>

                                <!-- Brush applied to surface of object-->
                                <GeometryModel3D.Material>
                                    <DiffuseMaterial Brush="#FF008000" />
                                </GeometryModel3D.Material>
                            </GeometryModel3D>

                            <!--Referenced Object -->
                            <GeometryModel3D
                                Geometry="{StaticResource SmallerBox}">
                                <GeometryModel3D.Material>
```

```
                                    <DiffuseMaterial Brush="Pink" />
                                </GeometryModel3D.Material>
                            </GeometryModel3D>

                            <!-- Light Source-->
                            <AmbientLight Color="#FFFFFFFF" />
                        </Model3DCollection>
                    </Model3DGroup.Children>
                </Model3DGroup>
            </Viewport3D.Models>
        </Viewport3D>
    </Panel.Children>
</Canvas>
```

Figure 4-12 shows the result of this code.

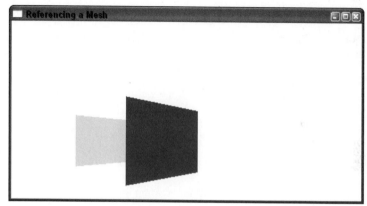

Figure 4-12

Materials

`Material` represents the surface of a 3-D object. With no material information, a model will most likely end up being rendered entirely black. Applying a material to a mesh is much like applying a brush to a 2-D object. The surfaces of the 3-D objects can be painted with brushes derived from the four brush base classes:

❑   `GradientBrush`

❑   `NineGridBrush`

❑   `SolidColorBrush`

❑   `TileBrush`

```
<GeometryModel3D.Material>
    <DiffuseMaterial Brush="Red"/>
</GeometryModel3D.Material>
```

`Viewport` is an additional property required when applying a brush from the `TileBrush` base class. It determines the location and dimensions of the tiles produced by the brush.

```
<GeometryModel3D.Material>
    <DiffuseMaterial>
        <DiffuseMaterial.Brush>
            <ImageBrush Stretch="UniformToFill" ImageSource="MyImage.jpg" />
        </DiffuseMaterial.Brush>
    </DiffuseMaterial>
</GeometryModel3D.Material>
```

Transforms

As with 2-D graphics, 3-D objects can also be transformed. In a 3-D scene, all objects are defaulted with an identity matrix, which means the object has a position value of 0,0,0 and has no rotation nor scaling applied. Transforms control the placement, orientation, and sizing and can also be used with animation to move the objects through the scene.

As with the rest of the APIs, when controlling multiple objects, they are held in a collection class. In 3-D the class is called a `Transform3DCollection`.

Following is the XAML syntax for creating a single transform for a 3-D object:

```
<GeometryModel3D Mesh="{StaticResource SmallerBox}">
    <Model3D.Transform>
        <TranslateTransform3D Offset="-10,3,30" />
    </Model3D.Transform>
</GeometryModel3D>
```

Next is an example of how to write the markup for creating multiple transforms within a `Transform3DCollection` for a 3-D object:

```
<GeometryModel3D Geometry="{StaticResource SmallerBox}">
    <Model3D.Transform>
        <Transform3DGroup>
            <Transform3DGroup.Children>
                <Transform3DCollection>
                    <TranslateTransform3D Offset="-10,3,30" />
                    <ScaleTransform3D ScaleVector="2 4 2"
                        ScaleCenter="0,0,0"/>
                    <RotateTransform3D Center="0,0,0">
                        <RotateTransform3D.Rotation>
                            <Rotation3D Axis="0,10,100" Angle="45" />
                        </RotateTransform3D.Rotation>
                    </RotateTransform3D>
                </Transform3DCollection>
            </Transform3DGroup.Children>
        </Transform3DGroup>
    </Model3D.Transform>
</GeometryModel3D>
```

Translation

A Translation transform moves an object's location through the scene. Instead of just shifting the 2-D graphic based on its X, Y coordinates, in 3-D it performs the transform to the X, Y, Z coordinates of each point listed in the 3-D object.

```
<TranslateTransform3D Offset="10 20 0" />
```

Scale

`ScaleTransform3D` is the transform used to make objects bigger or smaller. Based on the center point of the object, this transform applies the scaling to each of the mesh's points. The `ScaleVector` property individually scales the object based on its X, Y, Z values.

```
<ScaleTransform3D ScaleVector="2 4 2" ScaleCenter="0,0,0"/>
```

For example, in the preceding code fragment, the X and Z points will be two times the original size, and the Y points will be four times the original size. Values less than 1 will scale down the size of the object. If `ScaleCenter` has values other than 0,0,0, the stretching and the object's positioning will be altered.

Rotation

`RotateTransform3D` uniformly rotates all points of a mesh around its axis. The `Angle` property determines the amount of incline that will be applied (in degrees) to the object as it is rotated around the `Center` property. If the `Center` values are not centered to the object, the object will appear to spin around that point instead of spinning in one spot.

```
<RotateTransform3D Angle="45" Center="0,0,0" Axis="0,10,100"/>
```

Summary

This chapter introduced you to the basic concepts and requirements for creating rich interactive interfaces in the areas of styling, binding, interpolation, and 3-D.

In styling, there are three formats to applying styles to Avalon elements:

- ❑ Implicit styles
- ❑ Named styles
- ❑ Derived styles

In addition to learning about applying styles, you learned that styles can be applied with `Triggers`, such as on `MouseOver`, and how to override the Visual Tree of an Avalon element to completely change its appearance but still maintain the element's basic behaviors (for example, the gel buttons in the calculator project).

The next area was an introduction to how events work in Avalon. You learned that there are three methods of event handling:

❑ Direct

❑ Tunneling

❑ Bubbling

The next area covered in this chapter was resources. You learned that this section resides at the root of the document or application and acts like an encyclopedia by holding data about the defined elements of the application.

Next we covered binding, and you learned the three methods of binding data:

❑ One Way

❑ Two Way

❑ One Time

This led to the topic of interpolation and migration, which means that all the forms that you once created in WinForms aren't completely lost; with the use of a .NET control, the old form can be hosted within an Avalon document and vice versa.

In the "Serialization" section of the chapter, you learned that there are two modes of serialization:

❑ Binary, for when an object is used in more than one application (such as a library object).

❑ XML, for the creating and consuming of data.

The last area was an introduction to 3-D. You learned that you need Viewport3D, a camera, and lights when first creating a scene. You now know that 3-D objects must have a material and/or a texture for the light to illuminate them. You also learned that although the objects are made of meshes and textures, unlike the 2-D backgrounds and foregrounds, they can be rotated, scaled, and transformed similarly to the 2-D graphics.

Part II
Indigo

5

Introducing Indigo

The driving force behind software today, whether you are using a browser, e-mail client, or peer-to-peer program, is connectivity. Traditionally, the process of writing communication software has been difficult. In the Win32 world, you had to contend with Winsock. With .NET, there are over seven different ways of communicating with other systems. When you have to worry about reliability and security, making interoperable software can be a real challenge. Windows communication APIs have also grown, and it can take a great deal of time and effort to: (1) figure out which APIs will work best for you, and (2) learn how to effectively leverage them. For example, the System.EnterpriseServices namespace in the .NET Framework 1.1 has over 831 methods, 320 types, 294 fields, and 176 properties!

Indigo is a code name for Microsoft's new communication subsystem for Windows Longhorn. In architecting Indigo, Microsoft had specific design goals:

- ❑ Create a new unified communications API
- ❑ Base it on service-oriented architecture
- ❑ Provide a new and robust way of implementing Remoting and Web Services (WS)
- ❑ Support most WS-* specifications

> Kenny Wolf has an explanation of the early origins of the Indigo code name in his weblog (www.kennyw.com/indigo). The Indigo project was originally code named "Green." The story goes that product team members John Shewchuk and Robert Wahbe drove by an Apple Indigo iMac billboard, and the rest was history.

At the core of Indigo is the `System.Messaging` namespace. In this chapter, you will learn about the fundamental components of Indigo and how to leverage the new API to create connected software.

Service Orientation

Microsoft (and many other Fortune 500 companies) is placing big bets on Service Orientation. Service Orientation is centered on four primary tenets. (Don Box first presented these tenets in a presentation at the 2003 PDC.)

❑   **Boundaries are explicit** — In Service Orientation (SO), boundaries are well defined and formalized. You have a set contract and set endpoints. The most important thing to remember is that implementation of a service is hidden from a client and vice versa. This has huge implications. In the old DCOM way of doing things, you must create tightly coupled applications to be able to instantiate remote distributed objects. In these kinds of applications, the boundaries are all over the place. One of the problems of using this method is that the client and server implementation are so tightly bound to each other that any upgrades or changes to the code require a huge amount of work and cost. By hiding the implementation details, you have a great deal of flexibility about how you implement your services and your client applications. For example, if you perform enhancements or upgrades to a service, it won't break a client implementation as long as the service and expected endpoints are still accessible. On top of that, the service details are automatically transmitted using metadata, further simplifying your development. Be aware that whenever you need to cross any kind of boundary, you will have to pay a price in performance hits, increased complexity, or communication issues.

❑   **Services are autonomous** — Systems are in constant evolution. Rarely will you encounter a situation where you will install services and let them be for indefinite periods of time. When you use distributed objects, all parts of your application are interdependent. This means that any incremental changes to your system require you to completely rearchitect and redeploy your solution. With autonomous services, no such dependencies exist. You don't have to worry about a central authority or tight binding. Each service can be upgraded and versioned independently; it's a simple matter to add endpoints to your service once your service is upgraded.

❑   **Services share schemas and contracts, not classes** — Rather than use types and classes, services rely on schemas to represent data and contracts to represent behavior. The data and behavior are represented separately, which allows you to create communication software that doesn't rely on a particular execution environment or tight coupling. You can be assured of the consistency and stability of the schemas and contracts over time.

❑   **Service compatibility is determined based on policy** — The requirements and compatibility of a service is dependent on policy. A policy is simply a description of systems capabilities. Using policies, you can distinguish between service constraints and service interactions. Policies can help set a set of specifications to make it easy to gracefully degrade the service capabilities to match the service with the client.

Indigo Architecture

Here is an architectural overview of Indigo. At the bottom level is a wide variety of hosting environments. Then you have the connectors that implement the channels of communication and the service model at the API level. The messaging capabilities and services are baked into the API, as illustrated in Figure 5-1.

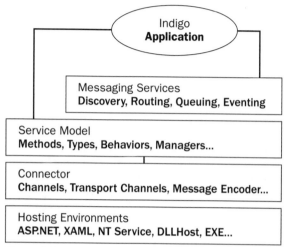

Figure 5-1

Contracts and Endpoints

If you look up the word *contract* in the dictionary, you will find it defined as "an agreement between two (or more) parties." Indigo contracts define how remote clients will agree to connect to your service through endpoints. In a nutshell, a contract is an abstract description of the methods, return values, and parameters of an endpoint.

In the old DCOM way of doing things, remote communication is difficult. You have to instantiate an object on a remote server, maintain refcounts, and track pointers. In the Indigo world, all transactions are message-based rather than object-based. All data transfers are loosely coupled, and message exchanges are mapped by value.

In code, you can create an Indigo contract by simply decorating your classes and methods with Contract attributes. Here is a simple example of a ServiceContract and an OperationContract:

```
[ServiceContract]
interface IConvertTemperature
{
[OperationContract]
void CelsiusToFahrenheit(TemperatureValue Temp);
}
```

The ServiceContract attribute creates an Indigo service from your IConvertTemperature interface. The OperationContract converts the CelsiusToFahrenheit method into a service endpoint, passing a parameter of the type TemperatureValue. The following section looks at three types of contracts:

Chapter 5

❏   `ServiceContract`

❏   `OperationContract`

❏   `DataContract`

Code-First, Contract-First and Late-Bound Development

You can develop with Indigo using one of these three programming styles:

❏   **Code-First** — With code-first development, you start by writing your code to represent a service contract, using common language runtime (CLR) types decorated with attributes. The service then in turn creates metadata (like a Web Service Description Language, WSDL, file). In most circumstances, this is the most intuitive way of creating contracts in Indigo. The plumbing is abstracted away from the developer: Indigo takes care of all the Simple Object Access Protocol (SOAP) messaging. One of the key advantages of the code-first approach is that the API will remain consistent even if there are changes to the underlying WS-* protocols.

❏   **Contract-First** — The contract-first approach involves writing out the metadata first and then generating code. To facilitate the code generation process, Indigo provides the Svcutil tool. Svcutil will read the service metadata and autogenerate the corresponding service or client code for you. (You can learn more about the Svcutil tool at the end of Chapter 7.) This approach requires a solid understanding of the Web Service specifications and protocols.

❏   **Late-Bound** — You can develop applications that send and receive messages without requiring the use of contracts. For example, what if you want to build an application that handles a wide variety of messages from different sources and you can't assume the contents of the message? Like contract-first programming, late-bound programming requires a strong knowledge of the structure of SOAP messages and a deep knowledge of the Web Services specifications and protocols. Late-bound programming provides you with the utmost of flexibility — however, it is the most error prone and requires the most expertise to implement.

With most of the examples in this book, you learn how to use the code-first approach; however, it is very important for you to map out the architecture of your application (including the contracts and the endpoints) before you start writing out a single line of code.

Service Contract

Service contracts are a very important concept in Indigo. They are used to define message exchange patterns between a client and service. A `ServiceContract` defines what application interface will be exposed as an Indigo service. Here is an example:

```
[ServiceContract]
interface IposEntry
{
[OperationContract(IsOneWay=true)]
void InsertOrder(CustomerOrder Order);
}
```

You don't necessarily need to use an interface. You can also define your `ServiceContract` using a class declaration, as follows. You might be asking yourself: Why implement an interface rather than a class? If you think of it, an interface perfectly represents the contract without exposing any of the implementation details. Interfaces provide for flexibility and portability without the hangups of tight binding — it's a natural fit.

```
[ServiceContract]
class PosEntry
{
[OperationContract(IsOneWay=true)]
void InsertOrder(CustomerOrder Order){...}
}
```

Each contract has a name and a namespace, which uniquely identifies the contract in the Metadata portion of the service:

```
[ServiceContract(Name="MyContract", Namespace="http://localhost:80/contracts")]
interface IPosEntry
{
[OperationContract(IsOneWay=true)]
void InsertOrder(CustomerOrder Order);
}
```

Operation Contract

An operation contract defines a message exchange operation. It can be an individual exchange or request/reply. It also specifies what methods will be available through the Indigo service. Here is a typical example of an `OperationContract`:

```
[ServiceContract]
interface IOrderEntry
{
[OperationContract(IsOneWay=true)]
void PlaceOrder(PurchaseOrder Order);
}
class OrderEntry : IOrderEntry
{
public void PlaceOrder(PurchaseOrder Order){...}
}
```

Data Contract

A data contract abstractly defines the types in the classes to be exchanged between the client and service. The types aren't exchanged — only the data contract. The data contract determines what parameters will be serialized. Here is an example of a typical data contract. Each of the parameters is decorated with a `DataMember` to specify which return types are to be serialized.

```
[DataContract]
public class Customer
{
[DataMember]
public string CustomerName;
[DataMember]
public int CreditCard;
}
```

In most cases, when the data arrives to the client, a corresponding type has to match the service types. The `KnownType` attribute typically decorates a structure or class and specifies that a type is known whenever any associated objects are deserialized:

```
[DataContract]
public class Order{}

[DataContract]
public class Cheque{}

[DataContract]
[KnownType(typeof(Order))]
[KnownType(typeof(Cheque))]
public class PosTracker
{
[DataMember]
Object[] trackingModule
;
}
```

Bindings

The bindings of an Indigo service define the communication stack specifications of the service. Specifically, it defines how an endpoint will communicate with an external client. A binding has several characteristics, including the following:

❑ **Transport protocols** — Some of the choices include HTTP, Named Pipes, TCP, and MSMQ.

❑ **Encoding** — You have three choices: Text, Binary, or Message Transmission Optimization Mechanism (MTOM). MTOM is an interoperable message format that allows the effective transmission of attachments or large messages (greater than 64K). You can learn more about MTOM at the following link: www.w3.org/TR/soap12-mtom.

❑ **Security** — Includes wire security (SSL) or schema-defined security (WS-Security).

> **Most non-Indigo software supports only one binding. Indigo can support multiple bindings.**

Bindings can also determine if you are using sessions or a transacted communications channel. You have the choice of creating custom channels or using prebuilt bindings. In this section, you'll learn how to work with both types. Here are the five standard Indigo bindings to handle most common message exchange patterns (MEPs):

❑ `BasicProfileBinding` (also referred to as BP 1.0) — `BasicProfileBinding` allows developers to communicate using SOAP standards such as SOAP and WSDL over HTTP. The `BasicProfileBinding` supports SSL but no Transactions sessions.

❑ `WsProfileBinding` — `WsProfileBinding` implements WS-Security and WS-Transactions (using sessions). Use the `WsProfileBinding` to implement Secure Reliable Messaging (SRM).

❑   `WsProfileDualHttpBinding`—`WsProfileDualHttpBinding` allows you to communicate over duplex channels on an HTTP channel.

❑   `NetProfileTcpBinding`—`NetProfileTcpBinding` supports streaming and duplex communication over TCP.

❑   `NetProfileNamedPipesBinding`—`NetProfileNamedPipeBinding` supports streaming and duplex communication using Named Pipes instead of TCP.

The Basic Profile 1.0 is used for interoperability with existing XML Web Services, and the WS Profiles allow you to implement Secure Reliable Messaging using `WS-*` specifications. Bindings are composed of an ordered set of binding elements. Each element and type must be placed in the correct order to correctly build the communication stack. Figure 5-2 shows the structure of the Basic Profile binding classes and elements.

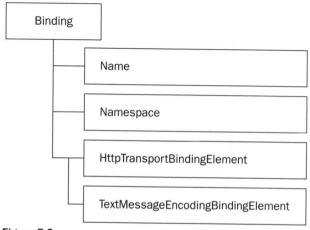

Figure 5-2

In the preceding example, the `BasicProfileBinding class` uses the HTTP transport (as defined by the `HttpTransportBindingElement`), and the message will be serialized as text (via the `TextMessageEncodingBindingElement`).

Standard Bindings

The following example demonstrates how you can incorporate one of the standard bindings into your application. To make use of the `basicProfileBinding` using SSL, we added a parameter to obtain secure communication by defining the `securityMode` as HTTPS. The endpoint defines the address of our service and the binding, and specifies that the communication should be configured to work according to our custom binding configuration settings.

```
<configuration>
<system.serviceModel>
```

```
<bindings>
<basicProfileBinding>
<binding configurationName="Secure" securityMode="Https" />
</basicProfileBinding>
</bindings>
```

```
<services>
<service serviceType="Pos">

<endpoint address="http://server:8080/PosServer"
                  bindingSectionName="basicProfileBinding"
                  bindingConfiguration="Secure"
                  contractType="Pos" />
</service>
</services>
</system.serviceModel>
</configuration>
```

While it is recommended that you put the binding information in your `.config` file, you can also place it inline in your code. In the following example, the `ServiceContract` and `OperationContract` attributes are added to a point-of-sale application. A runtime is generated using `ServiceHost<T>`, and the bindings are added programmatically to the endpoint.

```
[ServiceContract]
public class Pos
{
    [OperationContract]
    public int AddOrder(int OrderNumber) { ... }
}

public static void Main(string[] args)
{
    ServiceHost<Pos> host = new ServiceHost<Pos>("http://server:8080/PosServer");

    BasicProfileBinding binding = new BasicProfileBinding();
    binding.SecurityMode = BasicProfileSecurityMode.Https;
    host.AddEndpoint(typeof(Pos), binding, "BpEndpoint");
    host.Open); }
```

Custom Bindings

Custom bindings allow you to define com type, transport, and encoding. What if you need to do something that doesn't fit with the five standard bindings? You can create your own custom bindings by carefully stacking a set of available Binding Elements. The following table contains the common Binding Elements (which can be found in the `System.ServiceModel` namespace).

Binding Element Name	Element Description
ContextFlowBindingElement	Permits logical threads and flowing transactions.
ReliabilityBindingElement	Implements the reliability features found in the WS-ReliableMessaging specification.
SecurityBindingElement	Implements security features such as confidentiality, authentication, and authorization.
CompositeDuplexBindingElement	Enables communication between client and service where both are capable of transmitting and receiving unsolicited messages.

Binding Element Name	Element Description
TransportBindingElement	Enables protocol transports such as HTTP, Named Pipes, TCP, and MSMQ.
MessageEncoderBindingElement	Enables message encoding such as Text, Binary, and MTOM.

The following code sample creates a custom binding that allows a binary encoded message to be sent over TCP with a maximum message size of 10,024 bytes. The custom binding uses the `CompositeDuplexBindingElement`, the `TcpBindingElement` as the transport protocol, and message serialization using the `BinaryMessageEncoderBindingElement`.

```
public static void Main(string[] args)
{
ServiceHost<Pos> host = new ServiceHost<Pos>("net.tcp://server:8080/PosServer/");
CompositeDuplexBindingElement ComDuplexBind = new CompositeDuplexBindingElement();
TcpBindingElement TcpBind = new TcpBindingElement();
TcpBind.MaxMessageSize = 10024;
BinaryMessageEncoderBindingElement BinMes=newBinaryMessageEncoderBindingElement();
CustomBinding CustomBind = new CustomBinding(ComDuplexBind, TcpBind, BinMes);
host.AddEndpoint(typeof(Pos), CustomBind, "CustomEndpoint");
}
```

You can also define the custom binding in the `.config` file. The following example shows the parameters to be added between the `customBindings` tags:

```
<?xml version="1.0" encoding="UTF-8" ?>
<configuration>
<system.serviceModel>
<bindings>
<customBinding>

<binding configurationName="TestCustomBinding">
<compositeDuplex />
<tcpTransport maxMessageSize="10024" />
<binaryMessageEncoding />
</binding>
</customBinding>
</bindings>
</system.serviceModel>
</configuration>
```

> You can't mix and match all Binding Elements; some are simply incompatible. For example, avoid setting a large `TcpBindingElement MaxMessageSize` in conjunction with the `TextMessageEncoderBindingElement`. You will experience performance issues and other problems. Use standard bindings whenever you can.

Metadata

In object-oriented programming on the Windows platform, runtime metadata is quite important. Using .NET reflection (or a client application such as Reflector), you can extract classes, methods, and properties from any assembly. The inherent limitation of reflection is that it doesn't scale well in a distributed environment. Metadata formats such as Web Service Description Language (WSDL), XML Schema Definition (XSD), and the WS-MetaDataExchange (MEX) specifications are designed to effectively describe Indigo clients and services.

It is important to note that metadata semantically describes an Indigo service or client (as opposed to its implementation details). The schematic representation of a service is called a `ServiceDescription`. On the client, it's called a `ChannelDescription`. Metadata can be created in three ways:

❑ **By annotating your code with attributes in Visual Studio** — This is the code-first approach. Your metadata is represented by an in-memory representation using CLR types. This metadata representation of your contract and endpoints can be published as a WSDL or MEX.

❑ **Using tools such as Svcutil** — Your WSDL file can be converted into annotated proxy classes. Please refer to the "Consuming Static Metadata" section for more details.

❑ **Coding by hand** — You can create a representation of your contract using the contract-first approach. Indigo typically shields the developer from the plumbing details, but brave developers can build WSDL files by hand (or by using modeling tools). The obvious area to watch out for is structural and formatting errors in your code.

Publishing and Exporting Metadata

Metadata can currently be exported into two formats: WS-MEX and WSDL using HTTP GET. To enable Metadata export on an Indigo service, you have to add a few parameters in the service behaviors portion of your `.config` file. Here is an example:

```xml
<?xml version="1.0"encoding="utf-8"?>
<configuration xmlns="http://schemas.microsoft.com/.NetConfiguration/v2.0">
<system.serviceModel>
<services>...</services>
<behaviors>
<behavior configurationName="PosServerBehavior">
<metadataPublishing
  enableGetWsdl="true"
  enableHelpPage="true"
  enableMetadataExchange="true" />
</behavior>
</behaviors>
</system.serviceModel>
</configuration>
```

The Service Metadata behavior is enabled by default in Indigo. The service will use Scheme-Based Default Bindings (which are customizable). To disable publishing your service as metadata, simply set the parameter value to false. For example, enable `MetadataExchange="false"`.

The `EnableGetWsdl` parameter publishes your service metadata as a WSDL. Let's say that the base address of your service is `http://server:8080/PosServer/PosService.svc`; you can then retrieve the metadata by accessing the following address:

```
http://server:8080/PosServer/PosService.svc?wsdl
```

You can also define the location of a custom metadata file using `MetadataLocation`. Please note that WSDL will currently work only over HTTP and HTTPS. The `EnableHelpPage` parameter enables HTML Help pages — these pages are quite familiar if you are used to working with .NET Web Services.

`EnableMetadataExchange` publishes your service metadata in MEX format. To enable MEX, you have to perform two steps: First, you must define the MEX endpoint using an `IMetaDataExchange` contract. Then you have to enable `wsProfileBinding` in your `.config` file, as indicated in the following:

```xml
<configuration xmlns="http://schemas.microsoft.com/.NetConfiguration/v2.0">
<system.serviceModel>
<services>
<service serviceType="PosService">
<endpoint
address="http://server:8080/PosServer"
bindingSectionName="wsHttpBinding"
contractType="IPos"/>
</service>
</services>
<behaviors>
<behavior configurationName="POSServerBehavior">
<metadataPublishing
   enableGetWsdl="true"
   enableHelpPage="true"
   enableMetadataExchange="true" />
</behavior>
</behaviors>
</system.serviceModel>
</configuration>
```

When you are manipulating configuration files, please be careful about spelling errors and spacing. They may cause errors during execution.

Your MEX metadata is accessible at the following address (assuming that you are using the same base address as the WSDL example):

```
http://server:8080/POSServer/mex
```

There are two ways you can publish metadata in the current version of Indigo: using custom and default Metadata Exchange endpoints. You can download the WS-MetaDataExchange specifications in PDF format at the following link: `http://msdn.microsoft.com/ws/2004/09/ws-metadataexchange`.

Consuming Static Metadata

The Service Metadata Utility Tool (SvcUtil.exe) is a powerful and often-used Indigo tool. It retrieves metadata from an Indigo service and generates proxy code to allow you to access the service. It's very similar to the Add Web Reference functionality in Visual Studio when you are trying to connect to an XML Web Service. The following example retrieves the metadata from the Indigo service using Svcutil and creates a C# output file called posproxy.cs:

```
SvcUtil.exe http://server:8080/PosServer/PosService.svc?wsdl /out:posproxy
```

SvcUtil.exe will create both code and configuration information. You can add the addresses and bindings into the configuration file (or incorporate it in code). The contract proxy classes should be added in your own custom code. It creates contract proxies, contract interfaces, endpoint configuration information, and more. Here is an example of source code output from Svcutil:

```csharp
using System.ServiceModel;

class IndigoClientApp
{
public interface IPos
{
[OperationContract]
public int AddOrder(int OrderNumber)
{ ... }
}

public class PosProxy : IPos
{ ... }

void SendMessageToEndpoint()
{
PosProxy proxy = new PosProxy();
int result = proxy.AddOrder(12345);
}
}
```

The PosProxy class creates a channel behind the scenes. You must also add the following generated code into your .config file to define the address and binding:

```xml
<configuration xmlns="http://schemas.microsoft.com/.NetConfiguration/v2.0">
<system.serviceModel>
<services>
<service serviceType="PosService">
<endpoint
address="http://server:8080/PosServer"
bindingSectionName="netProfileTcpBinding"
contractType="IPos"/>
</service>
</services>
</system.serviceModel>
</configuration>
```

You can also communicate with an endpoint using a `ChannelFactory`. In the following example, a channel is created using `ChannelFactory.CreateChannel<T>`. The contract is passed as a type `T` (in this case, `IPos` interface). The address and binding are sent as parameters.

```
using System.ServiceModel;

class IndigoClientApp
{
public interface IPos
{
[OperationContract]
public int AddOrder(int OrderNumber)
{ ... }
}

void SendMessageToEndpointUsingChannel()
{
IPos channel=ChannelFactory.CreateChannel<IPos>(
"http://server:8080/PosServer",
new NetProfileTcpBinding());
int result=channel.AddOrder(12345);
}
}
```

For every contract, only one proxy class is generated. It will provide all the code you need to create a client contract that will communicate with the service endpoint. For more information about the `svcutil.exe` tool, refer to Chapter 7.

Handling Dynamic Metadata

There are circumstances where you would want to consume dynamic metadata. You might want to add new members, new endpoints, or operations to your service. You also might want to use a new binding to expose your existing contract. By creating several bindings, you can open up the service on many ports and to a diverse range of clients. When the service is static, it's quite easy to generate proxy classes. However, what do you do with your client code if your service changes during a period of time?

To successfully implement dynamic metadata binding in your application, your client has to know the target MEX endpoint address, the service binding, and the endpoint contract. From a best practices perspective, the changes that are made to the service should be geared towards compatibility.

> Please note that only the default MEX binding is supported in the current version of Indigo.

The Indigo SDK has a sample application called `RetrieveMetadata`, which demonstrates how to gather and resolve dynamic metadata. The application creates a proxy to the Indigo service via MEX and connects to all the endpoints.

Service Addresses

The service address is a Uniform Resource Identifier (URI) that specifies the location of a service. It's a globally unique location that identifies where to communicate to an endpoint. Usually, one service address is defined per transport scheme. Each host provides a series of base addresses and an endpoint defines a relative address.

Here is the typical structure of a service address:

```
http://wrox.com:80/POSService/WS
```

You must define both a host and an endpoint pattern. (Refer to the URI specifications for more details.) The endpoint addresses are usually included in your `.config` file (as seen in the following). You can also extract endpoint service addresses from metadata using the `Svcutil` tool.

```
<endpoint
   address="http://server:8080/PosServer"
   bindingSectionName="wsHttpBinding"
   contractType="IPos"/>
```

URI Specifications

The following table outlines the address URI specifications.

URI Components	Description
Transport Scheme	Specifies the transport protocol to be used (for example: http, https, net.tcp, net.pipe, and so on).
Host Name	Specifies your host name.
Port	This is an optional parameter. Specifies a port number. (Can't be used in conjunction with Named Pipes.)
Base Path	Specifies the base path of your service. For example, PosServer is the Base Path of `http://server:8080/PosServer`.
Endpoint Address	Specifies a targeted endpoint in an Indigo service.

Hosting

Indigo supports a wide variety of hosting conditions; the onus is on the developer to pick the right hosting model for the right application. It is important to note that Indigo services aren't tied to a specific application model and can support self-hosted to remotely hosted scenarios. In the context of Indigo, hosting means creating environments that support and control Indigo services. The two hosting models that we will be examining in detail include self-hosting and Web hosting. Following is a table with a comparison of the relative strengths and weaknesses of each hosting approach.

Self-Hosting	Web Hosting
Using ServiceHost<T>, you can host the application in any Windows based application.	On Internet Information Server (IIS), you must create a service (.svc) file in an accessible directory. The Web hosting option requires IIS.
Services are not automatically instantiated. You must instantiate them manually using the Open method, and dispose of the services using Close and Dispose.	Services are instantiated and managed automatically.
The application hosting the service must be compiled in a binary format in order to be used.	The application hosted on IIS can be in binary form or source code.
Indigo processes are not managed automatically.	For the most part, Indigo processes are managed automatically.
You define a standard address for your service. For example: `http://localhost:8000/IndigoService/`.	You must generate a virtual directory and a .svc file to make IIS aware of your Indigo service.

If you would like to create a Windows application (be it a Windows Forms application, Windows Service, Dynamic Link Library (.DLL) or console application) that hosts Indigo services, self-hosting is for you. At the core of self-hosting is the ServiceHost generic class. The service lifetime is under your full control. Here is an example of the configuration file for a self-hosted application — you have to define the endpoint address and binding (in this example, we chose the wsProfileBinding over HTTP):

```
<system.ServiceModel>
    <services>
        <service serviceType="ProWinFXBeta.SelfHostingDemo">

            <endpoint address="http://localhost:8000/SelfHostingService/"
                      binding="wsProfileBinding"
                      contractType="ProWinFXBeta.ISelfHostingDemo" />
        </service>
    </services>
</system.serviceModel>
```

Otherwise, you can define your endpoints in code. Here is an example of the Windows Forms application using self-hosting with the endpoint definitions inline:

```
Using System;
Using System.Collections.Generic;
Using System.ComponentModel;
Using System.Data;
Using System.Drawing;
Using System.Text;
Using System.Windows.Forms;

Using System.ServiceModel;
```

```
namespace WindowsFormsDemo
{
    public partial class SelfHostingDemo : Form
    {
```

You then create an instance of ServiceHost<T> called selfHost. This object will be used to instantiate, close, and dispose of your self-hosted Indigo service.

```
ServiceHost<SelfHostingService> selfHost = null;
public SelfHostingDemo()
{
    InitializeComponent();
}
```

You can then load the Windows Form and start the service using the selfHost.Open command. You'll notice that the address and binding are exactly the same as the configuration file outlined at the beginning of the section.

```
private void SelfHostingDemo_Load(object sender, EventArgs e)
{
    selfHost = new ServiceHost<SelfHostingService>();
    Uri address = new Uri("http://localhost:8000/SelfHostingService/");
    BasicProfileBinding binding = new BasicProfileBinding();
    selfHost.AddEndpoint(typeof(ISelfHostingDemo), binding, address);
    selfHost.Open();
}
```

To dispose of your self-hosted Indigo service once you are done, simply include:

```
private void SelfHostingDemo_FormClosing(object sender, FormClosingEventArgs e)
{
    selfHost.Close();
    selfHost.Dispose();
}
```

Now we have to wire up our interface and class. Here is the code for defining the ISelfHostingDemo interface. The following Indigo service will calculate Einstein's famous theory of relativity equation:

```
[ServiceContract]
public interface ISelfHostingDemo
{
    [OperationContract]
    integer RelativityCalculation(int matter, int speedoflight);
}
```

Next, we have to write out the class that will actually perform the calculation. Notice that the ServiceBehavior contains a parameter called RunOnUIThread. This parameter tells the Indigo service that the service will be run using a Windows Form thread. Indigo can then optimize the service for that particular.

```
[ServiceBehavior(RunOnUIThread = true)]
public class SelfHostingService : ISelfHostingDemo
{
     public integer RelativityCalculation(int matter, int speedoflight)
     {
          return matter * (speedoflight)^2;
     }
}
```

Using ServiceHost<T>, Indigo can host a number of self-hosted Windows applications, including console, Windows Forms, and Windows Services. For more examples, please refer to the MSDN documentation available as part of the WinFX Beta 1 SDK.

If you currently using Internet Information Server 5.1, please note that it will try to take over port 80. When you are defining binding addresses, pick a port number other than 80; otherwise, you are bound to experience connectivity problems and port conflicts with your self-hosted Indigo application. Web hosted Indigo hosted applications are not bound by this limitation.

Web Hosting

Internet Information Server (IIS) 5.1 and 6.0 can support Indigo hosting. The advantage of using version 6.0 over 5.1 is that the Indigo service runs using the IIS 6.0 process model (which means they have a dedicated AppDomain and Worker Processes).

Here are the steps to set up a Web hosted Indigo service:

1. Set up your desired virtual directory using the Internet Information Server Console. (You can access it by clicking Start ➪ Control Panel ➪ Administrative Tools ➪ Internet Information Services.) You can also define your endpoints in the Web.config file by adding the following section. Notice that the endpoint address is set to nothing (which means that the service will be accessible from your virtual directory — for example, http://localhost/CustomService/service.svc):

```
<system.ServiceModel>
   <services>
     <service serviceType="ProWinFXBeta.WebHostedDemo">

        <endpoint address=""
                  binding="wsProfileBinding"
                  contractType="ProWinFXBeta.IWebHostedDemo" />
     </service>
   </services>
</system.serviceModel>
```

When you are working out bugs in your service, you can enable the debug options in your system.web *settings within your* Web.config *file. It may help you track problems more easily.*

2. You can then create your service file. First, create a new file called service.svc in your virtual directory. Edit the file and add the following @Service directive:

```
<%@Service language="C#" Debug="True" class=" ProWinFXBeta.WebHostedDemo" %>
```

3. You then have two choices. You can bring in a code-behind file using the `@Assembly` directive. Your service source code can also be compiled into a .dll.

```
<@ Assembly src="service.cs">
```

4. Otherwise, you can include your service code inline. Here is the Einstein relativity example shown in the Self-Hosted section adapted for Indigo Web hosting:

```
Using System;
Using System.ServiceModel;

[ServiceContract]
public interface IWebHostingDemo
{
    [OperationContract]
    integer RelativityCalculation(int matter, int speedoflight);
}

public class WebHostingService : IWebHostingDemo
{
    public integer RelativityCalculation(int matter, int speedoflight)
    {
        return matter * (speedoflight)^2;
    }
}
```

Once your service is in place, you should test the service in your browser to make sure that everything is working well and you can create a number of clients to consume the service. You can use the Svcutil tool to create your proxy code and simplify your development process. You can host as many services as you want within a directory.

Windows Activation Services

Windows Activation Services (WAS) is a new message service found in IIS 5.1, 6.0, and 7.0. This service is primarily used for message-based activation. The version of WAS found in IIS 7.0 allows protocols such as TCP, Named Pipes, and MSMQ to be used. IIS 7.0 will be available to coincide with the final release of Windows Longhorn — stay tuned for more details.

Indigo from End to End

Indigo is built on the client/service model. Following is a sample end-to-end application designed to calculate and pass a temperature calculation between an Indigo service and client.

Building the Indigo Client

First we have to configure the endpoint in the `.config` file. The application uses the `wsProfileBinding` (which means the messages will be passed along reliably):

```
<?xml version="1.0" encoding="utf-8" ?>
  <configuration>
   <system.serviceModel>
     <client>
       <endpoint configurationName="TempCalculatorEndpoint"
              address="http://localhost/TempCalc/"
              bindingSectionName="wsProfileBinding"
              contractType="ITempCalculator, client" />
     </client>
   </system.serviceModel>
  </configuration>
```

Here is the code for our client software. The `TempCalculatorProxy` will act as a proxy to the `TempCalculator` service endpoint. Then a value of 30 Celsius is passed into the service. Finally, the results are displayed in the console screen, as shown in Figure 5-3.

Figure 5-3

```
class Client
{
   static void Main()
   {
     using (TempCalculatorProxy proxy =
     new TempCalculatorProxy("TempCalculatorEndpoint"))
     {
      int temp = 30;
      int result = proxy.CelsiusToFahrenheit(temp);
      Console.WriteLine("{0} Celsius equals {1} Fahrenheit", temp, result);
      proxy.Close();
     }
   Console.WriteLine();
   Console.WriteLine("Press Enter to close the console.");
   Console.ReadLine ();
   }
}
```

Building the Indigo Service

You will now define the contract and endpoints to configure our Indigo service. First, we must define our endpoints within the .config file.

```
<?xml version="1.0" encoding="utf-8" ?>
  <configuration>
   <system.serviceModel>
    <services>
     <service serviceType="TempCalculatorService"

       <endpoint address="http://server:8080/TempCalc"
                 bindingSectionName="wsProfileBinding"
                 contractType="ITempCalculator, service" />
     </service>
    </services>
   </system.serviceModel>
  </configuration>
```

Your Indigo service is defined as follows. You have exposed a method called CelsiusToFahrenheit, which can be remotely accessed by our Indigo client:

```
[ServiceContract]
public interface ITempCalculator
{
  [OperationContract]
  int CelsiusToFahrenheit(int temp);
}
```

In this example, you will use the ServiceHost<T> hosting model. The following code will host the Temperature Calculator Indigo service within the console application:

```
ServiceHost<TempCalculatorService> iserv = new
ServiceHost<TempCalculatorService>();
iserv.Open();
```

Finally, you have to build your interface to perform the actual calculation. You define the name of your assembly and the programming language of your service:

```
<%@Service language="C#" class="TempCalculatorService">
<%@Assembly Name="TemperatureCalculationService" %>
```

Then you create the interface with a method called CelsiusToFahrenheit, which will perform the calculation:

```
public class TempCalculatorService : ItempCalculator
{
  public int CelsiusToFahrenheit(int celsius) {
  return (celsius*1.8)+32;
  }
}
```

Summary

In this chapter, you were introduced to Indigo, including the concept of Service Orientation and the ABCs of building an Indigo service. It delved into the creation of Indigo contracts and endpoints, focusing on the service, operation, and data contracts.

You learned how to leverage standard bindings and build custom bindings. The chapter also explored metadata and the different types that can be published from an Indigo service.

Finally, you learned how to properly construct service addresses and the Indigo hosting options at your disposal. We wrapped up the chapter with an end-to-end Indigo application featuring both client and service code to help you gain an understanding of how everything fits together.

6

Transactions and Messaging

Effective transaction handling is one of the most difficult mechanisms to implement within an application. COM+ and MTS succeeded on a certain level but at a price — complexity. Everyone at one time or another has to figure out how to implement transactions in business logic.

In all real-world systems, the following tends to happens:

- ❑ Servers can fail.
- ❑ Messages get lost.
- ❑ Connected systems get out of synch.
- ❑ Messages get reordered.
- ❑ Messages cannot be safely retried.
- ❑ Messages are interconnected but processed individually.

The way to get around this is to create assurances that messages arrive exactly once, in the same order as they were sent. Assurances are provided by default in the following bindings:

- ❑ `NetProfileTcpBinding`
- ❑ `WSProfileBinding`

To implement Secure Reliable Messaging, here are the options you must configure in your custom bindings:

```
<bindings>
 <customBinding>
```

```
      <binding configurationName="ReliableTransportOverHTTP">
        <reliablesession/>
        <httpTransport/>
      </binding>
  </customBinding>
</bindings>
```

Indigo greatly simplifies messaging by using the WS-* specifications to implement Secure Reliable Transactions (SRT). The implementation details are abstracted from you. All SOAP plumbing is automatically generated. (Of course, you can work with XML if you are determined to use contract-first methodologies.)

Indigo uses a variety of standards including the following:

❑ WS-Transactions

❑ WS-Coordination

❑ WS-Security

❑ WS-Reliability

System.Transactions

System.Transactions, found in .NET Framework 2.0, handle all kinds of transactional operations. Unlike Enterprise Services (ES), System.Transactions doesn't require a tight coupling of the object state and transaction. Indigo takes System.Transactions to the next level with loose coupling and no object dependencies. In combination with WS-AtomicTransactions, you can communicate via Web Services with any other platform.

Using Indigo Transactions

You can indicate that you want a transaction to occur by using the OperationBehavior attribute. The behaviors leverage System.Transactions.

```
using System.ServiceModel;
[ServiceContract]
class CashTransfer
{
[OperationContract]

    [OperationBehavior(RequireTransaction=true,
                       AutoCompleteTransaction=true)]
    int Transfer(int)
    {
    ...
    }
}
```

Secure Reliable Messaging

If you have ever tried to create communication protocols or had to pass messages back and forth from remote points, one of the hardest things to program in is reliability. All kinds of disruptions may happen in the course of transmitting a message: The server may go down, the connection may hiccup, or you may experience periods when the service drops. Reliability entails three things: an expectation that the message will arrive at a destination, a mechanism to compensate for, recover, and resend the missing data if the message doesn't arrive, and a way of detecting when things go wrong.

Another difficult thing to implement is security. One of the issues you face is that you may have little control over how the messages are handled at each endpoint. You'll need to create a lot of custom code to implement a custom encryption scheme to make it work. Cross-platform security adds another layer of complexity.

Indigo provides solid tools to implement reliable secure communication. And even more surprising, it's dead easy to set up. Placing ReliableSessionEnabled in your binding will put all the infrastructure in place. Secure Reliable Messaging is available in the following bindings:

❑   WsProfile binding

❑   WsProfileDualHttp binding

❑   NetProfileTcp binding

❑   NetProfileDualTcp binding

You can also use ReliableSessionBindingElement to implement custom bindings. The following example shows how to enable secure reliable messaging in your configuration file. (You can also enable it in code just like other bindings.)

```
<?xml version="1.0" encoding="utf-8" ?>
<configuration xmlns="http://schemas.microsoft.com/.Netconfiguration/v2.0">
<system.serviceModel>
<client>
<endpoint
configurationName="customEndpoint"
address="http://localhost:8080/customService"
bindingSectionName="wsProfileBinding"
bindingConfiguration="customBinding"
contractType="ICustomService" />
</client>
<bindings>
<wsProfileBinding>
<binding
configurationName="customBinding"

reliableSessionEnabled="true"
orderedSession="true" />
</wsProfileBinding>
</binding>
</system.serviceModel>
</configuration>
```

The preceding code sample also ordered the session. To enable reliable sessions in code, simply add the `session` property to your `ServiceContract` attribute.

```
[ServiceContract(Session=true)]
```

Following is an example of how to implement SRM in a custom binding:

```
<bindings>
 <customBinding>
    <binding configurationName="CustomReliableMessagingOverTcp">

        <reliableSession/>
          <tcpTransport />
    </binding>
 </customBinding>
</bindings>
```

Indigo Queues

You can implement queues using Indigo. Indigo queues use the Microsoft Message Queue (MSMQ) infrastructure to create queued channels. The great thing about this integration is that if you are experienced with MSMQ, you'll feel very comfortable with Indigo queues. As outlined in the tenets of service orientation in Chapter 5, services are decoupled by default. Indigo queues also can assist in the decoupling services.

In many business circumstances, you may want one-way operations with high availability. From an administrative standpoint, you may also want to maintain and load balance your services without any downtime while keeping these operations invisible to the clients. Indigo queues provide all of these advantages and more; you can effectively handle many challenging demands made to the system.

Indigo doesn't support database-style operations in a queue. Instead queued messages wait for any kind of availability to push the message in the service code. Here is how you can create a vanilla one-way contract:

```
public interface IAirlineReservation
{

  [OperationContract(IsOneWay = true)]
  void AddReservation(int resID, string CustomerName);
}
```

Here is how you can write out the queue endpoint. This example uses `netProfileMsmqBinding`. Most queued communication is local; you'll notice that the address points to a private queue (denoted by `private$`):

```
<endpoint

  address ="net.msmq://MyServer/private$/MyQ/"
  bindingSectionName="netProfileMsmqBinding"
```

```
bindingConfiguration ="MyQueueBinding"
contractType="Queue.IAirlineReservation, Queues" />
```

In some circumstances, you will need to access public queues. You can write the public queue using an address such as net.msmq://MyServer/MyQ/:

```
<endpoint

address ="net.msmq://MyServer/MyQ/"
bindingSectionName="netProfileMsmqBinding"
bindingConfiguration ="MyQueueBinding"
contractType="Queue.IPurchaseOrder, Queues" />
```

In the endpoint, there is a referenced binding configuration called "MyQueueBinding". This binding information can also be found in your configuration file. You can configure the details of your queued communication, including the queue protection level and the authentication mode.

```
<bindings>

<netProfileMsmqBinding>
  <binding
   configurationName="MyQueueBinding"
   addressingMode="Native"
   assurances="ExactlyOnce"

   msmqProtectionLevel="EncryptAndSign"
   msmqAuthenticationMode="None" />
 </netProfileMsmqBinding>
</bindings>
```

You can also specify the use of NetProfileMsmq binding in the code by using the NetProfileMsmqProfile class. Here is an example:

```
Uri baseAddress = new Uri("net.msmq://localhost/private$/CustomService");
NetProfileMsmqBinding qBinding = new NetProfileMsmqBinding();
service.AddEndpoint(typeof(IAirlineReservation), qBinding, baseAddress);
```

To access queues, you have to preconfigure them using the Microsoft Management Console (MMC) Computer Manager snap-in. In some circumstances, you would want to enforce the use of queues in your application. You can do this in code using the QueuedDeliveryRequirements property within the BindingRequirement attribute. Here is an example:

```
[BindingRequirements(QueuedDeliveryRequirements = RequirementsMode.Require)]
class ReservationService : IAirlineReservation
{ ... }
```

Managing Queues and Transactions

You can combine queues and transaction to make sure that no messages get lost, especially when massive connectivity problems occur. It is also important to tie transactional operations in your queues when you are tying in a database or another external resource is used. Using the combination of transactions and queues, queued messages are handled a batch at a time.

Transacted queues share special characteristics:

- ❑ Transactions occur between the client, the service, and the queue. Any messages sent from an "outside" source will not be seen.

- ❑ All transactions are local.

- ❑ When the transaction is committed, messages are then removed from or added to the queue.

- ❑ If a message returns to the queue, another attempt will be made.

If you are interested in using transacted queues, you must perform the following steps:

1. Choose a queued transport, using one of the MSMQ bindings.

2. On the service side, enact the `AutoEnlistTransaction` and `AutoCompleteTransaction` parameters, using the `OperationsBehavior` attribute.

3. On the client side, use a transaction scope to send messages and complete the transactions.

Here is some client code for a transacted queue. First, you need to define a scope for the transaction, using the `TransactionScope` object. You can then perform a number of operations and end the transaction by using the `Complete` method:

```
TransactionScope transScope;
using (tranScope= new TransactionScope())
{
  AirlineSystem.AddReservation(transactionID, clientCode, credAuthID);
  commitData();

  transScope.Complete();
}
```

Your service uses a different transaction to read every message, despite the fact that the messages were sent within the same transaction on the client. The approach is really decoupled between the client and service. Here is a code sample of the service using the `OperationBehavior` attribute:

```
[ServiceBehavior(TransactionIsolationLevel=IsolationLevel.ReadCommitted)]
public class AirlineService:IAirlineService
{

  [OperationBehavior(AutoEnlistTransactions=True, AutoCompleteTransactions=True)]
  string GenerateReservation(int transactionID)
  {
    ...
  }
```

The `ServiceBehavior` basically does what it indicates: It sets the behavior for your service. The `TransactionIsolationLevel` in `ServiceBehavior` allows you to set the amount of isolation between transactions; this will greatly impact the way transactions affect one another. The accepted values for `TransactionIsolationLevel` include the following:

- ❏ Chaos
- ❏ ReadCommitted
- ❏ ReadUncommitted
- ❏ RepeatableRead
- ❏ Serializable
- ❏ Snapshot
- ❏ Unspecified

The default value for `TransactionIsolationLevel` is `Unspecified`. The level set in the preceding example is `ReadCommitted`. The `OperationBehavior` attribute sets the behaviors for all operations conducted by the service. The `AutoEnlistTransactions` parameter sets whether the `GenerateReservation` operation must execute as a transaction. The `AutoCompleteTransaction` parameter enables the transaction to be completed automatically after the service operation is completed. This autopilot feature is convenient from a programming standpoint, letting Indigo automatically manage the transaction details for you (rather than having you manually shut down a transaction).

Queues provide consistent transactions, but don't allow transactions using one-way operations because you can never know how they will turn out before the commit stage. All queued transactions are validated by the service model. (You have the option of removing the validator, but it's definitely not recommended.) Here is a code sample featuring the `IServiceValidator` collection:

```
ServiceDescription servdesc=...;

foreach (IServiceValidator validator in servdesc.Validators)
{

  ContextValidator context = validator as ContextValidator;
  if (context != null)
  {

     description.Validators.Remove(context);
  }
}
```

Handling Transaction Failures in Config

Transaction failures are commonplace, as is the way they are handled. After a transaction fails, retrying it is a logical step to take. But what happens if you don't want the application to retry sending the message or if you want to set the amount of times that a retry should occur? You can use retry patterns to cope with transaction failures very easily and with a lot of granularity.

Retry patterns let you control what to do with any messages that fail. You can control whether you want to automatically retry failed messages, configure the maximum number of retries, and set whether you want messages to appear in a Dead Letter Queue (DLQ) or Poison Message Queue (PMQ).

The following code shows you how to deal with transaction failure in your binding code, including some of the parameters you can set:

```
<netProfileMsmqBinding>
  <binding configurationName="CustomQueueBinding"
           msmqAuthenticationMode="None"
           msmqProtectionLevel="None"

           maxRetries="5"
           maxRetryCycles="3"
           retryCycleDelay="0:0:40"
           rejectAfterLastRetry="True" />
</netProfileMsmqBinding>
```

The `maxRetries` parameter is set to 5, which means that if a transaction fails it will be retried five times. The `maxRetryCycles` is set to the default value of 3. This controls the number of times the transaction is cycled in the retry queue and the application queue. `retryCycleDelay` sets the amount of time that should pass between each retry. Finally, the `rejectAfterLastRetry` parameter is set to `True`, which means that a message should be rejected (as opposed to being sent to the PMQ). The default value for `rejectAfterLastRetry` is `True`.

The PMQ is a subqueue of the application queue. It is a place where lost messages get sent to if they can't be sent otherwise. These messages are then passed back into the application queue on a schedule different from the primary application queue's schedule.

```
<endpoint

  address="net.msmq://MyServer/private$/MyPrivateQueue;Poison/"
  bindingSectionName="netProfileMsmqBinding"
  bindingConfiguration="CustomQueueBinding"
  contractType="Queue.IAirlineReservation, Queues" />
```

The `;Poison` at the end of the endpoint address indicates that the queue to be used is the PMQ rather than the application queue.

Using Sessions in Queues

What if you have to process groups of messages together? Breaking up the messages into smaller chunks is sometimes not the answer because this complicates the process of recovering the messages. The way to get around this problem in Indigo is to use Queue Sessions. What will happen is that your applications will not be able to recognize the message unless all of them end up in the message queue. Queue Sessions deliver all the messages within the same transactions, and there is no possibility of creating partial sessions. If there is more than one call to the service method, they are all accomplished in the same transaction. Keep in mind that if you end or abort a transaction, all the associated session messages revert back to the queue.

To use queues with sessions, you must first define Queue Session contracts. Here is some code demonstrating the mechanics of the contract in a client:

```
[ServiceContract(Session = true)]
public interface IAirlineReservation
{

[OperationContract(IsOneWay = true)]
void SetReservation(int reservationID);
}
```

To set a session in a `ServiceContract`, simply add a `Session=True` parameter in the `ServiceContract` attribute. You'll also notice that `OperationContract` is set to `IsOneWay=True`. The one-way service doesn't bother to send a response; the return value for this kind of operation is typically void. The following looks in more depth at the way that queue sessions are handled in a service:

```
[BindingRequirements(QueuedDeliveryRequirements=RequirementsMode.Require,
RequireOrderedDelivery=true)]
```

The `BindingRequirements` attribute sets what binding requirements must be met in a service contract. In this case, the `QueuedDeliveryRequirements` specifies that queuing is required and the delivery order of the messages has to be ordered.

```
[ServiceBehavior(InstanceMode=InstanceMode.PrivateSession)]
class AirlineReservationService:IAirlineReservations
{

[OperationBehavior(AutoEnlistTransaction=True, AutoCompleteTransaction=False)]
public void SetReservation(int reservationID) {...}
}
```

The `InstanceMode` attribute in the previous example is set to `PrivateSession`. This means that an instance of the service will be created for every client that connects. As explained before, the `AutoEnlistTransaction` parameter enables transactional support for the `SetReservation` operation. Since the `AutoCompleteTransaction` is set to `False`, you would typically have to define where you want to shut down the transaction somewhere in your code.

Handling Queue Delivery Errors

How can you find out when your message's delivery failed within a timeframe? You can set the delivery assurances to `Exactly-Once` (the default value). This is only available using reliable, transacted queues. You can define the time-to-live (TTL) for any bindings as opposed to relying on the default values. If the message is not processed in the correct amount of time (defined by the TTL), then it is sent to the Dead Letter Queue (DLQ).

To know when messages are sent to the DLQ, you have to write (or invoke) logic or contact the administrator.

Dead Letter Queues

You can define the DLQ for every client binding, and all queues using transactions use the same DLQ. To access the DLQ in your binding, you must use the following address:

```
net.msmq://SpecialQueue/system$;deadxact/
```

The default DLQ for queues not participating in transactions is set Null. Typically, you would want to use the default DLQ only for activities such as debugging. The DLQ sits on the queue manager on the client side. Here is the binding code for a deadLetterQueue:

```
<binding configurationName="CustomQueueBinding"
  ...

  timeToLive="0:1:0"
  deadLetterQueue= "net.msmq://MyClient/private$/myCustomDLQ" />
```

The DLQ endpoint for the client is written as follows:

```
<endpoint
  address ="net.msmq://MyClient//private$/myCustomDLQ/"

  bindingSectionName="netProfileMsmqBinding"
  bindingConfiguration ="CustomQueueBinding"
  contractType="Queue.IAirlineReservation, Queues">
</endpoint>
```

From a peripheral perspective, the DLQ behaves like other channels, but it can carry extra information on failures and so forth:

```
MsmqMessageProperty m = OperationContext.Current.IncomingMessageProperties
[MsmqMessageProperty.n] as MsmqMessageProperty;
Console.WriteLine("Failure Status:{0}", m.DeliveryFailure);
```

Synchronous versus Asynchronous Invokes

You can use sync and async methods to drive message operations. You can set sync and async decisions using local behaviors. These decisions will not affect the metadata. From a CLR implementation perspective, you must modify the local view of the contract. Keep in mind that the implementation varies, but the wire contracts are identical. In a nutshell, the choice in the way you want to go (synchronous or asynchronous) is decided in the same way you make determinations of how you would want your invocations handled.

```
  [ServiceContract]
public interface IAirlineReservation
  {

    [OperationContract(AsyncPattern=true)]
    IAsyncResult BeginAddReservation (int reservationID);
    int EndDoWork(IAsyncResult result);
  }
```

Indigo Sessions

Indigo sessions are used to allow your messages to maintain state over a period of time. Implementing sessions is quite easy; all you have to do is set the `Session` parameter to `True` within `ServiceContract`:

```
[ServiceContract(Session = true)]
public interface IAirlineReservation
{
 [OperationContract]
 int AddReservation(int reservationID);
}
```

You can enable an automatic session shutdown (to automanage your session) using the `AutomaticSessionShutdown` parameter. In the example that follows, the `BindingRequirements` attribute is set to require an ordered delivery of messages:

```
[ServiceBehavior(AutomaticSessionShutdown=true)]
[BindingRequirements(RequireOrderedDelivery=true)]
class AirportReservationService : IAirportReservation
{
 public int AddReservation(int reservationID) { ... }
}
```

In the configuration portion of the service, you can set the `reliableSession` parameter to send messages in an ordered or unordered fashion. Here is a custom binding example using a configuration file:

```
<bindings>
   <customBinding>

     <binding configurationName="MyCustomBinding">
       <reliableSession ordered="True">
       <tcpTransport />
     </binding>
   </customBinding>
```

You can also manipulate the standard bindings. The following example sets the `orderedSession` attribute to `True`:

```
   <wsProfileBinding>

         <binding configurationName="OrderedReliableMessaging"
                 orderedSession="true">
         </binding>
   </wsProfileBinding>
</bindings>
```

Initiating and terminating sessions can be accomplished using the `IsInitiating` attribute and `IsTerminating` attribute as shown in the following example.

```
[ServiceContract(Session=true)]
public interface IAirlineReservation
{
```

```
[OperationContract(IsInitiating=true,IsOneWay=true)]
public void Start();
```

```
[OperationContract(IsInitiating=false,IsTerminating=true,IsOneWay=true)]
public void End();
}
```

In the configuration file, you can set all sorts of connection management settings, including the inactivity timeout. The inactivity timeout is measured according to the amount of time it takes to send a message to and from a service and/or client. The timeout appears when no traffic is generated. The inactivity timeout has a set number of retries; messages are tried a number of times until they are acknowledged. The message acknowledgments in turn can be sent in batches. Here is a bit of binding code that sets the acknowlegment interval, the quota of buffered messages, and an inactivity timeout:

```
<reliableSession
```

```
acknowledgementInterval="00:00:00.20"
bufferedMessagesQuota="50"
inactivityTimeout="00:40:00"
maxRetryCount="6"/>
```

To configure the sessions on the client, you use the `TransactionScope` object. After the transaction has been completed, you can use the `Complete` method to end the transaction process:

```
TransactionScope transcope;
using (transcope=new TransactionScope())
{
Reservation.Add(reservationID);
Reservation.Close();

transcope.Complete();
}
```

As soon as a service runs, an instance of the implementation class is instantiated for any request message. The instance mode sets when implementation instances are instantiated and destroyed. The common instancing modes include the following:

❑   **Shared and Private Sessions** — A private session instance means that a class instance is created for every client request. The shared instance means that many clients can share the same instance.

❑   **Singleton** — Multiple callers rely on one service instance.

❑   **Per-call** — A single class is instantiated for each message request, and then it is destroyed.

Indigo Transactions

Indigo supports a variety of transacted communications. The following code demonstrates a transacted service operation. To enable a transaction in Indigo, use the transaction parameters within the `OperationBehavior` attribute:

```
    [OperationBehavior(AutoEnlistTransaction = true,
                       AutoCompleteTransaction = true)]
public bool RemoveReservation(bool transactionFlag);
```

To share a transaction in Indigo, simply use the `contextFlow` parameter within your binding, and set the `transactions` parameter to `Required`:

```
<bindings>
  <wsHttpBinding>
    <binding configurationName="CustomBinding">

      <contextFlow transactions="Required" />
    </binding>
  </wsHttpBinding>
</bindings>
```

To require a transaction flow, you can set the `TransactionFlowRequirements` within the `BindingRequirements`:

```
[BindingRequirements( TransactionFlowRequirements = RequirementsMode.Require)]
```

The possible enum values for `RequirementsMode` include the following:

❑   Required

❑   Disallowed

❑   Ignore

Please note that the default value is `Ignore`, which means that no transaction flow is required. You can also validate your transactions using the `IServiceValidator` interface. You can set the context using the `ContextValidator` object:

```
ServiceDescription description = ...;

foreach (IServiceValidator validator in description.Validators)
{

  ContextValidator context = validator as ContextValidator;
  if (context != null)
  {

    description.Validators.Remove(context);
    break;
  }
}
```

To flow a transaction from the client, you can set a transaction scope and complete the transaction using the following code:

```
TransactionScope transscope;
using (transscope = new TransactionScope())
```

```
  {
    proxy.Transfer(employeeID);
    UpdateLocalCache(employeeID);
    transscope.Complete();
  }
```

To control the transaction flow of your application, simply add the `TransactionFlowRequirements` parameter to your `BindingRequirements` attribute. The options you can set include: `Ignore`, `Require`, and `Disallow`.

```
  [BindingRequirements(TransactionFlowRequirements=RequirementsMode.Require)]
```

Using the `AutoEnlistTransaction` and `AutoCompleteTransaction` parameters, you can set up a transaction for your method:

```
  [OperationBehavior(AutoEnlistTransaction = true, AutoCompleteTransaction = true)]
  public void AddReservation(string myArg)
  {
   ...
```

If the transaction does not complete successfully, you can force a rollback using the `Rollback` method:

```
  if (AbortConditionToKillTheTransaction)
  {

    Transaction.Current.Rollback();
  }
  }
```

Otherwise, you can throw an exception to kill the transaction. The following code shows you how to accomplish this:

```
  if (AbortConditionToKillTheTransaction)
  {

    throw new Exception(...);
  }
  }
```

To complete a transaction, you can use the `SetTransactionComplete` method. If you know that you will be programmatically terminating the transaction, you can set the `AutoCompleteTransaction` attribute to `false`, as shown in the following example:

```
  [OperationBehavior(AutoEnlistTransaction = true, AutoCompleteTransaction = false)]
  public void AddEmployee(int employeeID)
  {
  // Do neccesary operations under the transaction.
    ...

    OperationContext.Current.SetTransactionComplete();
  }
```

Duplex Communication

Traditional remote procedure calls (RPCs) use in-and-out operations. Indigo supports multichannel in-out operations, otherwise known as duplex communication. These are implemented using duplex contracts. You should use `ServiceContract` to define your inputs and `CallContract` to define the outputs. See the following example:

```
[ServiceContract(CallbackContract = typeof(IPosCallback), Session = true)]
public interface IPos
{
    [OperationContract(IsOneWay = true)]
    void AddOrder(string itemID);

    [OperationContract(IsOneWay = true)]
    void commitTransaction();
}

public interface IPosCallback
{
    [OperationContract(IsOneWay = true)]
    void Confirmation(string status);
```

To set up a duplex sender, implement `CallbackContract` and provide `Callback` at proxy creation:

```
public class PosCallback : IPosCallback
{
    public void Confirmation(string orderStatus)

        Console.WriteLine(orderStatus);
    }
}
// ...
```

```
PosCallback posCBack = new PosCallback();
PosProxy proxy = new PosProxy(new ServiceSite(posCBack));
proxy.Add("Brown Shirt");
```

To set up a duplex receiver, you must first implement a `ServiceContract` and use the callback channel (from the `OperationContext`). Here is an example:

```
public class PosService : IPos
{
    List<string> items = new List<string>();
    public void AddItem(string item)
    {
        items.Add(item);
    }

    public void Complete()
    {
```

```
        IPosCallback posCallback =
        OperationContext.Current.GetCallback<IPosCallback>();
```

```
                    posCallback.Confirmation("Ok");
        }
   }
```

Duplex communications allow for rich message exchange patterns (MEPs). ServiceContract defines the in messages and CallbackContract defines the out messages.

Streaming

Indigo supports application-level chunking of messages. By default, messages are buffered before they can be accessed. You can also break one operation into many. Here is a code sample demonstrating streaming:

```
public Stream StreamData(string incomingStream)
{
  MemoryStream outgoingStream = new MemoryStream();
  XmlFormatter xFormat = new XmlFormatter();
  ...
  xFormat.Serialize(outgoingStream, incomingStream);
  outgoingStream.Seek(0, SeekOrigin.Begin);
  return outgoingStream;
}
```

To do streaming on the Indigo platform, you must use stream-oriented operations. The stream parameter will provide you with a return value. You can also use an XmlReader over a message body. All you need to do is set the binding's TransferMode to Streaming. When you use Streaming, you must not enable reliable sessions.

There are other streaming restrictions you should be aware of. You are limited to transport-based security (for example, SSL). If you want to add security to your bindings, add the security mode to None, TcpWithWindowsSecurity, or TcpWithSsl. HTTP-based bindings and nondual bindings are not supported. Custom bindings are required for any request-reply operations.

BizTalk Server and Indigo

In the near future, BizTalk Server and Indigo will integrate in a powerful way. It's the perfect mix: BizTalk provides services such as transformation, business process orchestration, and the capability for designers to model and track business activities. Indigo provides the low-level transport. Indigo will provide many additional features to BizTalk, including Secure Reliable Transactions and greater interoperability with third-party platforms. BizTalk server brings to the table business process management capabilities and rules.

Microsoft is planning to fully integrate BizTalk Server 2006 with Indigo via an Indigo connector. If you would like to start using the connector today, Scott Woodgate (the lead product manager for BizTalk) is working with members of his team on a prototype that works with BizTalk Server 2004. For a link to download the Indigo connector and for more information, please visit Scott's blog at http://blogs.msdn.com/scottwoo.

Please note that the adapter works only with the .NET Framework 2.0. (BizTalk currently interacts with the .NET Framework v.1.0.) The system requirements and installation details are available through the blog Web site.

Summary

Indigo has multiple ways of providing assurances about the delivery of your messages. The deterministic nature of Indigo makes it easy for developers to set the order and the number of messages sent. Indigo provides robust transaction and session management, and high availability for business applications.

In this chapter, you learned about transaction boundaries and the standards behind the transaction, security, and reliability features of Indigo. You then learned about the concept of compensation and how Indigo relates to `System.Transactions`. Next, you looked at secure reliable messaging in Indigo, including the bindings used to set it up. You also learned about Indigo queues and synchronization; how to effectively manage sessions and scopes; and how to deal with failures, critical communication errors, and Dead Letter Queues.

The next topic on the roster was sessions and the four types of instancing. You also looked at transactions in detail, including how to start, fail, and complete transactions. Then you examined duplex communication and streaming. Finally, you learned how BizTalk and Indigo will be integrated in the near future.

Speaking of integration, how does one port over existing applications to Indigo? In the next chapter, you learn how to port and connect existing COM+, ASMX, Enterprise Services, .NET Remoting, and MSMQ applications to Indigo.

7

Indigo Migration and Interoperability

Indigo is the new communication paradigm for the next generation of the Windows operating system. This chapter examines what changes you will be required to make to your existing code base to make your applications interoperable with Indigo. We will be examining all the major communication APIs that currently exist on the Windows platform, including the following:

- ❑ XML Web Services (ASMX)
- ❑ Enterprise Services (ES)
- ❑ Microsoft Message Queuing (MSMQ)
- ❑ NET Remoting
- ❑ DCOM/COM+

In many cases, you'll find that migrating your application to Indigo is quite simple. You can even leverage old, unmanaged COM+ components without too much difficulty. Toward the end of the chapter, you will find out what challenges lie ahead and how to avoid common migration pitfalls.

Indigo is interoperable not only with Microsoft technologies but also with other platforms through the `BasicProfile`, `WSProfile`, and `WSProfileDualHttp` bindings. This chapter primarily focuses on the integration of Indigo with existing Microsoft technologies and provides a migration path to port your applications to Indigo.

The Big Picture

Code rewrites are not pleasant experiences. The process can be prohibitively expensive and require a lot of time. Another challenge is justifying the costs from a business perspective.

Chapter 7

Fortunately, the developers on the Indigo team anticipated these challenges and created relatively simple mechanisms to migrate or wrap your existing code to make it work with Indigo.

Indigo interoperates on the wire level with Enterprise Services, Web Service Extensions 3.0, and ASMX. MSMQ and COM+ can also interact with Indigo using proxies and minor code modifications. Microsoft is currently working on plug-ins to integrate Indigo with BizTalk Server 2006 and the SQL Server Service Broker. (BizTalk Server/Indigo integration is covered in more detail in Chapter 6).

The only formats that will require extensive code changes are Web Service Extensions 2.0 and .NET Remoting. This isn't a small issue; these two communication technologies present a unique set of challenges. We will help guide you in the right direction.

Looking at the Scorecard

How can you prepare your current applications for Indigo? Here's a high-level overview of best practices for all the current Windows communications technologies. Later in the chapter, we will drill down through each of these technologies.

❑   **COM+** — If your infrastructure is primarily component-based, it makes a great deal of sense to try to keep your business logic in place. The simplest transition point between COM+ and Indigo is Enterprise Services. You can use unmanaged COM+ clients to transmit and receive Indigo messages; however, Enterprise Services will provide you with a solid and established framework that easily interconnects with Indigo.

❑   **Enterprise Services (ES)** — ES interacts well with Indigo, especially if your code is written in .NET. In most cases, your code will require only a few annotations.

❑   **.NET Remoting** — .NET Remoting does not interoperate well with Indigo. In most cases, you will have to rewrite large chunks of your code to make it work. However, .NET Remoting will be supported on the .NET Framework for the foreseeable future.

❑   **MSMQ** — If you use MSMQ, only small changes are required to make your code interoperable with Indigo. (Refer to Chapter 6 and the "Microsoft Message Queuing" section later in this chapter.)

❑   **ASMX** — Indigo can communicate on the wire with ASMX and requires the least amount of work to migrate. Both are based on the WS-* specifications. (You can find out more in the section that follows.)

> **Throughout the chapter, you'll find the terms *attribute* and *annotation*. Please note that they refer to the same thing — the terms are completely interchangeable.**

Web Service Enhancements and ASMX

Indigo is based on service-oriented architecture, most notably the Web Service standards ratified by the Organization for the Advancement of Structured Information Standards (OASIS). You can find out more about OASIS at the following location: oasis-open.org.

Note that the Web Service Enhancements (WSE) 2.0 are not wire-compatible with Indigo. For direct compatibility, use WSE 3.0 (which is slated to ship before the final version of Indigo).

Indigo is fundamentally compatible with ASMX using the `BasicProfileBinding` (which corresponds to the WS-I Basic Profile). It supports the HTTP/SOAP/WSDL infrastructure and SSL transactions over HTTP. `BasicProfileBinding` does not support WSE-based transactions. (Indigo's transactional infrastructure is provided by WS-Transactions.)

Indigo and ASP.NET support SOAP. If you are trying to port over a Web Service to Indigo, anything that contains ASP.NET sessions or ASMX SOAP code modifications (in other words, anything dependent on HTTP security or sessions) will require a rewrite. Security and session are now handled through Secure Reliable Messaging (SRM). Indigo provides fine-grained control and customization using simple annotations. Here is an example of an Airline Reservation Web Service client. The `AddRes` operation passes two variables into the Web Service (the customer name and the transaction ID):

```
using System.Web.Services;
public class AirReservationWSClient
{
public static void Main(string[] args)
{
AirReservation arc = New AirReservation();
AirReservationOperation NewRes = new AirReservationOperation("Jon Doe","ID132537");
arc.AddReservation(NewRes);
}
}
```

To convert this Web Service client to an Indigo client requires a few subtle changes. First, you must replace `System.Web.Services` with `System.ServiceModel` (the core Indigo namespace). Then you must create an Indigo proxy and explicitly close your communication channel, as illustrated in the following code:

```
using System.ServiceModel;
public class AirReservationIndigoClient
{
public static void Main(string[] args)
{
AirlineReservationProxy arc = New AirlineReservationProxy();
AirReservationOperation NewRes = new AirReservationOperation("Jon Doe","ID132537");
arc.AddReservation(NewRes);
arc.Close();
}
}
```

Now, look at the Web Service providing the airline reservation functionality. First, you need to define your Web Service variables within the `AirReservationOperation` class. You then define the `AirReservation` class and declare it a `WebMethod` using a simple annotation. The `TransactionOption` property is set to `RequiresNew`. This property will automatically instantiate a transaction for the Web Service method.

```
using System.Web.Services;
public class AirReservationOperation
{
```

```
public string CustomerName;
public string TransactionID;
}

public class AirReservation:WebService
{
[WebMethod(TransactionOption = TransactionOption.RequiresNew)]
public string AddReservation(AirReservationOperation NewRes)
...
}
```

Now, change this code to make it interoperable with Indigo messaging rather than default Web Services. As with the previous examples, you must first change the namespace to System.ServiceModel. Then you define an Indigo service contract for your class using the [ServiceContract] attribute. You can set the behavior of your Indigo service using the [OperationBehavior] attribute. The AutoEnlistTransaction property will allow the transaction to appear in the client window. AutoCompleteTransaction will report the client transaction's success when the service contract is completed. The [OperationContract] attribute exposes the method as an Indigo operation.

```
using System.ServiceModel;
public class AirReservationOperation
{
public string CustomerName;
public string TransactionID;
}

[ServiceContract]
public class AirReservation:WebService
{
[OperationBehavior(AutoEnlistTransaction = true, AutoCompleteTransaction = true)]

[OperationContract]
public string AddReservation(AirReservationOperation NewRes)
...
}
```

Enterprise Services (ES)

Indigo has many similarities to Enterprise Services. They both support asynchronous calls, publication/subscriber-like events, security contexts, reliable messaging, and much more. Using attributes (such as [Transaction]), you can allow an application using Enterprise Services to interoperate with Indigo. If your application doesn't use the .NET Framework, Indigo offers the service moniker to help connect to Web Services. (Refer to the section on COM+ for more details; use the same instructions to create an Indigo service for your ES component.)

You'll notice a lot of similarities between migrating an Enterprise Services application to Indigo and migrating ASMX code to Indigo. Both involve required attribute changes. Here is an example of a simple sales class using Enterprise Services:

```
Using System.EnterpriseServices;
[Transaction(TransactionOption.Required)]
public class Sales:ServicedComponent
{
public void AddSale(string salesAccount, int salesAmount)
{ . . . }
}
```

To migrate this code to Indigo, you must change the namespace from System.EnterpriseServices to System.ServiceModel. Using the [BindingRequirements] attribute, the TransactionFlowRequirements property set as RequirementsMode.Require makes sure that the bindings that are used support transactions.

You can set the behavior using the [ServiceBehavior] attribute. In the example that follows, the InstanceMode and ConcurrencyMode properties denote that there is a new instance of the service for each session (you can set the service to be shared by several sessions by using the InstanceMode.SharedSession value), and the service instance is single threaded. The ConcurrencyMode.Reentrant value indicates that service can accept reentrant calls; this is especially useful if your services will call other services.

You will notice that the AddSale method is decorated with two attributes: [OperationBehavior] and [OperationContract]. The AutoEnlistTransaction and AutoCommitTransaction properties will allow the service to be displayed on the client and indicate when the service starts and ends (these properties were also used in the Indigo code sample in the section on Web Services at the beginning of the chapter). The ReleaseInstance property makes sure that the service object is recycled after the call (via the ReleaseInstanceMode.AfterCall value). The [OperationContract] attribute sets the AddSale method as the primary Indigo operation in the following example:

```
using System.ServiceModel;
[BindingRequirements(TransactionFlowRequirements=RequirementsMode.Require)]
[ServiceBehavior(InstanceMode=InstanceMode.SharedSession,
                 ConcurrencyMode=ConcurrencyMode.Reentrant)]
[ServiceContract(Session=true)]
public class Sales:ServicedComponent
{
[OperationBehavior(AutoEnlistTransaction = true,
                   AutoCommitTransaction = true,
                   ReleaseInstance=ReleaseInstanceMode.AfterCall]
[OperationContract]
```

```
public void AddSale(string salesAccount, int salesAmount)
{ . . . }
}
```

> If you are unfamilliar with the Indigo Contract and Behavior properties, refer to the WinFX Software Development Kit (SDK) documentation available on the Microsoft MSDN Web site: http://winfx.msdn.microsoft.com. This online source is constantly updated and contains current API information.

Microsoft Message Queuing

Microsoft Message Queuing (MSMQ) is Microsoft's initial offering for reliable messaging. It contains a powerful API to queue messages on an enterprise level. A new version of MSMQ will be available in Longhorn; in fact, it is a core component of Indigo, providing all of its queuing capabilities. BizTalk includes a message queuing framework (codenamed MSMQ-T). Microsoft is currently developing interfaces to allow BizTalk and SQL Server Service Broker to interact with Indigo. To find out more about MSMQ, visit the Microsoft Message Queuing Center at www.microsoft.com/windows2000/technologies/communications/msmq/default.asp.

Indigo implements queuing using the QueueService component. QueueService supports Global XML Web Services Architecture (GXA) protocols. It enables you to implement your own Indigo queuing schemes or communicate directly to MSMQ using Web Services. Figure 7-1 illustrates the relationship between the GXA and Indigo.

The Global XML Web Services Architecture (GXA) and Indigo

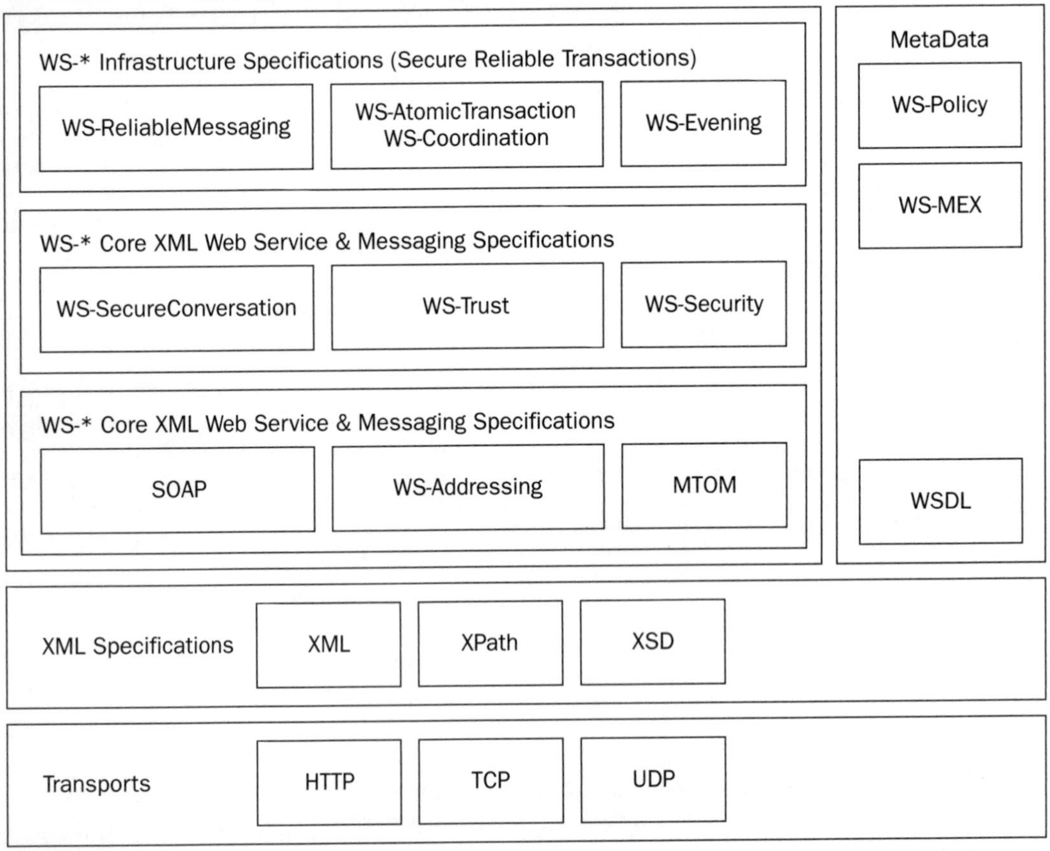

WS-* Infrastructure Specifications (Secure Reliable Transactions)			MetaData
WS-ReliableMessaging	WS-AtomicTransaction WS-Coordination	WS-Evening	WS-Policy
WS-* Core XML Web Service & Messaging Specifications			WS-MEX
WS-SecureConversation	WS-Trust	WS-Security	
WS-* Core XML Web Service & Messaging Specifications			
SOAP	WS-Addressing	MTOM	WSDL
XML Specifications	XML	XPath	XSD
Transports	HTTP	TCP	UDP

Figure 7-1

If you are used to creating MSMQ applications, you won't find that you can easily leverage your existing knowledge to create Indigo queues.

MSMQ is very useful in tackling service-oriented challenges such as load balancing or availability. Queues loosen the coupling between client and service, allowing you to add reliability in the process. Queued messages are passed to the code level based on the availability of the message. If you are unfamilliar with MSMQ, be aware that you can currently access MSMQ capabilities through the `System.Messaging` namespace.

Unsupported Features

There are several MSMQ features that are unsupported under Indigo. You will need to eliminate the code that references these features and use the Indigo analogues:

❑ **Request/response**

❑ **Simulating database-like operations** — In Indigo, database-like operations are not permitted.

❑ **Pragmatic General Multicast (PGM) protocol** — PGM is a reliable messaging protocol that allows an ordered or unordered transfer of messages. PGM is not supported under Indigo because it is not a standard service-oriented transport (and, therefore, is not included in the list of available channels). Secure Reliable Messaging is included within Indigo via the WS-* specifications.

❑ **Distribution lists**

❑ **Message priorities**

Working with Indigo Queues

Much of the code used to define the queue properties can be set in the `.config` file. Here is an example of how you can create a queued, one-way operation contract in Indigo. The following example demonstrates an interface for a Customer Entry program. As with any Indigo-enabled application, you must first add in a reference to the `System.ServiceModel` namespace. The `[OperationContract]` attribute exposes the `AddCustomer` method as an Indigo operation. The `IsOneWay` property indicates that the method should not deliver a reply; all messages to `AddCustomer` should be treated as one-way messages.

```
using System.ServiceModel;
public interface ICustomerEntry
{
 [OperationContract(IsOneWay=true)]
 void AddCustomer(string CustomerName, string Address, int CustomerCode);
}
```

Creating Queue Endpoints in Config

As previously indicated, Indigo queue properties such as addressing method and queue bindings can be defined in the configuration file. Here is an example of a private queue endpoint definition. You can set an endpoint as private by adding `private$` in the URI between the local server name and the queue. `Address` sets the base address and protocol (which is set to `net.msmq`). The `bindingSectionName` property is set to `netProfileMsmqBinding`, which allows you to select a standard queue binding. The `bindingConfiguration` property is set to the value of `usingDefaults`. This indicates that you want to use the default queue binding configuration settings. Finally, the `contractType` property generates a queue for the `ICustomerEntry` interface.

```
<endpoint
 address ="net.msmq://MyServer/private$/MyQueue/"
 bindingSectionName="netProfileMsmqBinding"
 bindingConfiguration ="usingDefaults"
 contractType="Queue.ICustomerEntry,Queues" />
```

If you want to instantiate a public queue, simply remove the `$private` value in the URI, as indicated in the following example:

```
<endpoint
 address ="net.msmq://MyServer/MyQueue/"
 bindingSectionName="netProfileMsmqBinding"
 bindingConfiguration ="usingDefaults"
 contractType="Queue.ICustomerEntry,Queues" />
```

Creating Queue Bindings in Config

You can define queue bindings in the `web.config` file using the following code:

```
<bindings>
 <netProfileMsmqBinding>
  <binding
     configurationName="usingDefaults"
     msmqProtectionLevel="None"
     msmqAuthenticationMode="None"
   />
 </netProfileMsmqBinding>
</bindings>
```

The `netProfileMsmqBinding` section defines the properties of the binding. This binding is referenced in the Endpoint section of the configuration file (see the preceding section). The `configurationName` property indicates that the binding should use default values. `msmqProtectionLevel` and `msmqAuthenticationMode` indicate if encryption should be added to the binding and if authentication is required. In the preceding example, both are set to `None`. You have four authentication types that you can use in Indigo including Anonymous, Certificate (using X.509), Username (also using X.509), and Windows (using NTLM/Kerberos).

You can enforce a queue by adding the `[BindingRequirements]` attribute to an interface. The `QueuedDeliveryRequirements` property is set to `RequirementsMode.Require`. This means that the delivery of messages from the service must be executed using Indigo queues.

```
[BindingRequirements(QueuedDeliveryRequirements=RequirementsMode.Require)]
class CustomerService:ICustomerEntry
{ ... }
```

For more in-depth information on the MSMQ features in Indigo, refer to Chapter 6.

.NET Remoting

.NET Remoting allows you to create custom communication channels. You can connect to remote .NET objects and remote processes can interact with the processes using any protocol you want. .NET Remoting uses CLR assemblies to map value types and can only operate on two (or more) systems using the .NET platform. By contrast, Indigo is designed to communicate with vendor-independent systems using Web Services. This very fact (and many others) highlights the difficulties in migrating .NET Remoting applications to Indigo.

With the release of Indigo, .NET Remoting has been deprecated. All the object-remoting semantics plumbing is included in Indigo. One of the core reasons that .NET Remoting will not easily interoperate with Indigo applications is the differences in the way that the SOAP headers are encoded. .NET Remoting uses an RPC variety of SOAP, whereas Indigo specifically adheres to the ASMX/WS-I Profile. Indigo also has no way of knowing how to handle custom infrastructure extensions. For example, Indigo is not compatible with non-WS features, unusual transports, and encodings. If you have built a proprietary system using custom extensions, you might want to look into Indigo's extensibility features to successfully port your custom protocols and code.

> If your .NET Remoting applications work as you want them to, you don't necessarily need to recode them to make them Indigo-compliant. .NET Remoting will continue to be supported in the .NET Framework 2.0 and for the foreseeable future.

One of the things to look out for is a client application that uses lease-based lifetime properties or `Singleton` objects. These will definitely need to be changed: the Leased-Based Lifetime Manager handles the task of garbage collecting when a lease expires. Indigo uses sessions to maintain state and has completely different mechanisms for maintaining sessions (see Chapter 6 for more details). Also be sure to respect the service boundaries and keep the calls local.

Client- and server-activated objects are not supported in Indigo. (In fact, they go completely against the fundamental principles of SOA, especially the boundaries tenet.) If you are using basic Web Services to access remote objects, you can easily create a proxy to the service using Indigo. However, if the activation code is not Web Service–based, you must do one of the following:

❑   Bypass Indigo and continue using the built-in support for .NET Remoting in the .NET Framework 2.0/WinFX. If your system works, there should not be any pressing need to change it.

❑   Rewrite the .NET Remoting code as Indigo. Instead of remotely accessing objects, use contracts and endpoints.

It is possible to port applications that use .NET Remoting to Indigo; however, you will need to manually recode portions of your application that relate to wiring (specifically custom formatters and sinks). The bulk of the work will involve changing your code to Indigo channel providers. There are advantages to doing this because Indigo abstracts a lot of the low-level plumbing (which will simplify your development efforts later).

If you want to simulate .NET Remoting using Indigo, use the extensibility model that allows you to manipulate the low-level calls much like remoting extensions. This will give you granular control over how the wire is handled. You can interoperate Indigo with a .NET Remoting application only if the application is used to communicate to a .NET Web Service over HTTP.

COM+

The great news with trying to integrate COM+ applications with Indigo is that you don't have to rewrite any code. Service monikers and proxies are used to wrap COM+ clients to allow them to receive Indigo messages. COM+ components can also become Indigo services. This means that you don't have to scrap any of the business logic you've built — a huge benefit from a cost perspective.

You can expose COM+ functionality to Indigo using an Indigo proxy. This proxy can be created easily and seamlessly using the comsvcutil tool. (You can learn more about the tool later in this chapter.)

Please note that Indigo doesn't use DCOM as a communication channel.

To consume Indigo services using COM+, you must create an Indigo service moniker. The Indigo service moniker can interoperate with COM-based development tools such as Visual Basic 6.0 and Office Visual Basic for Applications.

Preparing your COM+ Assemblies for Indigo

Microsoft has designed a mechanism to allow developers to access Indigo Web Services using strongly typed COM objects. This can be accomplished using the Indigo service moniker. The following instructions show you how to create COM-visible definitions of the Indigo Web Service contract and bindings. It is the simplicity of being able to set up client info from the config file that makes the solution very elegant — Indigo does all the plumbing work.

1. Use the Service MetaData Utility (svcutil.exe) to create the metadata contract from the Indigo Web Service. This will create a proxy assembly and a config file for your COM object. (The tool is covered later in the chapter.) The binding information should then be placed in a configuration file within your application directory (for a file called AirlineReservation.exe, create a config file called AirlineReservation.exe.config).

2. Next, your assembly must be made ComVisible. Add the following as the first line of code in your assembly file (if you are writing your application in C#, your assembly file will be called AssemblyInfo.cs):

```
[assembly: ComVisible(true)].
```

3. Your proxy has to be compiled as a strong named assembly. If you are unfamilliar with strong naming assemblies, you can obtain more information on the MSDN Web site at http://msdn. microsoft.com/library/en-us/cpguide/html/cpconstrong-namedassemblies.asp.

4. The assembly must then be registered in the Global Assembly Cache (GAC), and the assembly types must be registered with COM. You can use the GAC tool (gacutil.exe) and the Assembly Registration (regasm.exe) tool to pull this off. For example, type gacutil/ iAirlineReservation.dll and regsvcs AirlineReservation.dll.

Exposing COM+ Functionality Using Indigo Services

How can you expose a COM+ client as an Indigo service? First, you must configure the binding. In the following example, the `configurationName` of the binding is called `COMIndigoBinding`. The SOAP version that is used for the binding is version 1.2.

```
<configuration xmlns="http://schemas.microsoft.com/.NetConfiguration/v2.0">
    <system.serviceModel>
        <bindings>
            <wsProfileBinding>
                <binding configurationName="COMIndigoBinding" soapVersion="Soap12" />
            </wsProfileBinding>
        </bindings>
    </system.serviceModel>
</configuration>
```

For every COM+ class, Indigo generates a unique corresponding service. Indigo directly maps the interface of a COM+ component to a matching service contract. COM+ features, such as security and transactional support, are also reflected into the service using Indigo implementations. Here is the actual code for the airline reservation application. First, you must create a reference to the `System.ServiceModel` namespace. Then you define an Indigo service contract called `IAirlineReservation`. It, in turn, exposes a method called `BookFlight`.

```
using System.ServiceModel;
...
[ServiceContract]
public class IAirlineReservation
{
[OperationsContract]
public int BookFlight(int FlightID)
}
```

You can then use the `ComSvcConfig.exe` tool to expose Indigo endpoints on a COM+ service. The `IAirlineReservation` interface is exposed as an Indigo Web Service hosted within the COM+ container.

```
ComSvcConfig add /application:AirlineReservation /interface:
AirlineReservation.BookFlight,IAirlineReservation /hosting:complus
```

The Indigo service generated from the COM+ component can be hosted either by using Web hosting or standard COM+ (svchost) hosting. (See Chapter 5 for an overview of Indigo hosting.) The next section demonstrates how to consume Indigo services using COM+.

Consuming Indigo Services Using COM+ Clients

To consume an Indigo service using COM+, you must build an Indigo service moniker and call the `GetObject` method. Once the moniker is used, a typed Indigo channel is "invisibly" created. The first step in building a moniker is accomplished by constructing a moniker string. Here is an example:

```
service:address=http://localhost/AirlineReservation, binding=wsProfileBinding,
bindingName=MyBinding
```

In the preceding code sample, the base address is set to a service called `AirlineReservation` on local-host. The moniker will use the Web Service WS-I Profile binding (`wsProfileBinding`) to access the service. In the example, the binding has been named `MyBinding`. You can also reference an Indigo contract using a GUID, as shown in the following example:

```
service:address=http://localhost/AirlineReservation, binding=wsProfileBinding,
bindingName=MyBinding, contract={36ADAD5A-A944-4d5c-9B7C-967E4F00A090}
```

The next code sample features a VB6 example of an Indigo service moniker. If you want to reference an Indigo Web Service inside a VB6 application, simply add a reference to the assembly in your project and add in the following code:

```
Dim AirlineReservationProxy As IAirlineReservation
Dim process As Integer
Set AirlineReservationProxy = GetObject(_
        "service:address= http://localhost/AirlineReservation,_
        binding=wsProfileBinding,_
        bindingName=MyBinding")
process=AddService.BookFlight(5150)
```

You can also use Indigo service monikers to make COM clients "speak" to COM+ services using Indigo.

You will have to modify or rewrite any code that uses COM+ Loosely Coupled Events (LCE) or COM+ context dependencies.

Indigo Moniker Properties

The Indigo service moniker supports the properties shown in the following table:

Property Name	Description
wsdl	An alternate address for metadata contract information. Example: `http://localhost/MyService/?wsdl`
address	A link (URL) where the service is located. Example: `address=net.tcp://INTLIVE/BookService`
contract	The service contract Interface Identifier (IID). Example: `contract={39BABA7D-B543-5d7a-7A5B-235D2A85B121}`
binding	Specifies the binding type. Example: `binding=customBinding`
bindingName	Identifier for the binding — corresponds with binding specified in config. Example: `bindingName=MyBinding`

Other Vendors' Technologies

Interoperability can be a challenge if you try to connect a non-Microsoft system with a Microsoft application. One of the ways you can get over this limitation is by using the following WS-* protocols:

- ❑ WS-ReliableMessaging
- ❑ WS-I Basic Profile
- ❑ WS-AtomicTransactions
- ❑ WS-Security

From a .NET development perspective, Indigo abstracts the construction of the SOAP headers. As a .NET developer, all you need to worry about are changes in the API. Indigo was designed that way to minimize the impact of WS-* spec changes.

Integration Challenges

Microsoft has vowed that they will implement specs with full fidelity. However, many interoperability challenges lie ahead, including the following:

- ❑ Other vendors might not implement the Web Services protocols exactly as indicated in the specifications.
- ❑ Standards are in a state of flux and there are challenges in getting wide adoption of standards-based technology.

Indigo Tools

Indigo provides many tools. The following sections describe two of these tools.

ComSvcConfig

This tool helps you integrate Indigo with COM+ and Enterprise Services components by creating a Web Service. Here is an example of a typical ComSvcConfig command-line directive:

```
ComSvcConfig add /application:POS /interface:POS.AddCustomer, IPOS /hosting:was
/webDirectory:PosService /mex
```

The following table lists the command line options available for ComSvcConfig:

Option	Description
/application	Configure the selected the COM+ application. You can identify your application by application ID or Name.
/hosting	You can choose the hosting model that fits your needs. The available choices include: was and complus.
/interface	You can select the interface to configure using the /interface option. You can identify you interfaces using the ClassID, ProgID, InterfaceID, or Name.
/id	Shows IDs for all application interfaces and components.
/mex	Creates a metadata endpoint.
/nologo	Hides the ComSvcConfig logo.
/quiet	Hides all output with the exception of errors.
/webDirectory	Choose the target virtual directory for hosting.
/webSite	Choose the target Web site for hosting.

Otherwise, you can use ComSvcUtil to integrate COM+ with services For more information about both tools, refer to the COM+ integration section earlier in the chapter and the MSDN documentation.

Svcutil

Svcutil is an amazing tool that enables you to do automatic code generation based on a WSDL or Mex metadata. Svcutil can create source code from service metadata and assemblies. Here is how you can generate proxy code from an Indigo address:

```
svcutil http://localhost/CustomService
```

You can also create a .svc file form service assembly files:

```
svcutil CustomService.dll
```

Summary

In this chapter, you learned the relationship between Microsoft's existing communication technologies and Indigo. You also found out how to migrate or interoperate technologies such as ASMX, MSMQ, Enterprise Services, .NET Remoting, and COM+ with Indigo. Finally, you learned about the integration challenges in implementing Indigo and got an overview of some of the important tools to help you simplify Indigo development.

In the next chapter, you learn how data is handled in WinFX and how to integrate data-binding capabilities in Avalon forms.

Part III

Data and Web

8

Data
Services

Like so much in WinFX, one could make a compelling argument that the new features afforded to developers with respect to data binding are essentially the same as they've always been. One could also make an equally compelling argument that the new features are completely different. Depending on your perspective, both are equally true. To understand what is new, it's critical to understand what is in the current .NET Framework.

As someone who spends a good bit of time answering questions on various newsgroups and forums, I've seen a lot of confusion and misinformation about .NET and data binding, in particular. I can't count the times on my fingers that I've read a post by someone berating ADO.NET, for instance, because he can't get data to display and behave as he wanted in a `DataGrid`. ADO.NET is a technology that has absolutely *nothing* to do with user interface (UI) or visualization, yet it often gets blamed for any shortcomings in the display of data. Chapter 9 is titled "ADO.NET and ASP.NET," and given this, should give a pretty good clue that data binding (Data Services) and accessing data (ADO.NET) are two totally different areas. However, although they are two totally different areas, they are two technologies that can and should be used in conjunction with one another in many situations to meet business requirements for users.

Data Services

Data Services, stated simply, is merely the new name Microsoft has given the mechanism of setting properties based on values persisted to and retrieved from a data store somewhere. Under the current version of the .NET Framework, there are a few different ways you can bind data to a data store. The first is the most obvious and simple and entails using a given controls set accessor to specify the value, as in the following example:

```
tbBirdName.Text = "EDC";
```

Now, if you had a `DataTable` (retrieved from a database in most instances), and you wanted to set the value of `tbBirdName` to a value contained therein, you'd typically do something like this:

```
private void Form1_Load(object sender, System.EventArgs e) {
DataTable Cuckooz = new DataTable("CuckooBirds");
DataColumn CuckooFirstName = new DataColumn("CuckooFirstName",
typeof(System.String));
DataColumn CuckooLastName = new DataColumn("CuckooLastName",
typeof(System.String));
Customers.Columns.Add(CuckooFirstName);
Customers.Columns.Add(CuckooLastName);
//Fill Customers with a DataAdapter, XML etc
tbBirdName.Text = Cuckooz.Rows[0]["CuckooFirstName"].ToString() + "" " +
Cuckooz.Rows[0]["CuckooLastName"].ToString();
    }
```

At present, if you want to programmatically set properties, using the preceding code is the way you accomplish it. With the advent of .NET though, Microsoft gave us a few new tools to take advantage of. One of the more interesting ones is the configuration file. You can now use a configuration file (which is stored with your executable and ends in `.config`) and store the initial values for many features, controls being one, in a structured and easy to read XML Format. Once those are set, the application will use those values without any intervention on the developer's part. If you look at Figure 8-1, you can see how to instruct the Integrated Development Environment (IDE) to use a value in a configuration file for a given control.

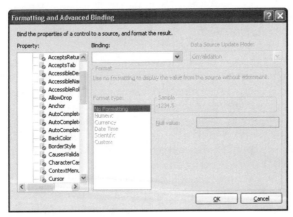

Figure 8-1

When using the designer, a configuration file will be generated for you if it doesn't already exist, and you set the value in the respective "value" section of the configuration file, as follows:

```
<?xml version="1.0" encoding="utf-8"?>
<configuration>
 <appSettings>
        <!--  User application and configured property settings go here.-->
        <!--  Example: <add key="settingName" value="settingValue"/> -->
        <add key="tbBirdName.Text" value="EDC" />
```

```
    </appSettings>
    </configuration>
```

Thus, using the code in the first two examples, where the value for `tbBirdName.text` is specified through the accessor, will have the same result as using the dynamic properties and specifying the value, as shown in the preceding code.

The final current alternative is to use the designer to drag a typed `DataSet` onto a form and then specify a mapping through the (Data Bindings) tool. An example of how this is accomplished is provided in Figure 8-2.

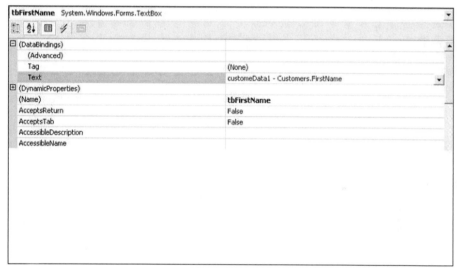

Figure 8-2

While any of the preceding methods will still be available under Avalon, Data Services is such a profound improvement that it's hard to imagine why anyone would want to use any of them.

Enter XAML

At the heart of Data Services is a mechanism known as Extensible Application Markup Language (XAML) and specifically, UI Binding. Stated simply, XAML and UI Binding allow a developer to do away with traditional approaches and define UI elements and layout declaratively. To be honest, the first time I heard this, my initial response was "big deal." I've been programming for a few years now, so declaring and instantiating an object (particularly when the IDE does so much of the heavy lifting for you in regard to controls) and setting a few properties is second nature. Even when I think back to the days when I was first learning programming, I still never thought it was all that difficult to specify `Control.Text = "ValueIWantToShowUp"`. So why is being able to set values declaratively a big deal? According to the WinFX SDK (found at `http://winfx.msdn.microsoft.com/library/default .asp?url=/library/en-us/wcp_conceptual/winfx/connecteddata/overviews/dataservices .asp`), Microsoft lists the following as potential benefits:

1. Inherent support for data binding in the core UI

2. Flexible representation of data

3. Clean separation of business logic from UI

4. A broad range of binding targets provided by the data access models available in Avalon

Revisit Figures 8-1 and 8-2. Figure 8-1 lists every property available for a given `TextBox` control, but mapping values to a configuration file makes sense only in a very specific set of circumstances. Figure 8-2 shows that you can map the fields to the values in a dataset; however, there's one major problem — you have only the Text and Tag properties available to you directly. You can use the Advanced DataBindings to specify properties such as BackGround color, but it won't work exactly as you'd expect.

Binding Types

There are three types of bindings available in Avalon and Data Services:

❑ **One Way Binding** — This type of binding occurs unidirectionally. The control receives a property value(s) from a given data source, but changes made to that control are not propagated or transmitted back to the originator in any fashion. This method works well for read-only scenarios but has limited viability in any scenario where the user has a need to manipulate or change the data.

❑ **Two Way Binding** — In this type of binding, the original property values for a given control are set from a given data source. However, unlike One Way Binding, any changes that the user makes to the control's properties are sent back to the data store.

❑ **One Time Binding** — Of the three, this is the most limited. When the control is originally bound, the value is retrieved from the binding source. After that, any changes that are made to this data are *not* shown in the control. Thus, the primary difference between One Way and One Time Binding is that One Way Binding is dynamic. (In the example, any changes made to the BirdName row that you've bound to will show up in the control.)

The best way to think of these is by way of example. If you retrieve a value from a configuration file (`app.config`/`web.config`) and you change any values in the file, they will *not* be seen by the application until it is restarted. This method is analogous to One Time Binding. If you have a typical ASP.NET application that queries a database at each page load and pulls back the current data, this is analogous to One Way Binding. If the data changes between page loads, it will be reflected the next time the page is refreshed. Two Way Binding is exemplified by a typical data entry screen where you query for data, make changes to it, and hit a Submit or Save button when you're finished.

As is the case with everything in Data Services, there are two ways you can define the binding direction: through code (C#, VB.NET, and so on) or through XAML. An example of doing both is provided here:

```
<TextBlock Name="FirstName"    TextContent="{Bind Path=FirstName, Mode=OneTime}" />
<TextBlock Name="FirstName"    TextContent="{Bind Path=FirstName, Mode=OneWay}" />
<TextBlock Name="FirstName"    TextContent="{Bind Path=FirstName, Mode=TwoWay}" />

Binding FirstNameDefinition = new Binding("FirstName");
FirstNameDefinition.Mode = BindingMode.OneTime;
```

```
Binding FirstNameDefinition = new Binding("FirstName");
FirstNameDefinition.Mode = BBindingMode.OneWay;

Binding FirstNameDefinition = new Binding("FirstName");
FirstNameDefinition.Mode = BindingMode.TwoWay;
```

So let's dive into a real example. I'm going to create a simple class called `BindingExample` that has one simple property, `DBValueProperty`. Now, this is a completely contrived example and wouldn't make much sense in the real world. However, this class could just as easily have been something from the Enterprise library, the Data Access Application block, or any other real-world class.

```
namespace WroxDemo
{
  public class BindingExample
  {
    private System.String m_DBValue = "I came from a Data base";
    public BindingExample() {}
    public System.String DBValueProperty
    {
     get
       {
         return m_DBValue;;
       }
       set{
          m_DBValue = value;
       }    }
  }
}

<DockPanel ID="root"
  xmlns="http://schemas.microsoft.com/winfx/avalon/2005"
  xmlns:x="http://schemas.microsoft.com/winfx/xaml/2005"
  Width="500"
  Height="500"
  Background="NavyBlue">

  <DockPanel.Resources>
    <ObjectDataSource x:Key="ExampleDataSource"
TypeName="WroxDemo.BindingExample,DemoApp" />
  </DockPanel.Resources>
  <TextBlock>
    <TextBlock.TextContent>
      <Bind DataSource="{StaticResource ExampleDataSource}" BindType="OneTime"
Path="DBValueProperty"/>
    </TextBlock.TextContent>
  </TextBlock>
</DockPanel>
```

Data Sources

Any notion of data binding is essentially untenable without the context of data. What I mean is that in order for data to be bound, there needs to be something for it to be bound to. With the advent of .NET, the objects that could be bound to were seemingly endless. Believe it or not, Avalon and WinFX take this up a notch.

The primary item that developers will concern themselves with in regard to data binding is a Data Item. When you think of a data source in the context of data binding, what you're thinking of is a Data Item. So is a Data Item essentially a fancy phrase for "business object that I might want to bind my data to?" Yes. When you think of data sources, in most instances, you are going to be using Two Way Binding, as mentioned in the previous section. This is because, in most cases, users need to see data, make determinations about it, and modify it as necessary. One-way data is essentially little more than a report.

Any real binding mechanism has to perform many tasks. For one thing, formatting needs to be performed. For example, if you are binding to data in a SQL Server database, there is no such thing as a purely "Date" datatype. If you want to store date data in a SQL Server database, you can choose `DateTime`, `SmallDateTime`, or a string representation, which will need to be type cast to be of much value. However, many times you don't want the time element associated with the date. (In fact, if not specified, it defaults to midnight.) Conversely, you may want a time but not really care about the date. Before, you would trap two events to handle this: `Format` and `Parse`. This worked, but it definitely lacked elegance. This shortcoming is handled much differently in Avalon/WinFX.

As previously mentioned, data can come from many sources, including but not limited to the following:

❑   A text file

❑   XML

❑   An Access database

❑   A Web Service

❑   Hard-coded values

❑   Resource files

❑   Configuration files

Notice in the previous example that I specified an `ObjectDataSource`. This is one data source that you can use, but there are others, one of the more popular being `XmlDataSource`. All data sources will implement a common interface, `IDataSource`. To understand more about how it works, let's look at the interface in detail. (The following table is taken directly from the current MSDN documentation on `IdataSource` — by the time of publication, it's likely to have been enhanced.)

Properties:

Visual Basic	Public ReadOnly Property Data As Object
C#	Public object Data { get; }

C++	public:
	property Object^ Data {
	    Object^ get();
	}

JScript	public function get Data() : Object

Methods:

Visual Basic	Public Sub Refresh()
C#	public void Refresh();
C++	public: void Refresh();
JScript	Public function Refresh();

Events:

Visual Basic	Public Event **DataChanged** As EventHandler
C#	public event EventHandler **DataChanged**;
C++	public: event EventHandler^ **DataChanged**;
JScript	In JScript, you can use events, but you cannot define your own.

Now, both `ObjectDataSource` and `XmlDataSource` have many more members; remember that this is just the interface implementation, so most classes implementing it are going to have more functionality.

So basically, you have two ways of specifying a data source:

```
<Binding Source="{StaticResource ExampleDataSource}" BindType="OneTime"
Path="DBValueProperty"/>
```

or

```
Objectnsame.DataSource = ExampleDataSource;
```

You can also use the `XmlDataSource` for XML data:

```
<DockPanel xmlns=" "
  xmlns:x=" ">

  <DockPanel.Resources>
    <XmlDataSource x:Key="Person" XPath="/Details">
      <Persons xmlns="">
        <Person SSN="072-00-0000">
          <FirstName>Bill</FirstName>
          <LastName>Ryan</LastName>
        </Person>
        <!-- ... other Book entries ... -->
      </Persons>
    </XmlDataSource>

    <Style x:Key="PersonDataStyle">
      <Style.VisualTree>
```

```
            <TextBlock FontSize="Large" Foreground="Blue">
               <TextBlock.TextContent>
                 <Bind XPath="Details"/>
               </TextBlock.TextContent>
            </TextBlock>
         </Style.VisualTree>
       </Style>
    </DockPanel.Resources>

    <ListBox ItemsSource="{Bind DataSource={StaticResource PersonData},
   XPath=Person}"
        ItemStyle="{StaticResource PersonDataStyle}"/>

  </DockPanel>
```

Pay close attention to the ItemStyle *example because it will be discussed in depth in the next section.*

So what do you see here? Fortunately, both the ObjectDataSource and the XmlDataSource provide pretty intuitive mechanisms for seeing and manipulating data, and once you've used one, the other one is the functional equivalent.

Data Styling

Data styling is the main mechanism that developers use to present their data to their users. The primary object used in styling is not surprisingly called a *style*. There is a ton of nuance involved in using styles, which is my way of saying that they can get quite complex. However, to get started using them, it's actually quite straightforward. The SDK has one of the most compelling examples of using and extending styles, so I'm going to borrow from it here. First, I'll show how to create a simple (which isn't so simple after all) button, and then apply a data style to it:

```
<Button ContentStyle="{StaticResource WroxStyle}">
    <Person Name="BillRyan" Picture="BillR.jpg"/>
</Button>
```

Notice here that under the ContextStyle, you specifically reference a StaticResource named TestSimpleStyle. Whether you are using a Button control, a TextBox, a ListBox, or any other Avalon control, you can use the same style that is specified in the following:

```
<Style x:Key="WroxStyled">
    <Style.VisualTree>
      <DockPanel>
        <Image Source="{Bind Path=Picture}/>
        <TextBlock TextContent="{Bind Path=Name}"/>
      </DockPanel>
    </Style.VisualTree>
</Style>
```

In the first example, see that the Person object has a Name and a Picture property, respectively. The Name property takes a simple string representing someone's name, and the Picture property takes an image. Now, it's important to note that the implementation (that is, how the picture is rendered) is completely determined by the class. With this particular example, the class could have a network path prepended in the accessor, so it would look for \\NetworkShareName\BillR.jpg. This is totally decoupled, though, from the binding and the style. For the sake of this example, assume that the class handles the image name and the person name correctly.

Now notice the defined style. In it, I am declaring a DockPanel and adding an image. The image's path is mapped to the Picture property. Similarly, the TextBlock control is added to the panel and the TextContent is set to the Name property.

This style, in case you're wondering, is totally decoupled from the Button that is declared. You can do whatever you want here to the TestSimpleStyle class. You can add other items to the DockPanel, for example. However, if you want to do anything meaningful, you have to map some additional properties. Take the original definition and assume the following modifications:

```
<Button ContentStyle="{StaticResource TestSimpleStyle}">
    <Person FirstName="Bill" LastName ="Ryan" Picture="BillR.jpg"/>
</Button>
```

And now assume this modification:

```
<Style x:Key="TestSimpleStyle">
    <Style.VisualTree>
      <DockPanel>
        <Image Source="{Bind Path=Picture}/>
        <TextBlock TextContent="{Bind Path=FirstName}"/>
        <TextBlock TextContent="{Bind Path=LastName}"/>
      </DockPanel>
    </Style.VisualTree>
</Style>
```

Would this behave as expected? Sure. Could you also use the original implementation? Sure, assuming that you still had a property named Name. Now this is where things get pretty cool. Assume that you had a ListBox that you wanted to bind and use the same styling — how would it work?

```
<ListBox ItemStyle="{StaticResource TestSimpleStyle}">
    <Person FirstName="Bill" Picture="Bill.jpg"/>
    <Person FirstName="Jean-Luc" Picture="Jean-Luc.jpg"/>
  </ListBox>
```

Why specify ItemStyle in the second example and ContentStyle in the first? That has to do with Simple versus Complex Binding. A ListBox, for instance, is bound via Complex Binding. A button is bound using Simple Binding. So if you wanted to apply this style to another control, a TextBox for example, it would be as simple as this:

```
<TextBox ContentStyle="{StaticResource TestSimpleStyle}">
    <Person FirstName="Bill" LastName ="Ryan" Picture="BillR.jpg"/>
</TextBox>
```

*If you are unfamiliar with the terms Simple and Complex Binding, a quick way to distinguish between
the two is that objects that contain collections of other objects are typically Complex Binding objects.
The* ListBox *shows the binding multiple of* Person *objects, whereas only one is being bound in the*
Button *example.*

While this is pretty cool, applying the same style to a ListBox or a TextBox, the real coolness in my
opinion is in the style itself. Not only can you specify a name by which to apply styles, but you can
dynamically add them based on object type. For example, if you modify the first style slightly, you could
have something like the following:

```
<Style x:Key="*typeof(Person)">
    <Style.VisualTree>
      <DockPanel>
        <Image Source="{Bind Path=Picture}/>
        <TextBlock TextContent="{Bind Path=FirstName}"/>
        <TextBlock TextContent="{Bind Path=LastName}"/>
      </DockPanel>
    </Style.VisualTree>
  </Style>
```

So what does this do? Well, anytime the Data Item object is of the type specified in the Key declaration,
this style can be applied, allowing for great flexibility.

*I've played with just about every variation of this that I can think of and it behaves exactly as expected.
About the only shortcoming I've found is due to the nature of markup itself; because the object type
must be known in advance to specify it, you can't really use reflection, for instance, to make determinations about an object type and create styles accordingly, at least not through markup.*

Conversion

Previously we discussed binding to data, in a SQL Server database, that was of DateTime datatype
when you just wanted to display the date component and not the time. Previously, there was little support for such operations, and while you could essentially get where you wanted to go, your ways of getting there were very limited. With the advent of Avalon and WinFX, this conversion and transformation
ability has been greatly enhanced. The primary mechanism used to change data to display differently is
a Converter. You could use a Converter to take the first five numbers of a Social Security number and
replace their values with Xs so that critical information won't be displayed. This is one of the simpler
uses for Converters, but it's a pretty good starting point example for how they can be used.

In a nutshell, a *Converter* is a mechanism you can use to change the way source data is displayed.
Structurally, between building correctly normalized database tables and then business objects, the data
you get back is often not in the most user friendly format. SQL Server for instance has no notion of either
a Date or Time; it only has DateTime types. However, having an erroneous 12:00:00 at the end of every
date where you really just needed a date is inelegant at best and confusing at worst. Many people, for
instance, might think that they were supposed to add a time there and waste time over and over putting
it in, when in fact it will never be used. And if they did this incorrectly, it would cause the database to
bark at it, and they may have to reenter a record. My point is simply this: A lot of times, the optimal way

to store and maintain data is markedly different from the way you want to present it to the user. Key values, which are often integers, are of little value to users but are critical to the database system. So showing the users the CustomerName while tracking it internally with the key value is critical. But more importantly, often proper database design dictates things that make it very difficult for users to deal with. You'd never (at least it's really really hard for me to imagine a case) want to store City, State, and Zip Code in one field in a database. It would make it impossible (or really difficult) to sort and search on states and zip codes. But for presentation purposes, Miami, FL 33133-3433, is a typical representation of the way we'd show that information to users.

As mentioned, you would previously trap the format and parse events when you wanted to convert data. The current mechanism intuitively follows the same flow. However, as much as it stays the same, it differs.

The primary way you handle this mechanism is by implementing the IValueConverter interface. It's an extremely simple interface that implements two main methods: Convert and ConvertBack. The interface definition is provided in the following table:

Convert:

Visual Basic	Public Function Convert(_
	    ByVal *value* As Object, _
	    ByVal *targetType* As Type, _
	    ByVal *parameter* As Object, _
	    ByVal *culture* As CultureInfo _
	) As Object

C#	public object Convert(
	    object *value*,
	    Type *targetType*,
	    object *parameter*,
	    CultureInfo *culture*
	);

C++	public:
	Object^ Convert(
	    Object^ *value*,
	    Type^ *targetType*,
	    Object^ *parameter*,
	    CultureInfo^ *culture*
	);

JScript	public function Convert(
	    value : Object,
	    targetType : Type,
	    parameter : Object,
	    culture : CultureInfo
	) : Object;

ConvertBack:

Visual Basic	PublicFunctionConvertBack(_ ByVal *value* As Object, _ ByVal *targetType* As Type, _ ByVal *parameter* As Object, _ ByVal *culture* As CultureInfo _) As Object
C#	public object ConvertBack(object *value*, Type *targetType*, object *parameter*, CultureInfo *culture*);
C++	public: Object^ ConvertBack(Object^ *value*, Type^ *targetType*, Object^ *parameter*, CultureInfo^ *culture*);
JScript	Public function ConvertBack(*value* : Object, *targetType* : Type, *parameter* : Object, *culture* : CultureInfo) : Object;

So how would you make this work? It's pretty simple. Take your `Telephone` object, which represents Telephone Numbers. The `TelephoneNumber` class is pretty straightforward for the purposes here. Assume that it has a `CountryCode` property, an `AreaCode` property, a `FirstThree` property and a `LastFour` property. Furthermore, assume that none of them can be null, so there are default values specified in the accessors to ensure that you don't deal with null values. Thus, you want to have a conversion routine that formats instances of `TelephoneNumber` objects like `CountryCode(AreaCode)FirstThree-LastFour` ie `011(305)555-1212`.

```
public class PhoneConverter : IValueConverter
  {
public object Convert(
object o,
Type type,
object parameter,
      System.Globalization.CultureInfo culture)
    {
    TelePhoneNumber testPhoneNumber = o as TelePhoneNumber;
    return testPhoneNumber.CountryCode.ToString() + "(" +
testPhoneNumber.AreaCode.ToString() + ")" + testPhoneNumber.FirstThree.ToString() +
"-" + testPhoneNumber.LastFour.ToString();
    }
```

```
public class AddressConverter : IValueConverter
  {
    public object Convert(
      object o,
      Type type,
      object parameter,
      System.Globalization.CultureInfo culture)
    {
      Address testAddress = o as Addressr;
      return testAddress.City + ", " + testAddress.State + " " +
testAddress.ZipCode.FirstFive + "-" + testAddress.ZipCode.LastFour;
    }
```

Then you'd apply it like this:

```
<TextBlock.TextContent>
      <Bind Path="FormattedTelephoneNumber" Converter="{StaticResource
PhoneConverter}"/>
</TextBlock.Content>

<TextBlock.TextContent>
      <Bind Path="FormattedAddress" Converter="{StaticResource AddressConverter}"/>
</TextBlock.Content>
```

Of course, as with most everything else, you don't need markup here; you can specify it through code as well:

```
TestBindingDefinition.Converter = PhoneConverter;
```

Data Collections

Binding in Avalon can be accomplished through both Simple and Complex Binding mechanisms. A summary of both is provided here:

❑ *Simple Binding* is used, for the most part, exactly as its name implies. It is the mechanism by which you bind a single data element to a single property of a given control. Take a traditional TextBox object, for instance; you may want to set the BackGroundColor property or something else, but typically the property most people concern themselves with is the Text property. If you have a collection of sorts, be it a HashTable, DataTable, or custom collection that contains multiple Names, it only makes sense to bind the Text property to one of them at a time. Now, you could argue that an object was created such that it had many properties and that you'd use those properties to set multiple properties on the TextBox, but even this would still be Simple Binding because you are binding one property at a time.

❑ *Complex Binding*, in contrast, is what you'd typically see when you deal with a control like a DataGrid, ListBox, or ComboBox. Both the ListBox control and the ComboBox control, for example, have an indexer property called Items, which allows multiple things to be added to them. There are certainly times when you may have only one item in a ListBox or ComboBox, but in those cases the power of the controls pretty much is wasted. The only time you see the value of the control is when you are binding to multiple items. And if you had a DataTable with a list of states in it for instance, and you had to iterate through it, adding an item one at a time, it would be simple to do but it would be rather monotonous. To accommodate this, Complex Binding is available.

So the distinction is that you use Simple Binding when you are binding one value at a time and Complex Binding when you want to bind multiple values at one time.

Another important concept is that of *collections* — simple groups of objects. Collections can be strongly typed, meaning that every member of the collection is of the same type, or they can be weakly typed, meaning that all sorts of stuff can be included in the collection. For binding purposes, you are typically dealing with strongly typed collections, and enumerable ones at that. Why? Because if you had a collection that allowed Customers, Trades, Integers, and HashTables to be included in it, can you imagine what binding to such a thing would look like? First off, it would take a tremendous amount of work to accommodate just those few objects. After all, you'd need to know what you were going to bind to in a HashTable as opposed to a Trade. (HashTables don't have BrokerName properties after all.) But more troublesome is that a developer could intentionally or accidentally insert something you never anticipated into the collection, and your code wouldn't have any idea how to deal with it. At best you would get some unpredictable results, but in all likelihood, you'd have a bug that would be a deal breaker. As far as enumerability goes, an enumerable collection is simply a collection that can be iterated by type as opposed to index. In .NET, an enumerable collection will normally be enumerated via the for each construct. This type of iteration has many benefits, the main one being that it's very easy to see what the intent of the code is. Moreover, since there is an instance of the object in the loop already, you can reference its properties directly, which gives you IntelliSense support and makes coding a lot cleaner. If you used index-based iteration, it would provide better performance, but you'd have to reference the collection using the index, then type cast it and do all sorts of other things that are a pain to deal with. (Which way to iterate is a subject people argue ad nauseum — there's merit to both approaches, and I doubt the "right" way will ever be settled definitively.)

One problem with enumeration is that you can't remove or add items when using it. Suppose that you had a strongly typed collection and wanted to remove every item in it that had a FirstName property beginning with W. Using a for each construct, this would be impossible. Thus, you'd need to resort to an index-based approach and respond accordingly.

With this in mind, you can iterate through and bind to any collection that implements the IEnumerable interface. If you inherit from CollectionBase, for example, it already implements IEnumerable, so there's no need to implement it manually.

There's another interface, INotifyCollectionChanged, which is used to handle insertions and deletions. It has only one member, an event for CollectionChanged.

One of the more interesting new mechanisms is the notion of a view of your collection. In previous versions of the framework, you've no doubt used a DataTable object. This object is at the heart of ADO.NET and is the primary object used when manipulating, binding, or doing anything else with data. Although it's unbelievably powerful, it does have some shortcomings; for example, sorting is not possible.

For many other behaviors, such as sorting, the DataView object was created. For custom collections that need functionality such as sorting, the CollectionView object was created, and the ICollectionView interface was created for you to implement in your own collections.

The `ICollectionView` interface provides a tremendous amount of functionality, but most of it is concerned with either sorting or filtering. It also concerns itself with positioning.

The `ICollectionView` is an interface that you have available to make it possible and easy to manage positions within a collection of objects. Functionality that is commonly needed in collections, such as sorting and filtering, are provided as well. It's easy to overlook this fact and just assume that because you stick something in a collection, it can be sorted. But take, for example, a `TradesCollection` that has a group of securities trades in it. How many ways might you want to sort such a thing? By ticker symbol? By date? By broker? By dollar amount? By number of shares? In all likelihood, you'd probably want to do all of the above and more, depending on what all was in the collection. You might also want to filter things out. For instance, you may want to deal with trades from only one broker at a time and then iterate through those trades. If you didn't do this (filtering), you'd have to use some detection mechanism to decide when you reached another broker in cases when you wanted to deal with only one broker (or less than everyone), and you'd need to add additional logic to break out of the loop at some point. Difficult to do? Probably not in most cases. But it would be cumbersome and the type of monotonous programming task that takes some of the fun out of work.

The current version of the MSDN documentation lists the following properties/methods of the `ICollecionView`.

Properties:

CanFilter	Indicates whether or not this ICollectionView can do any filtering.
CanSort	Whether or not this ICollectionView does any sorting.
Culture	Culture contains the CultureInfo used in any operations of the ICollectionView that may differ by Culture, such as sorting.
CurrentItem	Return current item.
CurrentPosition	The ordinal position of the CurrentItem within the (optionally sorted and filtered) view.
Filter	Filter is a callback set by the consumer of the ICollectionView and used by the implementation of the ICollectionView to determine if an item is suitable for inclusion in the view.
IsCurrentAfterLast	Returns true if CurrentItem is beyond the end (End-Of-File).
IsCurrentBeforeFirst	Returns true if CurrentItem is before the beginning (Beginning-Of-File).
Sort	Set/get Sort criteria to sort items in collection.
SourceCollection	SourceCollection is the original unfiltered collection of which this ICollectionView is a view.

Methods:

Contains	Returns true if the item belongs to this view. No assumptions are made about the item. This method will behave similarly to IList.Contains(). If the caller knows that the item belongs to the underlying collection, it is more efficient to call Filter.
DeferRefresh	Enters a Defer Cycle. Defer cycles are used to coalesce changes to the ICollectionView.
MoveCurrentTo	Moves CurrentItem to the given item.
MoveCurrentToFirst	Moves CurrentItem to the first item.
MoveCurrentToLast	Moves CurrentItem to the last item.
MoveCurrentToNext	Moves CurrentItem to the next item.
MoveCurrentToPosition	Moves CurrentItem to the item at the given index.
MoveCurrentToPrevious	Moves CurrentItem to the previous item.
Refresh	Re-creates the view, using any Sort.

By implementing this interface, virtually everything you'd ever need to do with your data — sort it, filter it, or navigate it — is provided.

Following is a basic example of navigation:

```
public void OnButton(Object sender, RoutedEventArgs args)
{
  Button btnSample = sender as Button;

  switch (btnSample.ID)
  {
    case "Previous":
      if (MyCollectionView.MoveCurrentToPrevious())
      {
        FeedbackText.TextContent = "";
        o = MyCollectionView.CurrentItem as Order;
      }
      break;
    case "First":
      if (MyCollectionView.MoveCurrentToFirst())
      {
        FeedbackText.TextContent = "At First Record";
      }
      break;

    case "Next":
      if (MyCollectionView.MoveCurrentToNext())
      {
```

```
        FeedbackText.TextContent = "";
        o = MyCollectionView.CurrentItem as Order;
    }
    break;
        case "Last":
    if (MyCollectionView.MoveCurrentToNext())
    {
        FeedbackText.TextContent = "At Last Record";
        o = MyCollectionView.CurrentItem as Order;
    }
    break;


    }
}
```

You can do a lot more. You can call the MoveCurrentTo method passing in an index, and you'll move to that record if it's available. If you overshoot the boundary, fortunately you won't raise an exception; you'll just be taken to the last record. Similarly, you can move ahead by a given number. This type of functionality is analogous to absolute versus relative references in Excel. You might in some instances know for sure that you want to move to position 50. Or you might know that you want to find a given record and look to the record two positions ahead of it, wherever that may be.

You can also use it to test for a value. By calling the Contains method and passing in the value you are looking for, you can return either true or false, depending on whether or not the value exists. Again, this makes life a lot easier. Otherwise, each time you wanted to do this, you'd have to loop through the collection, object by object, check for the value you were looking for, and if it was found, set a True flag and break out of the loop, and if it isn't found, walk through the entire collection for nothing. Behind the scenes, this is what's being done, but the elegance of it is that you don't have to do it each time, and you can specify how this is accomplished. So, with the trading example discussed earlier, you could call Contains in such a way that it took into account Broker, TradeDate, and Number of Shares. You could specify this any way you wanted using whatever rules you wanted. And, of course, you could overload it to accommodate many different scenarios, something that in real life is often necessary.

The main point here is that while none of this stuff is necessarily "hard" to code, by any means, it's painfully monotonous.

Summary

Avalon is without a doubt a major leap forward in creating compelling software applications that involve user interface elements. While many things can be done just as they have traditionally been in .NET, there are many new methods that will fundamentally reshape your relationship with UI programming. Traditionally, if you wanted to create a TextBox control, you did this just as you would any other object. In fact, other than the object name, there was absolutely no distinction between creating a TextBox and creating a Foo. ObjectType objectName = new ObjectType() was the predominant metaphor when dealing with Windows applications.

In contrast, more and more applications needed to become Web-based. Traditional HMTL programming was declarative, and instead of using the "new" object paradigm, visual elements are now markup-based. This is probably the most notable feature of Avalon programming.

Since almost any nontrivial application involves the use of both a user interface and a data store, data binding has always been an important issue. In Avalon, you now have Data Services — ostensibly the biggest step forward in connecting data to user interface elements in a long time. Not only is the new approach more intuitive, but it also works like you've always wanted it to. Data binding in the past has been so problematic that many developers today still refuse to take advantage of many of .NET's binding features just because of problems they had in the past. Now with the advent of Avalon and Data Services, I suspect much of this ambivalence will dissipate quickly. Finally, you have an easy-to-use and -understand mechanism that works well and does exactly what it purports to do — enables developers to create more compelling data-driven applications in a much better way.

9

ADO.NET and ASP.NET

ADO.NET and ASP.NET are two core technologies of the .NET Framework. Many people think that ASP.NET and ADO.NET are languages, but indeed they are not — they are technologies. On a regular basis, I write both ADO.NET and ASP.NET code in both Visual Basic.NET and C#. Increasingly, I'm writing a lot in C++ as well.

Just about any application that you can think of has some need for data manipulation. In most real-world scenarios, data manipulation is not only a side note, but the crux of an application. While ADO.NET has expanded the notion of a data store extensively, at the end of the day, it's simply a mechanism to retrieve and manipulate data. If you've worked with previous versions of ADO or technology such as Java Database Connectivity (JDBC), ADO.NET is a huge leap from what you're used to. For instance, with very little experience, you can invoke a Web Service, populate a `DataSet` object with the results, and using the same dataset, you can populate a SQL Server or Oracle database, to name two. You could also fire up your application to retrieve data from a Web Service or database, pull the network cable out of your computer, manipulate the data as you see fit, and then plug the network cable back in and submit the changes. If you were to do this in old-school ADO, all you'd have on your hands would be a mess.

The Evolution of ASP.NET

The evolution of ADO.NET is amazing. Having used it for four years now and being involved in both the Visual Studio 2005 and Windows Longhorn Beta programs, I've seen the maturation of the technology. The first evolutionary step is in the .NET 2.0 (Whidbey) Framework and then ultimately the change to WinFX/Longhorn. Longhorn's release date is still in the future, but we are well into the beta phase and have a pretty good idea of what WinFX and the 2.0 Framework are going to look like.

So what's so amazing? Well, that's what this chapter is going to be about, but a few general points come to mind. I have heard various claims that ASP.NET 2.0 for instance, will allow developers to provide the same functionality they did in the 1.x frameworks with 70 percent less code. That's a pretty bold statement, but so far I think it's pretty close to accurate. There are enhancements in so many areas that some things that used to be painfully monotonous are now done automatically. On a typical ASP.NET project, for instance, my company will have a custom configuration file section for each module. We then need a `ConfigurationSectionHandler` and a class to hold those settings. The `Handler` class is virtually identical across modules, varying only in the specific properties being managed. But it's not uncommon to have these classes span a few hundred lines of code. Some projects have 10–15 of these. None of it is hard, but it's certainly monotonous. Now in ASP.NET 2.0, that's done just about automatically. So what took an hour or two to do (and test/debug correctly) now takes a few minutes at most.

Transaction processing is another area that's been enhanced. There's a new `TransactionScope` object that is used to handle transaction processing. It's very intelligent in the sense that it begins things as lightweight transactions and then promotes them to distributed transactions as the need arises. So now, you can accomplish in just a few lines of code what took quite a bit of code and a tremendous amount of knowledge of COM+ and distributed transactions to complete. It is no understatement to say that distributed transactions used to be items that those faint of heart would be well advised to avoid. Now the same functionality can be learned and used in just a few minutes. (When I say a few minutes, I'm assuming that you know and understand distributed transactions. Obviously, distributed transactions are something you could write an entire book on (and in fact people have.) So it's not something you just jump into. My main point is that the `transactionScope` makes using them a lot easier. There are new `MasterPage` controls in ASP.NET 2.0 that give your sites a common look and feel. And while these were available in previous versions, they took a little getting used to. Features for giving your site a consistent look and feel have been so enhanced in 2.0 that you'll need to see them to believe it. There's plenty more, but these are just a few of the examples that come to mind.

ASP.NET is no less amazing. Ten years ago, if you wanted dynamic content, you had to be a computer guru, not just a casual user. Most people used dialup back then and the whole Web experience was, well, amazing by old standards but painful by modern standards. The original Active Server Pages (ASP) changed things quite a bit. It allowed people to learn Visual Basic Script, for instance, and parlay an existing skill set (or one that you could easily gain due to the abundance of books and training on the subject) in VB6 into a Web developer career. Pretty soon market forces came into play and static content just didn't cut it any more.

As cool as ASP was, though, it was still very awkward. For one thing, you had to use scripting languages. While flexible, scripting languages were often weakly typed, and code reusability was accomplished by copying and pasting. The physical separation of presentation layer objects and business and data objects was difficult to accomplish and was often not done. When ASP.NET came out, everything changed in this regard. Microsoft boasted huge savings in terms of code. (It was pretty common to hear about people who recreated their ASP Web sites in ASP.NET with half the lines of code.)

I've been involved with ASP.NET 2.0 since the first Alpha release, and although I'm probably considered an advanced ASP.NET developer, I had a lot to learn. I wouldn't go so far as to say that the leap from 1.x to 2.0 is as big as the original leap from ASP to ASP.NET, but it is quite profound. If a developer started learning ASP.NET 2.0, he/she would be every bit as productive as an experienced 1.x developer in a mere fraction of the time. I know I keep emphasizing this point, but 2.0 is a full paradigm shift, not just a modest version change.

ADO.NET

The new features in ADO.NET under the 2.0/WinFX Framework can essentially be broken down as follows:

- ❑ Accessing data
- ❑ Transaction processing
- ❑ XML processing

The sections that follow discuss each in turn.

Enumerating SQL Server Instances

Chalk this one up in the "could do before but greatly simplified category." Previously, if you wanted to list all of the SQL Server instances on a network, you had to use either SQLDMO or you had to do some significant P/Invoke. Currently, this is all that it takes:

```
using System.Data;
using System.Data.Sql;
using System;
public class Wrox.DeveloperBeta
{
 public static int Main(string[] args)
 {
 SqlDataSourceEnumerator MyDbEnumerator = SqlDataSourceEnumerator.Instance;
 DataTable DBInstances = MyDbEnumerator.GetDataSources();
 foreach (DataRow row in DBInstances.Rows)
 {
        Console.WriteLine("Server Name:"+row["ServerName"]);
Console.WriteLine("Instance Name:"+row["InstanceName"]);
Console.WriteLine("Is Clustered:"+row["IsClustered"]);
Console.WriteLine("Version:"+row["Version"]);

 }
 return 0;
 }
}
```

That code just declared an instance of the SqlDataSourceEnumerator class and called its GetDataSources method. You'll notice that the DataTable object declared didn't have any columns added to it. In the same way that a DataAdapter object creates the schema, the GetDataSources method returns a DataTable object, which you set equal to DBInstances. Thus, there's no need to really do anything else. What I mean by this is that you are simply declaring a DataTable object but not instantiating it. The return value from the call to GetDataSources is a DataTable, so when it returns, DBInstances will no longer be an uninstantiated object.

SqlBulkCopy

While ADO.NET makes for a superb, scalable data access environment, one of its shortcomings has been manipulating data en masse. In previous versions of ADO.NET, this was true across the board, whether one was talking about bulk loading data or item-by-item updates to a database. Previously, if you wanted to move data from one table to another, you had to use very convoluted means. For example, you could set the `AcceptChangesDuringFill` property of the `DataAdapter` to `false`, so the `Rowstates` of each of your rows were added. Then you could call `Update` on the `Adapter`, pointing to an entirely new `DataTable`, as follows:

```
Private Sub Form2_Load(ByVal sender As System.Object, ByVal e As System.EventArgs)
Handles MyBase.Load
daSource.AcceptChangesDuringFill = false
End Sub

Private Sub btnImport_Click(ByVal sender As System.Object, ByVal e As
System.EventArgs) Handles btnImport.Click
  MessageBox.Show("DataSet currently has Changes: " & ds.HasChanges.ToString) 'True
  Dim i As Integer = daDestination.Update(ds, "TransferData") '203 records
  Label2.Text = "Transferred Records: " & i.ToString 'i = 203
End Sub

Private Sub btnLoadData_Click(ByVal sender As System.Object, ByVal e As
System.EventArgs) Handles btnLoadData.Click
ds.HasChanges() 'false
daSource.Fill(ds, "TransferData")
MessageBox.Show("Source Table has " & ds.Tables(0).Rows.Count.ToString & " rows")
'203
ds.HasChanges() 'true
Label1.Text = "Source Table: " & ds.Tables(0).Rows.Count.ToString
End Sub
```

Can you see what's wrong with this approach? You are pulling the data over a network in most cases, because all the data involved is probably sitting on the same server. Even if it's not, you are still essentially caching the data locally just so you can send it back, row by row, to another table. Because most such operations will involve a large amount of data, you can easily see that's something's very wrong with this picture. Now, look at the new way to handle the same operation. (The code is very different because they are fundamentally different approaches.)

```
//Declare a few variables...
private SqlConnection cn;
private SqlDataAdapter da;
private SqlCommand cmd;
private DataSet ds;
//Instantiate everything we need
private void Form1_Load(object sender, EventArgs e)
{
SqlConnection.ClearAllPools();//Cool new feature!
cn = new SqlConnection("integrated security=SSPI;data source=x;initial catalog=x");
cmd = new SqlCommand("SELECT TOP 200000 * FROM Source", cn);
da = new SqlDataAdapter(cmd);
}
//Load the DataSet/DataTable and Bind it to a DataGridView control.
```

```csharp
private void btnLoad1_Click(object sender, EventArgs e)
{
ds = new DataSet();
try
{
 DateTime dt = DateTime.Now;
da.Fill(ds, "MyTable");
 TimeSpan ts = DateTime.Now - dt;
lblStart.Text = ts.TotalSeconds.ToString();
}
    catch (SqlException ex)
      {
        System.Diagnostics.Debug.Assert(false, ex.ToString());
      }
      finally { cn.Close(); }
}
private void btnLoadDb_Click(object sender, EventArgs e)
{
    System.Data.SqlClient.SqlBulkCopy bc = new SqlBulkCopy(cn);
    bc.DestinationTableName= "Destination";
    try
    {
      DateTime dt = DateTime.Now;
      lblStart.Text = "Start Time: " + DateTime.Now.ToLongTimeString();
      cn.Open();
      bc.WriteToServer(ds.Tables[0]);
     TimeSpan ts = DateTime.Now - dt;
     lblDone.Text = "End Time" + ts.TotalSeconds.ToString();
    }
    catch (SqlException ex)
    {
      System.Diagnostics.Debug.Assert(false, ex.ToString());
    }
    finally { cn.Close (); }
}
```

Not only is this new mechanism more intuitive, but the speed difference is blinding. To be honest, in the first example, if you were dealing with more than a couple hundred rows, or using a slow network (and heaven help you if you were using a Web service), the speed would probably end up being prohibitive.

UpdateBatchSize

As far as bang for the buck goes, this is probably one of the hottest new features. Basically, by inserting one line of code, you can change the entire behavior of your DataAdapter so that performance is greatly increased. Currently, when you call Update, the adapter loops through your DataSet/DataTable and checks each row's rowstate. If it's Added, Modified, or Deleted, it looks for the corresponding command and sends the Update, one at a time. By specifying this property, you can gather them all up (or chunk them) and send them in batches. It's honestly this easy to use:

```csharp
System.Data.SqlClient.SqlDataAdapter da = new
System.Data.SqlClient.SqlDataAdapter(someCommand);
Da.UpdateBatchSize = 100;//Or whatever number you want.
```

AcceptChangesDuringUpdate

One of the common problems many new ADO.NET developers run into is regarding transactions. Remember that when you call the Update method of a DataAdapter, it walks through the rows, checks the Rowstate, and then calls the corresponding command. Well, there's one more thing that happens. After the update is complete, it calls AcceptChanges individually on the row.

However, there is a ContinueUpdateOnError property for each Adapter implementation, which, if an error is caused, will just proceed with the next row. So if you had 100 rows with a changed Rowstate and the 98th caused an error, you'd have 97 successful changes in the database and only three rows in your dataset without changes (assuming that you were not inside a transaction). If you specified ContinueUpdateOnError, you'd have 99 successful updates, and only one row with changes in it.

However, if this was inside a transaction, you'd have a serious problem. From the client side, nothing would be different, but in the first examples, you'd have 97 rows with AcceptChanges called on them, which would reset their Rowstate to Unchanged. But when the transaction rolled back, no changes would be present in the database. This would cause those changes to be effectively lost.

How do you get around this? First, you need to use the GetChanges() method of a dataset and then pass in the result to your DataAdapter. If successful, commit your transaction and call AcceptChanges on the entire dataset. This has some potential problems, because it's possible that the power could go out between the commit statement and the AcceptChanges, but fortunately, this all happens so fast that such a situation is highly unlikely. Here is an example of how to do this:

```
public void TransactionExample()
{
    SqlDataAdapter da = new SqlDataAdapter(BusinessClass.GetBusinesses());
    DataSet ds = new DataSet("WroxExample");
    DataTable dt = new DataTable("ExampleTable");
    ds.Tables.Add(dt);
using(SqlConnection cn = new
SqlConnection(ConfigurationSettings.AppSettings("ConnectionString"))))
{
SqlTransaction tx = null;
  try
  {
  tx = cn.BeginTransaction();
  da.Update(ds.GetChanges());
  tx.Commit();
  ds.AcceptChanges();
  }
  catch (SqlException ex)
  {
  tx.Rollback();
  System.Diagnostics.Debug.Assert(false, ex.ToString());
  }
  //The using block will ensure the connection is closed
  //but it's here for illustration.
  finally
  {
  cn.Close();
  }
  }
```

Now you can do away with the intermediary step of getting the changes and just set the `AcceptChangesDuringUpdate` property of the `Adapter` to `false`. This will prevent the adapter from calling `AcceptChanges` on each row as it updates them. Here's an example of how this works:

```
        private void button1_Click(object sender, EventArgs e)
{
        SqlDataAdapter da = new SqlDataAdapter(BusinessClass.GetBusinesses());
        DataSet ds = new DataSet("WroxExample");
        DataTable dt = new DataTable("ExampleTable");
 ds.Tables.Add(dt);
 //Make changes here.
 SqlConnection cn = new
SqlConnection(ConfigurationSettings.AppSettings("connectionstring"))");
 SqlTransaction tx;
 try
 {
 tx = cn.BeginTransaction();
 da.AcceptChangesDuringUpdate = false;
 da.Update(ds);
 tx.Commit();
 ds.AcceptChanges();
 }
 catch (SqlException ex)
 {
 tx.Rollback();
 System.Diagnostics.Debug.Assert(false, ex.ToString());
 }
 finally
 {
 cn.Close();
 }
```

SqlDependency

Another one of my favorite features is the `SqlDependency` and notification. If you spend any time in the .NET newsgroups, you'll no doubt see people wondering how to detect changes to their source data in a disconnected data scenario. As previously mentioned, with ADO.NET, you could query your database and then pull the network cable until you needed to update. A lot could happen in the interim. Okay, if you want to detect changes, you need a network cable plugged in, or at least you need to be running on the same machine as the DB server.

Just because you have an object to do something doesn't mean that it becomes inexpensive. And think about how you would implement detecting changes if you didn't have an object to take care of it. One way was to use SQL Server notification services. Another is to use `Triggers` and `Message Queues`. Do either of those sound cheap? Nope. And neither is the dependency. Again, if you are planning on using this feature as a mechanism to circumvent the underlying architecture of ADO.NET, don't do it. This is a *magnificent* feature when used correctly, but it wasn't intended to be used by 10,000 client applications. Also, the fact that you need the network cable plugged in should be a great hint about what's going on, right?

Enough preaching; let me provide an example:

```
System.Boolean CreateDependency()
{
  SqlConnection MyConnection = new
SqlConnection(ConfigurationSettings.AppSettings("connectionstring"));;);

  // Create a new SqlCommand object.
  SqlCommand cmd=new SqlCommand( "SELECT * FROM Cuckooz", MyConnection );

  // Create a dependency and associate it with the SqlCommand.
  SqlDependency dep=new SqlDependency( cmd );
  // Maintain the reference in a class member.

  // Subscribe to the SqlDependency event.
  dep.OnChanged+=new OnChangedEventHandler( OnDependencyChanged );

  // Execute the command.
 SqlDataReader dr =  cmd.ExecuteReader();
  // Process the DataReader.
}

// Handler method
void OnDependencyChanged( object sender,
                          SqlNotificationEventArgs e )
{
  MessageBox.Show(e.Info.ToString ());
}
```

Note that if you are using the code in the SDK documentation, the documentation is wrong. There is no such thing as an `SqlNotificationsEventArgs` *— it's* `SqlNotificationEventArgs`.

Anyway, it's that simple to use. The only real code is that for hooking up the event handler and then deciding what you want to check for. The `SqlNotificationEventArgs` class has three properties, no methods, and, of course, one event. The properties are listed in the following table.

Info	Gets a value that indicates the reason for the notification event.
Source	Gets a value that indicates the source that generated the notification.
Type	Gets a value that indicates whether this notification is generated due to an actual change or by the subscription.

SQL Server Provider Statistics

This is another feature that makes life a lot easier in the new framework:

```
using(SqlConnection cn = new SqlConnection("Data Source=xxxxxx;Initial
Catalog=xxxxxxxxxx;Integrated Security=SSPI;")){
 using (SqlCommand Cmd = cn.CreateCommand())
```

```
cn.Open();
        Cmd.CommandText = "sp_who";
        Cmd.ExecuteNonQuery();
        IDictionary result = cn.RetrieveStatistics();

        foreach (DictionaryEntry entry in result)
        {
            System.Diagnostics.Debug.WriteLine(entry.Key + " = " + entry.Value);
        }
        cn.Close();
    }
}
```

This code yields the following result:

```
BytesReceived = 6261
UnpreparedExecs = 1
SumResultSets = 0
SelectCount = 1
PreparedExecs = 0
ConnectionTime = 699
ExecutionTime = 0
Prepares = 0
BuffersSent = 1
SelectRows = 1
ServerRoundtrips = 1
CursorOpens = 0
Transactions = 0
BytesSent = 18
BuffersReceived = 1
IduRows = 0
IduCount = 0
```

Remember that when you try this, you are going to get different results because you are using a different machine, a different database, a different table, and a different query. Now, you probably are having the same reaction I first had: "This is cool and all, but why would I use it?" Well, all of the provider statistics aren't necessarily useful, but a few are. ServeRoundTrips, for instance, probably isn't the most useful statistic because you should have a pretty good idea about this in the first place. ExecutionTime, though, is pretty helpful and is certainly going to yield more accurate results than would be measuring execution time by creating two TimeSpan objects and comparing the differences between them.

DataTables Are Now Real Objects

Being the ADO.NET fanatic that I am, one of my ultra-pet peeves was that DataSet objects were required to do things when you didn't really need them. If you had only one Datatable and you wanted to write it to XML, you'd have to create a DataSet object and insert the DataTable into it before using the WriteXml method. This has always seemed wasteful and required a bunch of extra code for no real reason. Similarly, if you wanted to determine if a DataTable had changes, you couldn't use the HasChanges method because it didn't exist. You'd have to again stick the DataTable into a DataSet and check it. The same went for GetChanges.

Well, those days are over, as shown in the following code:

```
DataTable dt = new DataTable();
if(dt.HasChanges()){
MessageBox.Show("Yep, It has Changes");
}
SomeDataAdapter.Update(dt.GetChanges());// Yep, it works.
dt.WriteXml(@"C:\testtable.xml");
```

Essentially, if you can do it with a `DataSet`, chances are good that you can now do it with a `DataTable`, too.

Installed Data Providers

This is one of the other interesting new features. Essentially, you can use a `DBProviderFactory` object to enumerate (list) providers installed on a given machine. Using it is easy enough. In software development, there are a lot of tradeoffs, and this is particularly true with data access providers. There are two schools of thought. The first is to make things as generic as possible so if the back-end database changes, you aren't tightly coupled to it. Advocates of the other position would argue that you should always use the most specific provider you have available because this will afford you the best performance and feature sets. The decision on which way to go is dependent on a lot of factors, so there aren't any real hard-and-fast rules. On the one hand, if you're 100 percent sure that you'll never need your code to talk to a different database, using a generic provider gives you little benefit. On the other hand, if you think you may have to talk to a bunch of different databases, which is not uncommon in large distributed environments, it is probably well worth any performance loss.

```
public class ProviderTest
{
    public static void Main()
    {
        DataTable ProviderTable = DbProviderFactories.GetFactoryClasses();

        foreach (DataColumn col in Providetable.Columns)
            Console.Write(col.ColumnName + "\t");
        Console.WriteLine();

        foreach (DataRow row in ProviderTable.Rows)
        {
            foreach (DataColumn col2 in ProviderTable.Columns)
                Console.Write(row[col2] + "\t");
            Console.WriteLine();
        }
    }
}
```

Multiple Active Result Sets

Ostensibly the most hyped feature that I've ever encountered, Multiple Active Result Sets (MARS) is the ultimate solution to a subtle annoyance. In the previous versions of the framework, `1 command + 1 connection = DoublePlusGood 1 Command > 1 Connection = Exception`. What this means is that if you tried to fire a command using a connection that was already opened, you got the dreaded open and available connection error message. It was very easy to fix. If your problem was that you had left a connection open, you needed to write code to close it. If your problem was that you needed another connection, you needed to create one. So while iterating a `SqlDataReader`, for instance, you couldn't hit the same database (using the same connection) with values retrieved from the reader. With MARS that all changes. Now you can fire more than one command on the same connection. Again, you don't get something for nothing, so don't think this "enhances" performance by any means. Any performance benefit is merely perception, just like threading. And like threading, there may actually be additional overhead associated with this. But if you want to simplify your code, it's easy enough to do:

```
SqlConnection cn = new SqlConnection("SomeConnectionString");
SqlDataReader dr;
SqlCommand cmd = new SqlCommand("Select * From someTable where KeyField =
WhateverField", cn);
if(cn.State != ConnectionState.Open){cn.Open();}
dr = cmd.ExecuteReader();
while (dr.Read())
{
dr2;
SqlCommand cmd2 = new SqlCommand("Select * from ChildTable where KeyField =
@KeyField", cn);
cmd2.Parameters("@KeyField").Value = dr.GetString[0];
while (dr2.Read())  //DoSomething else
}
```

Transaction Processing

This topic could provide at least an entire chapter to itself, but the real news in transaction processing is in regard to the `TransactionScope` object

In most of my examples so far, I've referenced the SqlClient library, which is the native library for SQL Server. However, that library isn't of much use in distributed transaction scenarios because you probably aren't working with SQL Server across the board. Do you think that if you called an Oracle database that it would have any clue what `@@Error` is? Given this, the starting point here is the `System.Transactions` namespace. Out of the box, this isn't a referenced assembly, so you'll need to add a reference to it to use it. You can do this by selecting Project ➪ Add Reference, and then selecting `System.Transactions` under the .NET tab, as shown in Figure 9-1.

At the time of this writing, Oracle, SQL Server, and MSMQ are the only data sources that are provided under the `TransactionScope` object. If you need to use another DB, it's COM+ for you, although in all likelihood, it's virtually assured that other vendors will provide support for this.

For this to work correctly, remember that the following order should be adhered to:

1. Create your transaction.
2. Create the connection.
3. Dispose of the connection.
4. Call `TransactionScope`'s `Complete()` method.
5. Dispose of the transaction.

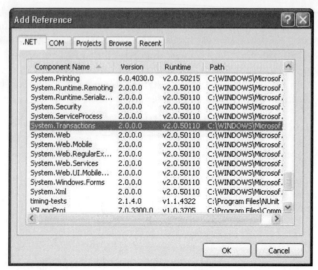

Figure 9-1

How do you create a simple transaction? An example follows:

```
const string ConnectString = @"Data Source=.\SQLExpress;Integrated
Security=True;AttachDBFilename=C:\Visual EmptyDatabase1.mdf";

private void btnTryTransaction_Click(object sender, EventArgs e)
{
  TimeSpan ts = new TimeSpan(0, 0, 5);
//Didn't do this yet - should have taken it out.
  TransactionScope scopeObject = new TransactionScope();
  string sql = "INSERT INTO tb_Customers(Customer_ID, Customer_FirstName,
Customer_LastName) VALUES (@CustID, @FirstName , @LastName)";
 using (scopeObject)
 {
 using (SqlConnection cn = new SqlConnection(ConnectString))
 {
 SqlCommand cmd = new SqlCommand(sql, cn);
 cmd.Parameters.Add("@CustID", SqlDbType.Int, 4).Value = 8;
 cmd.Parameters.Add("@FirstName", SqlDbType.VarChar, 50).Value = "William";
 cmd.Parameters.Add("@LastName", SqlDbType.VarChar, 50).Value = "Gates";
 cn.Open();
 cmd.ExecuteNonQuery();
 cmd.Parameters.Clear();
 cmd.CommandText = "SELECT COUNT(*) FROM tb_Customers";
 int i = (int)cmd.ExecuteScalar();//7 Records after Successful Insert
 cn.Close();
   //Open a connection to a Different Sql Server database,  MSMQ, Oracle etc and do
something there.
     }
```

```
scopeObject.Complete(); //At this point, the transaction is committed
    }
MessageBox.Show(GetTotalCount().ToString());
}

private int GetTotalCount()
{
using (SqlConnection cn = new SqlConnection(ConnectString))
{
SqlCommand cmd = new SqlCommand("SELECT COUNT(*) FROM tb_Customers", cn);
cn.Open();
int i = (int)cmd.ExecuteScalar();
cn.Close();
return i;
}
}
```

The default `Isolation` that will be used is `Serializable`, and the default timeout on the transaction is 60 seconds. However, you will probably come across scenarios where you want completely different settings. For this, the `TransactionOptions` class comes in handy.

```
TransactionOptions transactionOption =          new TransactionOptions();
transactionOption.IsolationLevel = System.Transactions.IsolationLevel.Snapshot;

//Set the transaction timeout to 30 seconds.
//In reality, you'd probably want to get this from a .Config setting
//or resource file.
transactionOption.Timeout =  new TimeSpan(0, 0, 30);
TransactionScope ts =
new TransactionScope(TransactionScopeOption.Required, transactionOption);
```

Other than `Timeout` and `IsolationLevel`, is there much you can do with this? Not that I've been able to find, but it is a straightforward way to manipulate these settings.

Back when I first loaded the alpha bits of Whidbey, things were a little more complex, and hats off to the ADO.NET team for making it ever easier. Previously, there was a property (actually the property is still there but you don't have to constantly set it) named `Consistent`. At each pass through your code, you'd set it to false if something failed. At the end, when the code exited the block and the scope was disposed of, if the `Consistent` property was set to true, everything would be committed. If `Consistent` was false, it would be rolled back. Compared to what you had to do previously, this was a walk in the park, but it was still a little short on elegance. Now, when you are done and you are sure you want to commit everything, you simply call the `.Complete` method and, voilà, everything is committed.

Presently, you can/should call `Complete` to finish off the transaction. You can still set the `Consistent` property, but the latest build I have of Whidbey indicates it has been deprecated already.

In this example, there is only one data store being used; thus, this transaction is operating as a local transaction. However, let's assume that we made a slight modification to this code, so that another data store was used:

```
using (SqlConnection cn = new SqlConnection(ConnectString))
        {
        SqlCommand cmd = new SqlCommand(sql, cn);
        cmd.Parameters.Add("@CustID", SqlDbType.Int, 4).Value = 8;
cmd.Parameters.Add("@FirstName", SqlDbType.VarChar, 50).Value = "William";
        cmd.Parameters.Add("@LastName", SqlDbType.VarChar, 50).Value = "Gates";
        cn.Open();
        cmd.ExecuteNonQuery();
        cmd.Parameters.Clear();
        cmd.CommandText = "SELECT COUNT(*) FROM SomeTable";
                int i = (int)cmd.ExecuteScalar();//7 Records after Successful Insert
                cn.Close();
    //Open a connection to a Different Sql Server database,  MSMQ, Oracle etc and do
    something there.}
      ts.Complete(); //At this point, the transaction is committed
    }
    MessageBox.Show(GetTotalCount().ToString());
    }
```

What would happen is very interesting. At first, a local transaction would be created. When the second connection was created and opened, it would be automatically enlisted into a distributed transaction.

Now, if you don't want to use the TransactionScope and you want to do things manually, there's a great new feature that simplifies things:

```
IDBConnection.EnlistTransaction
```

Each derivation of this, SqlConnection, OracleConnection, and so on, has the capability of manually enlisting the transaction, although as far as I know, SqlClient is the only provider in beta that has actually implemented it.

Monitoring Transactions and Their Performance

There's an inverse relationship between performance and accuracy in respect to isolation level. Another thing to remember is that distributed transactions require a lot more monitoring, so obviously there is more overhead associated with them. You will no doubt want to monitor them at some point.

The easiest way to accomplish this is visually. Select Start ⇨ Control Panel ⇨ Administrative Tools ⇨ Component Services ⇨ Component Services (under Console Root) ⇨ Computers ⇨ My Computer ⇨ Distributed Transaction Coordinator. Once you're there, you should see the screen shown in Figure 9-2.

From there, you can select either the Transaction List (which will show you all currently running distributed transactions) or Transaction Statistics (which will show you the performance statistics of any given transaction). In most instances, the latter, shown in Figure 9-3, will be of much more use.

Keep in mind that what you are viewing here are distributed transactions, not local ones. If a local transaction has been promoted/enlisted, it will become visible. But remember that this is the Distributed Transaction Coordinator, hence it's used for monitoring distributed (not local) transactions.

Figure 9-2

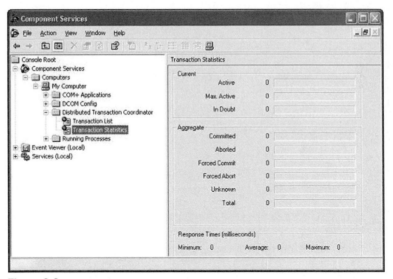

Figure 9-3

Transactional Web Services

Because Web Services are being used increasingly as a data source, it is worth mentioning them. If you want your Web Service to participate in a transaction automatically, you simply need to decorate the `WebMethod` with an additional attribute, as illustrated in the following code:

```
using System;
using System.Data;
using System.Data.SqlClient;
using System.Web.Services;
using System.Web.Util;
using System.EnterpriseServices;

public class WroxTest : WebService
  {
      [ WebMethod(TransactionOption=TransactionOption.RequiresNew)]
      public System.Boolean DoSomething(System.Boolean shouldComplete)
      {
        String cmd = "INSERT INTO SOMETABLE VALUES @Value)" ;

 SqlConnection cn = new SqlConnection
ConfigurationSettings.AppSettings("connectionstring")););
SqlCommand cm = new SqlCommand(cmd,cn);
cmd.Parameters.Add("@Value", SqlDbType.Bit);
cmd.Parameters["@Value"].Value = shouldComplete;

      // If a Web Service method is participating in a transaction and an
      // exception occurs, ASP.NET automatically aborts the transaction.
      // Likewise, if no exception occurs, then the transaction is
      // automatically committed.

cn.Open();
Boolean Result = cmd.ExecuteNonQuery() == 0;
 Cn.Close();
return Result
}
}
```

XML Processing

These days, it's almost impossible to read anything tech related and not hear the letters XML. Although the changes/enhancements in this area are the least substantial, they are definitely worth mentioning.

ASP.NET

With the changes from the 1.x Framework to the 2.0+ Frameworks in ASP.NET being so substantial, entire books could be written about both the new features in ADO.NET and ASP.NET, so at best I'm going to be able to scratch the surface. However, some really cool features are highlighted in the following sections.

Multi-Language Support

You can now use multiple languages in the same project, and it will work well. Before continuing, let me mention the Code folder, a new feature that simplifies things. In each ASP.NET application, there is a reserved folder called Code. You can insert classes in here, and they will be visible throughout your application. This is the primary mechanism that allows you to use both languages. Before doing so you need to specify some settings in your configuration file (and one could honestly write the good part of a book on the enhancements in configuration under the new frameworks, as well), as shown in Figure 9-4.

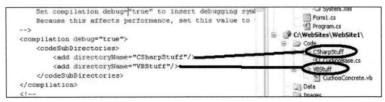

Figure 9-4

Once you have this in place, the stage is set for using dual languages. Think about the ramifications of this. For once, both VB.Net and C# developers can have their own way and no one will be the wiser. Figure 9-5 shows a simple example where I created a `Base` class in VB.NET and a derived class from C#, and they are both in the same project.

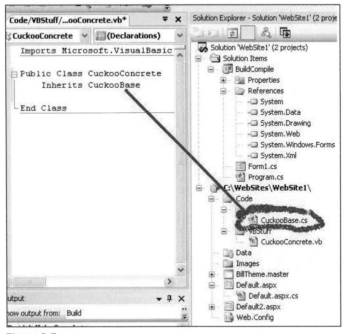

Figure 9-5

FTP Support

As a rule, I prefer stubbing my toes really hard over deploying ASP.NET applications. Fortunately, this is one area that has been greatly enhanced.

Once you are ready to deploy, you simply select Publish from the Build menu. You will be prompted with a dialog box that looks something like that shown in Figure 9-6 (which is intuitive enough not to need much explanation).

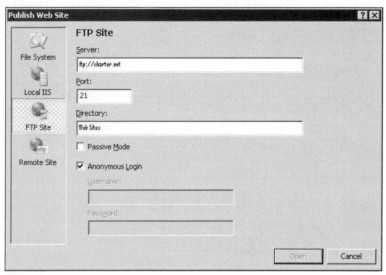

Figure 9-6

Master Pages

Master pages are definitely one of the more exciting features of ASP.NET 2.0, but they aren't necessarily new. At my current place of employment, we've been using them for well over a year and a half now. To see a master page in action, take a look at Figure 9-7.

The callouts show the actual `MasterPage`. This is static content that each page will have. If you think of a template, you're conceptually in the right place, but you have a lot more power here. Another callout shows the `ContentRegions`. These are the areas you specify that change from page to page.

There is now an actual `MasterPage` type that you can add to your project. The definition for a typical `MasterPage` looks something like this:

```
<%@ Master Language="C#" CodeFile="MasterPage.mymaster.cs" AutoEventWireup="false"
Inherits="MasterPage" %>
```

You layout your `MasterPage` just as you would any other page, except that you specify `ContentRegions`.

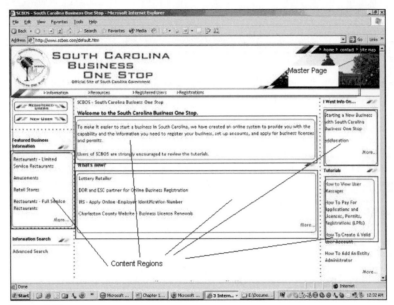

Figure 9-7

The pages containing `ContentRegions` reference the `MasterPage` as follows:

```
<%@ Page Language="C#" MasterPageFile="MySite.Master %>
```

Now one of the really interesting features about `MasterPages` is that you can nest them. One `MasterPage` can derive from another one, and another one from that, and so on. To do this, you simply change the declaration to the "child" master page and nothing more.

Themes

In similar capacity to that of `MasterPages`, *themes* can be used to provide a consistent look and feel. Themes are really easy to use and make life a lot easier, particularly in situations where consistency is critical.

To define a theme, you simply create a text file with a `.skin` extension or select Theme from the Add New Item Menu in Visual Studio .NET.

Here's a sample theme for a `TextBox` and `Button` control, respectively:

```
<asp:TextBox runat="server" BackColor="#FFFFFF" ForeColor="Black"
Font-Name="Tahoma" Font-Size="11px" SkinID="WroxTextBox" />
<asp:Button runat="server" BackColor="#FFFFFF" ForeColor="White"
Font-Name="Verdana" Font-Size="11px" SkinId="WroxButton"/>
```

When you have a control that you want to apply this to, you simply specify the `SkinID` value:

```
<asp:TextBox runat="server" ID="tbFirstName" SkinID="WroxTextBox" />
<asp:Button runat="server" ID="btnSubmit" SkinID="WroxButton" />
```

You can make life even easier by creating a custom control, setting a theme for it, and then using the custom control in place of the standard ones.

Base Pages Now Work

Probably the biggest annoyance that I've encountered in the past with ASP.NET has been when using inheritance (which I use constantly). Suppose that you create a given base page that has some properties available that will be used throughout a given segment of your application. Assume for the moment that you have the following page definition. (Some of it is truncated for the sake of brevity — but nothing related to this discussion has been removed.)

```
/// <summary>
/// Summary description for WebForm1.
/// </summary>
public class WebForm1 : System.Web.UI.Page
{public System.String CustomerLastName
{
get
{
        return Session["CustomerLastName"];
}

set
{
Session["CustomerLastName"] = value;
    }
}

public System.String CustomerFirstName
{get
{
return Session["CustomerFirstName"];
}

set
{
Session["CustomerFirstName"] = value;
}
}
```

Under the 2.0 Framework, the public properties show up, as do all the other properties of the page (see Figure 9-8). In previous versions, you had to use `this` keyword to get IntelliSense. This (no pun intended) greatly convoluted the intent of your code.

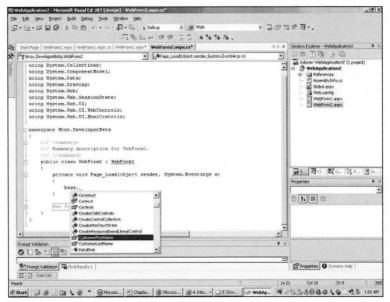

Figure 9-8

Data Binding

One area that typically threw developers familiar with only WinForms programming for a loop when coming to ASP.NET was data binding. Because HTTP is a stateless protocol, many people could not get used to module-level variables that were previously set, losing their values when a button was clicked. In essence, this hasn't changed. ASP.NET didn't make HTTP a stateful protocol out of the blue. However, it did make the way you interact with ASP.NET a lot more intuitive.

To begin with, there's a new object called the SqlDataSource that you can use. Take a look at the following declaration:

```
<asp:SqlDataSource ID="WroxDataSource" runat="server"
 SelectCommand="select * from TestTable"
 ConnectionString="<%$ MyAppSettings:MainConnectionString %>">
</asp:SqlDataSource>
```

Now, to use this DataSource, you simply specify it to a given control:

```
<asp:GridView ID="GridView1" runat="server"
 DataSourceID=" WroxDataSource ">
</asp:GridView>
```

While this seems cool, how many times do you really have a straightforward bind situation where you aren't specifying and restrictions? Well, it's easy as pie:

```
<asp:sqldatasource id=" WroxDataSource " runat="server"
connectionstring="server=xxxx;database=xxxx;trusted_connection=yes"
selectcommand="SELECT * From Cuckooz Where CuckooName = @CuckooName">
    <selectparameters>        <asp:controlparameter name="CuckooName"
controlid="tbCuckooName"        propertyname="Text"/>    </selectparameters>
</asp:sqldatasource>

What Cuckoo are you looking for? <asp:textbox id="tbCuckooName"
runat="server"></asp:textbox>
<br>
<asp:gridview datasourceid=" WroxDataSource" runat="server"/>
```

The same can be accomplished programmatically with the following:

```
if(Page.IsPostBack)
{WroxDataSource.SelectParameters.Add("@CuckooName", tbCuckooName.Text);
}
```

You could also take the value from a `QueryString` parameter and use it instead of a given control, as follows:

```
if(!Page.IsPostBack)
{WroxDataSource.SelectParameters.Add("@CuckooName",
Request.QueryString("CuckooName");
);
}
```

There is one subtle distinction between the two. When using a `TextBox`, you obviously want a value in most cases. This value probably isn't supplied when the page first loads unless you hard-code it or set it somewhere. However, when you use a `QueryString`, the exact opposite is the case; it typically has little value after the initial page load. As such, I have a Not (!) symbol in the second example.

Cookieless Forms Authentication

A while back, I was invited to Microsoft's Mobius conference in Redmond, Washington. I was pretty excited, but there was one problem. The night before I left, our company went live with an ASP.NET Web application that I was lead developer on. We had tested it thoroughly and all was well, until I got to the Atlanta airport. All of a sudden, the whole authentication scheme broke down and the application no longer worked. What was worse is that this was a HIPAA-compliant application, so we couldn't just loosen security.

What had happened was that right before we put the application in the wild, our network administrator ran some patches on the Web server, IIS Lockdown, and a few other tools. And he shut off cookies. That was the source of a very big problem for a few hours.

In the past, if you were using `FormsAuthentication`, you'd simply specify it and a username and a second parameter indicating whether you should persist cookies across sessions. Many people think this means "Don't use cookies," but it doesn't.

Take a look at Figure 9-9.

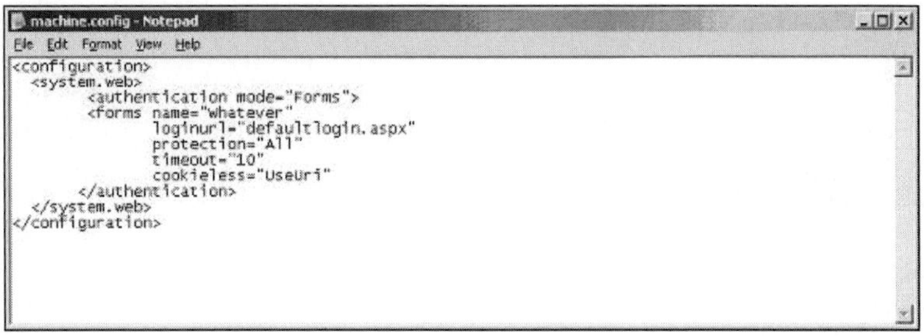

Figure 9-9

Personalization

Another slick feature in ASP.NET 2.0 is personalization. This allows you to build a class that you can reference throughout an application. Typically, this was done through Session variables in the past or included in a base page as previously illustrated. However, this is a much more straightforward, object-oriented, and type-safe way to handle things. There's no chance of spelling errors, and you have full IntelliSense support. In addition, the properties are strongly typed, and equally important, it's very easy to use.

Take a look at the following configuration file:

```
<configuration>
  <system.web>
 <personalization>
 <profile>
 <property name="FullName"/>
        <property name="LastLogIn"
                type="System.DateTime"/>
 </profile>
 </personalization>
  </system.web>
</configuration>
```

This is greatly simplified, but it creates two properties, `FullName` and `LastLogIn`.

You can set either of them like this:

```
Profile.FullName = "William Ryan";
Profile.LastLogIn = DateTime.Now();
```

Now, throughout the entire application, you can reference the `FullName` or `LastLogin` in both a typo-safe and type-safe manner.

Summary

So as would be expected, WinFX and Longhorn definitely change the developer landscape, particularly in regard to data access and display. Data access, of course, is addressed via ADO.NET, and the presentation layer, in part, is addressed by ASP.NET (not to mention XAML). Both of these technologies are wonderful and were marked advances when they came out, but both left a lot to be filled in. When the framework moved from 1.0 to 1.1, there were very few feature improvements, but the ones that were there were pretty cool. However the situation isn't the same with the next leap forward. Everything is getting better—a lot better. Everything is getting cooler—a lot cooler. Things like distributed transactions that used to be nightmarishly difficult are now accessible to even beginner programmers. And like everything else, these advances not only will lead to a lot greater developer productivity, but also will make coding in .NET a lot more fun.

10

Windows Services

It seems like almost yesterday that Windows Services were indeed rare. Today, most of the projects I work on or install on my computer entail a service or three. It wasn't too long ago that you needed to use C++ to write a Windows Service and it took a good bit of Windows API savvy to make it worthwhile. .NET has made creating services exponentially easier than it used to be, and it's only getting easier going forward. If you aren't familiar with a Windows Service, the best way to think of it is as a program that doesn't require a user to be logged in to run. Services can start, stop, and pause themselves. Think about a typical database implementation such as SQL Server. Imagine that the power went out. If it weren't for services, someone would have to physically approach the machine, log in, and start the program. Sure, you could stick the program in a Start Up folder, so you wouldn't actually have to start it, but you'd still have to log in. Moreover, many such items require specially privileged accounts, so in all likelihood, only a few people would know the credentials. This could cause a major problem if the person/people who knew those credentials weren't available.

To use, create, and manage Windows Services under Longhorn, you need be familiar with only one additional namespace, `System.ServiceProcess`, as well as `System.ServiceProcess.Design`, which is a subset of the preceding namespace.

Creating Services

The first step to easily creating services is to create a blank solution and then add a new project of type Windows Services to it. A template is already provided that does 95 percent of everything you need to actually create the service for you, as shown in Figure 10-1.

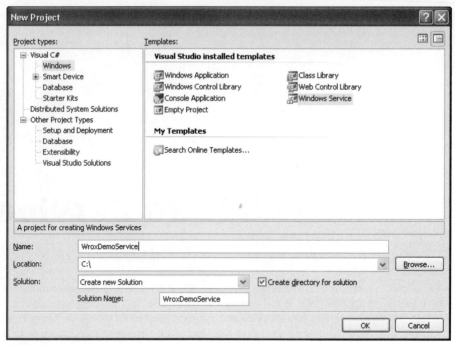

Figure 10-1

Visual Studio 2005 will go ahead and create a class for you that can be installed as a service. However, just like a Windows Form or ASP.NET application, it won't do anything at this point. The code that's created for you is provided here:

```
        // The main entry point for the process
        static void Main()
        {
System.ServiceProcess.ServiceBase[] ServicesToRun;

ServicesToRun = new System.ServiceProcess.ServiceBase[] { new Service1() };

System.ServiceProcess.ServiceBase.Run(ServicesToRun);
}

/// <summary>
/// Required method for Designer support - do not modify
/// the contents of this method with the code editor.
/// </summary>
private void InitializeComponent()
{
components = new System.ComponentModel.Container();
this.ServiceName = "DemoService";
}

/// <summary>
/// Set things in motion so your service can do its work.
// </summary>
```

```
protected override void OnStart(string[] args)
{
// Whatever you want to
// happen when the service starts


        /// <summary>
        /// Stop this service.
        /// </summary>
        protected override void OnStop()
        {
                // Whatever you want to
                // happen when the service stops
        }

    }
}
```

I intentionally left out some of the generated code irrelevant to Windows Services, but this is the majority of what you should see. First, you'll see the System.ServiceProcess namespace reference. You don't technically need this but you'll have to fully qualify your names for all ServiceProcess objects if you don't. The next important line is:

```
public class MyService: System.ServiceProcess.ServiceBase
  {
```

This indicates that the class inherits from ServiceBase, which provides all the functionality that you need to create a service. Now, out of the box, two methods are stubbed out for you, OnStart and OnStop. OnStart takes an Array of Strings that you can use to instruct your process on how to behave when it starts. The Main method also allows for parameters, and this affords a great opportunity for us. Services can't just be XCopied or double-clicked; they must be installed. However, if they must be installed, then debugging them can be a pain. A handy way to work around this shortcoming is to create a WinForm that calls the exact same functionality that the service will, but that has buttons or other UI elements that allow you to manually control it. Then check the startup parameters, and if the parameter you send in to indicate it's a debug scenario is present, call the WinForm as the startup object instead of the service code. It's amazingly simple and can save you a lot of hassle:

```
// The main entry point for the process
static void Main(string[] args)
{
  if (args.Length == 1) {
        System.ServiceProcess.ServiceBase[] ServicesToRun;
        // More than one user service may run within the same process. To add
        // another service to this process, change the following line to
        // create a second service object. For example,
        //
        //
        ServicesToRun = new System.ServiceProcess.ServiceBase[] { new MyService()
};
        System.ServiceProcess.ServiceBase.Run(ServicesToRun);
  }
  else {
        System.Windows.Forms.Application.Run(new ServiceForm());
  }
}
```

Another helpful trick applies to configuration files. When using a configuration file, the app looks to the `bin` directory, but with Windows Services, it uses the `Windows\System` folder. Thus, your configuration information won't be found unless you specify the following:

```
string ConfigFile =
AppDomain.CurrentDomain.SetupInformation.ConfigurationFile;
RemotingConfiguration.Configure(ConfigFile);
```

At this point, we've addressed just about all of the common stuff you'll run into when creating a service. Other than the installer, everything you need to create, start, stop, test, and configure a service has been addressed in just a few pages, but don't let this apparent simplicity fool you. Services are *very* powerful, and you can do quite a bit with them. Actually, I glossed over something. In the preceding example, the code to handle what occurs when the process stops or starts is addressed, but how you specifically stop or start the service isn't. So how do you start or stop the service? You can create a Service controller and use it, or you can use the tools provided in Windows. Under XP, you can select Start ⇨ Control Panel ⇨ Administrative Tools ⇨ Services. After selecting this, a dialog box similar to the one shown in Figure 10-2 should appear.

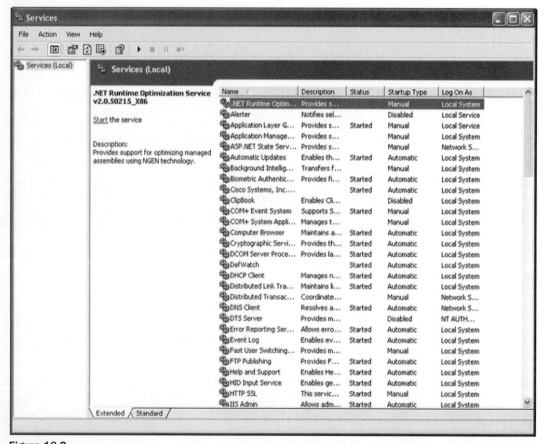

Figure 10-2

To actually run a service, you can call `ServiceBase.Run` and pass in a service name, as in the following example:

```
ServiceBase.Run("SqlService");
```

There are a few other methods and properties, but they are all, by and large, very intuitive and don't lend much to the imagination. For reference purposes, a complete set of the methods afforded by `ServiceBase` is provided in the following table.

Dispose	Disposes of the resources (other than memory) used by the ServiceBase.
Equals	Determines whether the specified Object is equal to the current Object. Inherited from Object.
Finalize	Releases unmanaged resources and performs other cleanup operations before the Component is reclaimed by garbage collection. Inherited from Component.
GetHashCode	Serves as a hash function for a particular type. GetHashCode is suitable for use in hashing algorithms and data structures such as a hash table. Inherited from Object.
GetLifetimeService	Retrieves the current lifetime service object that controls the lifetime policy for this instance. Inherited from MarshalByRefObject.
GetService	Returns an object that represents a service provided by the Component or by its Container. Inherited from Component.
GetType	Gets the Type of the current instance. Inherited from Object.
InitializeLifetimeService	Obtains a lifetime service object to control the lifetime policy for this instance. Inherited from MarshalByRefObject.
MemberwiseClone	Creates a shallow copy of the current Object. Inherited from Object. Also inherited from MarshalByRefObject.
OnContinue	When implemented in a derived class, OnContinue runs when a Continue command is sent to the service by the Service Control Manager (SCM). Specifies actions to take when a service resumes normal functioning after being paused.
OnCustomCommand	When implemented in a derived class, OnCustomCommand executes when the Service Control Manager (SCM) passes a custom command to the service. Specifies actions to take when a command with the specified parameter value occurs.
OnPause	When implemented in a derived class, executes when a Pause command is sent to the service by the Service Control Manager (SCM). Specifies actions to take when a service pauses.

Table continued on following page

OnPowerEvent	When implemented in a derived class, executes when the computer's power status has changed. This applies to laptop computers when they go into suspended mode, which is not the same as a system.
OnSessionChange	When implemented in a derived class, executes when a change event is received from a Terminal Services session.
OnShutdown	When implemented in a derived class, executes when the system is shutting down. Specifies what should happen immediately prior to the system shutting down.
OnStart	When implemented in a derived class, executes when a Start command is sent to the service by the Service Control Manager (SCM) or when the operating system starts (for a service that starts automatically). Specifies actions to take when the service starts.
OnStop	When implemented in a derived class, executes when a Stop command is sent to the service by the Service Control Manager (SCM). Specifies actions to take when a service stops running.
ReferenceEquals	Determines whether the specified Object instances are the same instance. Inherited from Object.
RequestAdditionalTime	Requests additional time for a pending operation.
Run	Provides the main entry point for an executable that contains multiple associated services. Loads the specified services into memory so that they can be started.
ServiceBase	Creates a new instance of the ServiceBase class.
ServiceMainCallback	Registers the command handler and starts the service.
Stop	Stops the executing service.
ToString	Returns a String containing the name of the Component, if any. This method should not be overridden. Inherited from Component.
UpdatePendingStatus	Sets the wait hint in the status for a service in a pending state.

These should all be pretty clear because they do exactly what their names imply. The properties of the `ServiceBase` class are very similar to the methods. In fact, most of them simply indicate whether or not a given method can be called, as described in the following table:

AutoLog	Indicates whether to report Start, Stop, Pause, and Continue commands in the event log.
CanHandlePowerEvent	Gets or sets a value indicating whether the service can handle notifications of computer power status changes.
CanHandleSession ChangeEvent	Gets or sets a value that indicates whether the service can handle change events received from a Terminal Server session.

CanPauseAndContinue	Gets or sets a value indicating whether the service can be paused and resumed.
CanRaiseEvents	Gets a value that indicates whether the component can raise an event. Inherited from Component.
CanShutdown	Gets or sets a value indicating whether the service should be notified when the system is shutting down.
CanStop	Gets or sets a value indicating whether the service can be stopped once it has started.
Container	Gets the IContainer that contains the Component. Inherited from Component.
DesignMode	Gets a value that indicates whether the Component is currently in design mode. Inherited from Component.
ExitCode	Gets or sets the exit code for the service.
ServiceHandle	Gets the service control handle for the service.
ServiceName	Gets or sets the short name used to identify the service to the system.

Controlling Services

To control a given service, the ServiceController class is used. Virtually everything that you need to do with or to a service can be done from just dragging a ServiceController onto a form and manipulating it from there. ServiceControllers are available under the Components tab of your Visual Studio .NET 2005 Toolbox, as shown in Figure 10-3.

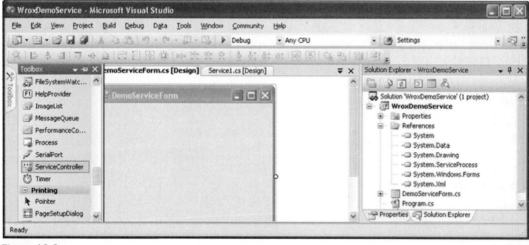

Figure 10-3

After dragging a `ServiceController` component onto your form and naming it (sc), add four buttons to control the service: Stop, Start, Pause, and Refresh. The code to handle each of these is as follows:

```
private void btnStart_Click(object sender, System.EventArgs e) {
        sc.MachineName = "BillRyan";
        sc.ServiceName = "DemoService";
        sc.Start();
}

private void btnStop_Click(object sender, System.EventArgs e) {
        sc.MachineName = "BillRyan";
        sc.ServiceName = "DemoService";
        sc.Stop();
}

private void btnPause_Click(object sender, System.EventArgs e) {
        sc.MachineName = "BillRyan";
        sc.ServiceName = "DemoService";
        sc.Pause();
}

private void btnReset_Click(object sender, System.EventArgs e) {
        sc.MachineName = "BillRyan";
        sc.ServiceName = "DemoService";
        sc.Refresh();
}
```

At each pass, you specify the `MachineName` and the `ServiceName`, but those can be set once and used just like any other property. (I simply reiterated this for illustrative purposes.)

As far as permissions go, starting services on someone else's machine is a big security no-no in most cases, so you can't use the `ServiceController` to do anything that you don't have permission to do already. However, you can use the `ServiceControllerPermission` class to specify declarative security permissions on what your code does. Any discussion of declarative security is beyond the scope of this chapter, but in today's environment, it's the height of insanity (and irresponsibility in my humble opinion) to write code that isn't secure. Do you really want to leave it to chance that no one will misuse your service?

If you want to enumerate each of the services running on a given machine and then leave a UI cue to manipulate them, you can do so with the following:

```
private void Form1_Load(object sender, System.EventArgs e) {
        ServiceController[] allServices;
        allServices = ServiceController.GetServices();
```

```
Console.WriteLine("Services running on the local computer:");
foreach (ServiceController svc in allServices) {
        listBox1.Items.Add(svc.ServiceName);
}
```

This code will yield the results shown in Figure 10-4.

Figure 10-4

Figure 10-5 is the Services dialog provided by the operating system. As you can see, they are identical, showing that each of the installed services can be discovered using the API.

You have probably noticed by now that both images bear a striking similarity, proving essentially that the GetServices method is working exactly as expected.

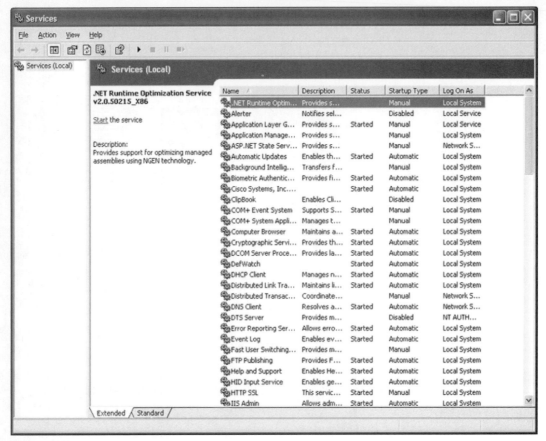

Figure 10-5

Installing Your Windows Services

There's only one somewhat tricky element in the whole area of processes, and that's installation. It's not really complicated, but it may seem so the first time around. The good news is that it's actually pretty easy after you've done it once or twice.

1. You need to create an Installer class. Simply create a new class that inherits from the Installer Class, or select Project ➪ Add New Item, and then select Installer, as illustrated in Figure 10-6.

2. Ensure that the RunInstaller attribute is set to true:

```
[RunInstaller(true)]
  public class Installer1 : System.Configuration.Install.Installer
  {

}
```

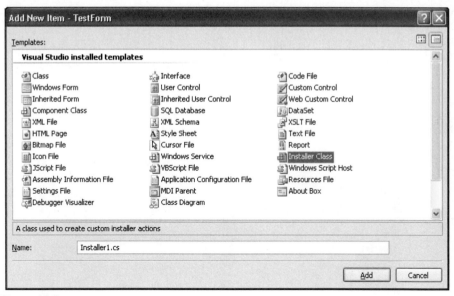

Figure 10-6

3. Create your `ServiceInstaller` and a `ServiceProcessInstaller`, as shown in Figure 10-7, and you are pretty much off to the races.

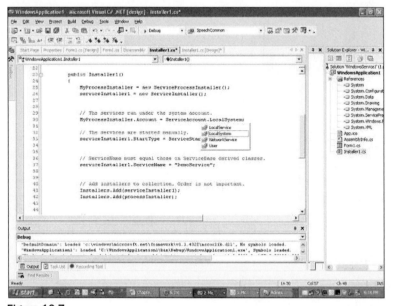

Figure 10-7

Notice that this is all pretty straightforward. Create a `ServiceInstaller` and a `ServiceProcessInstaller` object, specify the account that you want it to run under (`LocalService`, `LocalSystem`, `NetworkService`, `User`), select the Start Type (`Automatic`, `Manual`, `Disabled`), and you are ready to go.

All that needs to be done now is to call `InstallUtil.exe`, passing in the name of the assembly of the service, and it should take care of the rest. To get to `InstallUtil`, I recommend going to the Visual Studio .NET command prompt, navigating to your project directory, and calling `InstallUtil.exe` from there, as illustrated in Figure 10-8.

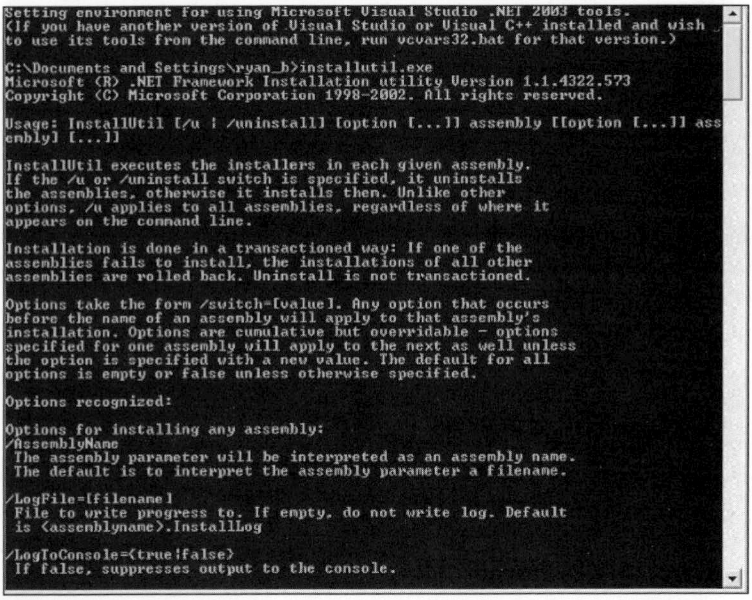

Figure 10-8

Summary

Just like most of the other new features that .NET has brought us, Windows Services are now easily accessible to most any developer. Far from being the complex beasts that most programmers feared, they are easy to create, maintain, and deploy. It wasn't very long ago indeed that very few programs ran as services, and now it's rather amazing how many do. (Just look at your services dialog box; I'm sure you'll be quite surprised at how many there are.)

Resources

Websites

Microsoft's Developer Center: `http://winfx.msdn.microsoft.com/library`

Xaml.net: `xaml.net`

XAMLshare.com: `xamlshare.com`

Newsgroups

Hosted by Microsoft Developer Center: `http://msdn.microsoft.com/longhorn/community/newsgroups/default.aspx?dg=microsoft.public.windows.developer.winfx.avalon&lang=en&cr=US`

Hosted by Mobiform Software: `http://groups.yahoo.com/group/XAML`

Hosted by MyWinFX.org: `http://groups.yahoo.com/group/mywinfx`

Tools

Aurora, Xaml Designer for WinFX: `mobiform.com/Eng/aurora.html`

AvPad: `http://blog.simplegeek.com/avalon/avpad.application`

Index

Index